IRISH RAILWAYS SINCE 1916

Irish Railways
since 1916

MICHAEL H. C. BAKER

LONDON

IAN ALLAN

First published 1972

SBN 7110 0282 7

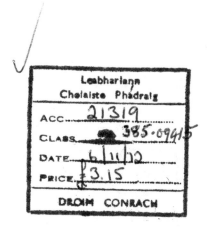
© Michael H. C. Baker, 1972

Published by Ian Allan Ltd, Shepperton, Surrey, and printed in the
United Kingdom by A. Wheaton & Co, Exeter

Contents

Appendices

Introduction

AN ENGLISHMAN writing about the railways of Ireland approaches the subject with some trepidation, for many Irishmen are better qualified than I am to carry out such a task. Yet, while much has been published on various aspects of the subject, there has not been a complete history since Conroy's *History of Railways in Ireland* of 1928. I have attempted to strike a balance between the many facets, but for a variety of reasons, not least the laws of libel, I have had to leave out a great deal that I would like to have included.

It may be thought that much of the fascination disappeared from the Irish railway scene with the end of the narrow-gauge and the run down of steam, but this is not so. In the first place the narrow gauge has not entirely disappeared, for the extensive systems of Bord na Mona (the Irish Turf Board) are still kept busy and employ a fascinating selection of rolling stock, including some former West Clare railcars which are known officially as the "Percy French cars", surely a unique tribute to a poet. In any case the narrow-gauge was only a very small proportion of the entire system, and there was much that was of interest but largely neglected on the broad-gauge lines, particularly on the Great Southern, and which is only now being appreciated. I hope that this book may lead readers to explore further in this direction.

I must apologise to the Irish reader for reiterating a number of political, economic and historical facts of which he will be well aware, but it is surprising how many people in Britain, despite recent events in Ulster, know practically nothing of Ireland's struggle for independence, the Civil War, and the economic war of the 1930s. Thus I felt that certain basic facts should be clearly understood, and the effect that these had on railway affairs better appreciated.

The English visitor will find many aspects of railway practice in Ireland which are familiar to him, and some that are not, and this mixture can be a source of great fascination. A word of warning is that the long familiar names of the Dublin terminal stations, Kingsbridge, Amiens Street and Westland Row, officially have vanished. In 1966 these stations, and a number of those in the Provinces, were renamed after leaders of the Irish independence movement, to celebrate the fiftieth Anniversary of the 1916 Rising, Kingsbridge becoming Heuston, Westland Row Pearse, and Amiens Street Connolly. The old names however, are still in common usage and no doubt will persist for some time to come.

My thanks for help in the preparation of this book are due to many people: to Mr B. d'Arcy Patterson, the Rail Control Officer (Personnel) of CIE, who could hardly have been more helpful; to Mr Devereux, Mr Tighe, Mr Hines, Mr Tier, Mr Willoughby, and many others at Inchicore who have always attempted to make my frequent visits there as interesting as possible; to the former Assistant CME of CIE, Mr J. J. Johnston, a great friend of the Irish

Railway Record Society; to my friends in the Society, particularly Mr Tim Moriarty; to Mr John Coulthard, formerly head of the UTA; to a great many railwaymen of CIE and the NIR; and finally to my wife, who by insisting on visiting her family in Ireland as often as possible has provided me with the opportunity to get to know something of the country.

The theme of the book is the effect the worsening financial situation, from World War I to the mid-1960s, had on the railways, and its eventual solution through systems of permanent aid from the Dublin and Stormont Governments. Although there are some chapters which are not strictly relevant, I have attempted in the main to hold to this brief. Whether I have succeeded is for you, the reader, now to decide.

MICHAEL H. C. BAKER

Oxted, Surrey
December 1971

IRISH RAILWAYS SINCE 1916

CHAPTER ONE

Irish Railway Beginnings

THIS, IF YOU LIKE, is a tale of suspense, of how the railways of Ireland which had never even in the competition-free days of the 19th century possessed a particularly robust constitution, so declined through the first half of the 20th that by the early 1960s death seemed to be upon them; and how a fairy godmother, first in the unlikely shape of the Irish Government and then, somewhat reluctantly, the Stormont one, stepped upon the stage and in the very nick of time waved a magic wand of money, so bringing about a remarkable restoration to health.

The very first railway in Ireland was opened in 1834. It connected Kingstown, where the mailboat from Holyhead docked, with Dublin, and thus helped to speed up communications between the Irish and English capitals, although it was some sixteen years before the rail link on the other side of the Irish Sea was complete. The gauge of the Dublin & Kingstown was the same as that of most English lines, 4ft 8½in, but the next railway to be opened in Ireland, the Ulster Railway from Belfast southwards to Armagh in 1839, decided to opt for something very much grander. While not approaching Brunel's 7ft it came up with the very fair compromise of 6ft 2in. The third Irish line, the Dublin & Drogheda, not wishing to be accused of lack of originality, thought up something between the two, 5ft 3in, and at this point the government decided to step in. A Railway Commission decided in 1846 that all railways in Ireland should be built to a gauge of 5ft 3in, and that those that were not of this width already must be altered. Why Ireland should be different from the rest of the British Isles was not made clear, but the decision was made and acted upon, and has involved the Irish railways in a lot of unnecessary expense ever since.

Some ten years earlier another Royal Commission had been set up to enquire into the best method of introducing railways into the country. In its first report, presented in the year Queen Victoria ascended the throne, it offered no great prospects of anyone making a quick fortune, and while in one respect it was unnecessarily pessimistic, in general the network it envisaged was very similar to, if somewhat simpler than, that which exists today. The report suggested that there should be a line from Dublin to Cork with a branch at Maryborough going down to Kilkenny, and two more at the small village of Holycross, one leading to Limerick the other to Waterford. There should also be a line from Dublin to Belfast taking a circuituous route through Navan, Kells, Cavan, Enniskillen and Armagh. As there were two canals from Dublin to the West the commission considered a railway line to Galway an unnecessary duplication. The report offered the pious hope that the Government might build these lines, but it did not; as was to happen so often down the years with both British and Irish administrations, after much goading and long after it was obvious that it would have to, the Government stepped in with a certain amount of financial assistance.

Up until 1846 the dividends paid by the Irish railways steadily increased. Then for two years running the potato crop failed. Potatoes were the staple diet of the Irish population, mainly small farmers, and the result of the supply dwindling drastically was the most awful famine. Men, women and children died in their thousands. Many would have been saved if the vast amount of grain exported each year to England had been diverted on to the home market, but the Westminster Parliament either through ignorance of the conditions or indifference to them, refused to sanction this. Many of the Irishmen and women who survived the famine somehow scraped together enough money to buy a ticket on an emigrant boat to the United States, and in three years the population of Ireland fell from 8m to 6½m. Partly for this reason the construction of 290 miles of railway line was held up through lack of funds until the Government, realising the strategic necessity of a railway system able to transport large numbers of troops rapidly about the country, particularly in view of the ugly mood of the people, arranged loans to enable the lines to be completed.

Not that the Irish themselves objected to railways. As in England the worthies in country towns throughout the land considered it a catastrophe if a projected line missed them out. So anxious were they to secure rail communications and so sure were they of the benefits, financial and social, to be gained, that in some cases they agreed to pay a fixed percentage to investors *ad infinitum*, whether the line made a profit or not. In later years when it had become obvious that most of these lines would never make money for anyone they became considerable millstones around the necks of local authorities.

Despite difficulties railway construction went on apace all over Ireland, only slackening off as the end of the 19th century approached. As in England, while the capital was in the south the principal centre of industry was in the north and most railway lines radiated from two focal points, Dublin and Belfast.

The original Dublin & Kingstown Railway had twice changed its title as it had expanded southwards, becoming first the Dublin, Wicklow & Wexford and then the Dublin & South Eastern; by 1916 it extended along the coast to Wexford and westwards from there by a rather circuituous route to Waterford. The shortest route to the latter city and the one most commonly used by travellers from Dublin was over Great Southern & Western metals along the Cork main line as far as Maryborough and then southwards through Kilkenny. There was actually a second alternative by way of Kildare, Athy and Carlow, and this situation made Waterford pretty well unique in Ireland, for there was seldom sufficient traffic between any two centres of population for anyone to fight over, and although a number of places were served by more than one company they almost invariably kept well clear of each other's territory. Apart from the Dublin–Waterford route the only important exceptions to this rule were the Belfast–Derry lines of the Great Northern Railway and Northern Counties Committee, and the GS&WR and Midland Great Western Dublin to Athlone lines.

These latter four railways, together with the D&SER, were by a comfortable margin the biggest in Ireland. Largest of all was the Great Southern and Western. Starting operations in August 1846 it provided the through route from Dublin to Cork recommended in the 1837 report. It had a monopoly of the routes between Dublin and Kilkenny, Cork, Limerick and Killarney, and it also worked three of the few important cross-country lines in the country, those from Rosslare by way of Waterford to Mallow on the Dublin–Cork line, from Waterford to Limerick, and northwards from the latter city up to Sligo in the heart of MGWR territory. These last two lines had been the property of the Waterford, Limerick & Western Railway, a fairly important company which the GS&WR had taken over in 1901.

The Midland Great Western connected Dublin with the west coast towns of Galway, Westport, Ballina and Sligo, and over on the eastern side of the country it approached GNR territory at Navan, Kingscourt and Cavan. Strictly speaking the latter three towns hardly produced enough traffic to justify a main line and the lines which served them were more in the way of lengthy branches. The hub of the MGWR was Mullingar, fifty miles from Dublin, just as Limerick Junction was the principal meeting-point of the various GS&WR lines.

The Great Northern, whilst second in size to the GS&WR, could lay fair claim to being the *doyen* of the Irish lines in most other respects. It provided the main line between the two principal cities, Dublin and Belfast, as well as owning the Belfast to Derry line via Portadown and Omagh and serving a number of other important northern towns. Its schedules were generally faster, its locomotives and carriages more up-to-date and its financial position sounder than those of any other lines.

The most northerly of the large railways was the Northern Counties Committee, whose principal line ran from Belfast to Derry by way of Antrim, Coleraine, the north coast and the shores of Lough Foyle; and it possessed a second route of almost equal importance, that from Belfast to the port of Larne. While the Irish and British companies had always done a great deal of business together of one sort and another the NCC had the closest relationship of all with a company on the other side of the Irish Sea, for as the Belfast and Northern Counties Railway it had been taken over in 1903 by the Midland. The Midland had a quarter share in the line from Carlisle to Stranraer over which its boat trains were worked, and from Stranraer the steamers of this consortium sailed to Larne, from which BNCR trains covered the 24 miles to Belfast. This, with the Midland's Heysham–Belfast service, no doubt prompted the Midland's interest in the BNCR. The latter was a well-run concern, and during the 1870s paid as high a dividend as $7\frac{1}{2}$ per cent on its ordinary stock. It owed its prosperity largely to the man who was its Traffic Manager (in effect General Manager) for 42 years, Edward John Cotton.

Born in Rochester, he had come to the Belfast & Ballymena, as the line was originally entitled, in 1857, and proved himself one of those almost larger than life characters with which railways seemed to abound in early and mid-Victorian times. He devoted the greatest part of his time to the well-being of the company and its employees, and in the days before trade unions had really established themselves as an effective force he did much for the men under him, setting up a provident and insurance fund and helping to found the first retirement pension fund for lower grades in Ireland. Some 35 years after his death he was still remembered and the Northern Ireland Prime Minister said of him in 1934, at the opening of the Greenisland Loop, "Every servant of the company had taken his cue from that kindly old man". Cotton was a great one for light railways and consequently the NCC possessed a considerable amount of narrow gauge mileage. Cotton claimed that the narrow gauge had a great part to play in the "amelioration of the lot of farmers, peasantry and fishermen of those hitherto inaccessible parts of the country", and during the latter years of the 19th century and the first 30 or so of the present one this undoubtedly held true.

Just about as far south as one can go from Larne is Rosslare, and it was there that another English company bought an interest in an Irish railway. This was the Fishguard & Rosslare Railways and Harbour Company. Authorised in 1895 to operate one steamer a day in each direction the nautical side of the business was worked by the Great Western Railway, but although the English company was also joint owner with the GS&WR of the new railway constructed from Rosslare Harbour to Waterford, and on to Mallow and Cork, the working of this was entirely the preserve of the GS&WR. The latter company built a splendid bogie restaurant car train for the service so that it would not be disgraced by the 70ft "Dreadnought" stock then current on the GWR, which it certainly would have been if it had used the flat-roofed six-wheelers which worked nearly all the GS&WR trains of the time. The restaurant car of the former train survived until recently, and there was talk of it being restored to its original condition and put on display in Cork, but nothing came of this proposal and the car has been scrapped. An equally magnificent vehicle from the boat train, a 12-wheel clerestory brake tri-composite, does still exist and is used on the Inchicore Works train. Although rather tatty now, it is basically little changed from when it was new nearly 70 years ago, and one may hope that either CIE or the Railway Preservation Society of Ireland will find a permanent home for it when it is finally withdrawn.

The opening of the Rosslare route proved of considerable benefit to the South-West for until then passengers to Cork or beyond had either to make a very long detour through Dublin, or else expose themselves to the rigours of a 96-mile sea voyage from New Milford to Waterford or an even longer one to Cork. Fishguard was actually laid out as much to serve Transatlantic liners as the Irish boats, and although the *Mauretania* did call there on her way from New York to Liverpool in 1909 the substitution of Southampton for Liverpool as the chief liner port after World War I ended Great Western ambitions in that direction.

If we go back up the coast again, beyond Dun Laoghaire and Dublin, we come to another port which operated a regular steamer service across the Irish

Sea. This was Greenore in County Louth, and it provided the third example of an English railway taking a financial interest in an Irish one. Two lines ran from Greenore to the nearby GNR line, one to Dundalk, and the other to Newry. Both were owned by the LNWR, and to work them six 0–6–0 STs, based on Ramsbottom's DX 0–6–0 goods engines, had been built at Crewe for the 5ft 3in gauge and shipped across, together with a number of six-wheeled carriages and some goods wagons. The Dundalk, Newry & Greenore Railway was seldom in a very happy financial position; most of what traffic it carried was cattle bound for England, and in 1916 it finished up with a deficit of £2,222.

The DN&GR was one of the many small lines which found the going tough, and although it was just about the least remunerative of them all there were others which ran it close. Their plight had long been recognised, and in 1910 a Viceregal Commission had recommended that all the 28 railway companies in Ireland should become one. Such a suggestion had a lot to recommend it, but the Government in its usual lethargic manner did nothing until World War I forced it to act. Nevertheless, the Irish Railways on the eve of the outbreak of the war were at their most prosperous. The small ones serving sparsely populated areas were unable to share in the general boom, but the big ones paid around 5 per cent, which if nothing startling, was quite acceptable. To the middle-class shareholder who travelled to his office each day on the 9.40 from Kingstown, where he lived with his wife and children and the cook and the maid, there probably seemed no reason why this situation should ever end. Three factors ensured that it did. One was the war, another the motorcar, and the third the rise of the Trade Unions.

In those far-away days when a business was not doing too well the easiest solution to its immediate problems was to sack some of the employees and reduce the wages of the others. This applied particularly in Ireland, where there were never enough jobs to go round and trades unions were weak in numbers and funds, so that both employers and employees had come to accept this as the natural order of things. Two men set out to change things, and as public transport was the only large industry outside Belfast, it was in this field that they made their greatest impact. Their names were James Larkin and James Connolly.

Larkin was the son of an emigrant working in Liverpool. His early career reads like something out of *David Copperfield*. Dismissed by an employer who, despite being a Roman Catholic, refused to let Larkin have time off to go to Mass, he tramped the country looking for work, sleeping in barns and under hedges. Eventually he became a seaman and then a docker, working his way up to foreman, but only to be sacked for siding with the men under him during a strike. In 1907, at the age of 31, Larkin moved from Liverpool to Belfast and plunged into trades union affairs there. Belfast had a population but little smaller than that of today and in many ways was more prosperous, with the shipyards and mills working to capacity. This prosperity benefited only the middle and upper classes, but women and children worked for rates ranging from 1d to 3d per hour, while men in unskilled jobs earned around 10s per week after working a 16-hour day.

The result of Larkin's activities was a strike by most of the manual workers in the city. Catholics and Protestants united, much to the surprise of the employers, and the strike spread even to the Police Force; eventually considerable concessions were gained by the strikers.

It need hardly be said that Larkin and Connolly were Socialists, and this at a time when the word aroused the same horror in the ranks of the establishment as did Communism in the late 1940s and 1950s. Like Larkin, James Connolly had been born of Irish emigrant parents, in Scotland. He served for a considerable time in the British Army and then went to America before coming to Dublin in 1910 to work with Larkin. The previous year the latter had formed the Irish Transport and General Workers' Union, and had immediately set out to build it up into an organisation powerful enough to force the employers into improving the lot of the working man. There was certainly a great deal which needed improving.

The average wage for an adult male worker was 18s per week, rather less than £10 in present day values. The death rate in Dublin, 27.6 per thousand, was equal to that of Calcutta, and the slums were the worst in the United Kingdom. In a book subsidised by the employers themselves and published in 1913 the author wrote, "The Dublin slum is a thing apart in the inferno of social degradation". In 1911 some GS&WR workers were involved in a lock-out; their union, the Amalgamated Society of Railway Servants, then called a national strike, and when the GS&WR directors refused to negotiate Larkin threatened to call out all ITGWU members. This brought about a settlement and nearly all the workers got their jobs back. But this was only the prelude to what was to happen in 1913.

The rise of the Trades Unions under the leadership of Larkin and Connolly was seen as a direct threat to the authority of the management and the prosperity of the directors and shareholders. One can sympathise with them up to a point for they lived in a world where few men, whatever their station, doubted that it was ordained by God that the rich would always be rich and the poor would always be poor. For a worker to step forward and proclaim publicly that he considered himself the equal of his master in all respects was a shockingly bold action and the Church, both Catholic and Protestant, along with practically everyone else, did not hesitate to call it a sin. Larkin and Connolly were no soft-spoken gentle persuaders. They were intelligent men who had knocked about the world and had no illusions and who were engaged in a fight to take away some of the advantages from the minority which had cornered them; they did not expect this to be a sporting contest between equals in which each side observed the rules and respected its opponent!

To counteract Larkin's growing power William Murphy, owner of three newspapers and of the Dublin Tramways, formed a Dublin Employers' Federation. He denounced the Transport and General Workers' Union, and on August 21, 1913, he gave notice to the employees of the Parcels Department of the Tramways that because of their membership of the Transport Union they were dismissed. If they liked to leave it they could have their jobs back. The next week was that of the Dublin Horse Show, the highlight of the social calendar. On the first day of the show, at 10 o'clock, the tram crews deserted their vehicles where they stood and announced they were on strike. Soon the strike spread throughout the various trades in the city, and although the main line railways continued to run, many of the carters who carried goods to and from the termini ceased work.

The strike dragged on into the autumn and the winter of 1913. Murphy and many other employers pledged themselves not to take back any man who was a member of the ITGWU and singled out Larkin as the instigator of the strike. He was said to be "indescribably foul of mind and tongue", and it was claimed of his followers that "if they were rich tomorrow, debauchery would soon have them into poverty again". There is considerable evidence of police brutality against strikers and their families, and during a meeting at the Inchicore tram depot a pitched battle between thousands of police, the military and strikers ensued after pickets had tried to prevent non-union men driving trams. Keir Hardie came to Dublin and spoke outside Liberty Hall, the Union headquarters, and much assistance was expected from England. But the TUC rejected boycotts and sympathy strikes, and although the Archbishop of Dublin declared that the unions' proposals were "eminently reasonable", the men were gradually forced to return to work. By the end of February, 1914, the strike was over.

The result could not be described as a victory for either side, and it did not involve the railways to any great extent, yet its long term effect on them was immense. The Transport Union was established and its members knew that they now had it in their power to go on pressing for and achieving a decent standard of living. If this might in the far-off future help to bring the railways to a state of insolvency one can hardly blame the workers for not putting the avoidance of such a happening at the top of their list of priorities.

CHAPTER TWO

Dublin, 1916

ON EVEN the dullest day the seaward approach to Dublin is worth coming out on deck for, and if one has been fortunate enough to choose an early spring morning when the sun has just risen, and is catching the domes and spires of the city emerging out of the mist as one's boat enters Dublin Bay with the Wicklow Hills showing faintly behind them, then one has had a fitting introduction to a very beautiful island. In 1916, just as today, the most popular rail/sea route from London to Dublin was from Euston by way of Chester and the North Wales Coast to Holyhead. From there one took the mailboat to Kingstown, and finally another train for the last six miles into Dublin.

If one chose to do the crossing during the day it would have been possible, given very clear weather, to see both Anglesey and the Hill of Howth, at the northernmost tip of Dublin Bay, simultaneously. Let us imagine, however, that we are crossing at night.

We have come down from Euston in the splendid coaching stock built especially by the LNWR for the "Irish Mail" some ten years earlier, hauled by a Precursor or a George V 4–4–0, or perhaps a brand new Prince of Wales 4–6–0. At Holyhead we board the *Munster*, an elderly twin-screw steamer, coal-fired of course, with two tall funnels and an abundance of polished mahogany and engraved glass. Whether or not we have travelled first-class on the train we shall be wise to do so on the boat, for the third-class will be packed to overflowing, mostly with soldiers on leave from the Western Front going to their homes in various parts of Ireland. They will all be volunteers, for although there has been talk of introducing conscription in Ireland many people are violently opposed to the idea and nothing as yet has been done about it. There will also most likely be troops on duty, congratulating themselves on their luck in securing a posting far away from the slaughter of the trenches, and perhaps there are one or two sailors going down to their base at Cork to rejoin their ships engaged on protecting merchant vessels from U-boat attack off the south-west coast.

Dawn is breaking as Howth looms up ahead, and we go out on deck and stand at the rails as the *Munster* heads towards the mouth of the Liffey. Then she swings away to the south, reduces speed as she comes up level with the lighthouse at the end of the long breakwater protecting Kingstown Harbour, and finally eases her way amongst the anchored yachts to tie up alongside the mailboat pier.

A group of porters comes scurrying up the gangway and our Welsh steward obtains the services of one of them, a slight, red-haired fellow who appears to think nothing of our substantial leather cases and assorted hat-boxes. He conducts us down the platform and seats us in a second-class compartment of a modern-looking bogie coach with very high elliptical roof, places our luggage on the rack and seems well pleased with the threepenny piece we give him for his trouble. We have some ten minutes before the train departs so we take a walk along the platform to have a look at the engine. It is a not very large 2–4–2T, in a livery of black with red-and-gold lining and the coat-of-arms of the company, the Dublin & South Eastern, on its tank sides. Looking back down the train it would seem that our porter has secured for us accommodation rather superior to that provided for most of the passengers, for while there are two more bogie coaches similar to ours (a third and a composite), all the rest are flat-roofed six-wheelers, decidedly antique-looking even by 1916 standards.

Back in our compartment we settle ourselves and are soon off, moving out slowly over a level crossing, then into a short tunnel, the wheels grinding against the rails as we swing sharply to the right and emerge on to the Wexford to Dublin main line and the single platform Kingstown station. The latter is lined with passengers waiting for a stopping train close behind ours bound for the city centre. Although the D&SER works a frequent service of suburban trains along the coast to Bray and Greystones it has had to be curtailed somewhat since the beginning of the war, and the tramways, already locked in a fierce battle with the trains, have been quick to take advantage of the situation. Once clear of Kingstown our 2–4–2T takes a hold of the train and accelerates steadily along the shore of Dublin Bay, pounding along at a steady 35–40mph. Behind us the funnels and masts of the *Munster* can be seen rising above the harbour buildings, whilst ahead across the strand is Ringsend Power Station and a collier heading towards it under a pall of black smoke.

Gradually the line straightens out whilst the coastline continues its eastward curve, and we now find ourselves passing suburban back gardens. Past a siding leading to the grounds of the Royal Dublin Horse Show, over the River Dodder, and the landscape becomes more industrial. There is a large flour mill, then a canal, followed by the works of the D&SER where our engine was constructed some dozen years earlier, with a number of engines in steam and the carriage sidings, and finally Westland Row station, under whose arched roof we come to a halt.

Whilst the bogie carriages, painted in a livery similar to that used by the (English) Midland Railway, are soon emptied of their occupants, the six-wheelers seem to possess some peculiar attraction not immediately apparent, for all their passengers remain ensconced in them. What this is becomes clear when an 0–6–0T of the Midland Great Western Railway couples up to them and conducts them off in the direction of Broadstone. This is the MGWR's terminus, and the mail train to Galway and the West will be waiting there to make a connection with the passengers from the boat.

Apart from Westland Row and Broadstone there are three other main

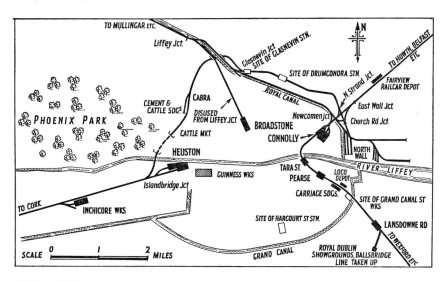

Dublin, 1972

line stations in Dublin—Kingsbridge, which belongs to the Great Southern & Western; Amiens Street, which is shared by the D&SER and the Great Northern; and Harcourt Street, which is the sole property of the D&SER. The two busiest are Westland Row and Amiens Street, most of the suburban traffic being handled at one or the other. The City of Dublin is already expanding northwards and southwards along the coast, and whilst much of the traffic thus created is the preserve of the tramways, a fair slice of it comes the way of the GNR and the D&SER. The GS&W and the MGW share the disadvantage of termini situated some distance from the city centre, and of main lines which lead south-west and west, well clear of the expanding suburbs. The MGWR does run a suburban service out to Maynooth, some 15 miles distant, but it does not amount to much. Nevertheless Broadstone and Kingsbridge are well worth visiting, and if we choose a busy period we shall find a great deal to interest us.

The GS&WR, the premier Irish railway, possesses almost a thousand miles of route and works it with some 340 engines. Its trains will take you to Valentia in the far west, Sligo in the north-west, Queenstown in the south, and Rosslare in the east. It is fairly prosperous by Irish standards, paying 5 per cent dividend in 1913, and makes a good deal of its profit from its principal main line, the $165\frac{1}{2}$ miles from Dublin to Cork. If we had been really ardent enthusiasts we could have taken a first look at this line immediately on disembarking at Kingstown, for there is a second boat train which is composed of two GNR vehicles bound for Belfast, and a number of GS&W coaches which are worked round to Kingsbridge and attached to the morning Cork Mail.

Kingsbridge station, standing close to the Liffey and within a few minutes walk of both the Phoenix Park and the Guinness Brewery, so that lovers of nature in both its natural and its processed state are equally well catered for, is a very fine piece of architecture and quite the most imposing station in Ireland. When it was erected in 1844 it was close to the business centre of Dublin and the principal markets, but the former has gradually moved down the Quays towards O'Connell Bridge, leaving Kingsbridge somewhat isolated. In contrast to its impressive façade the business end of the station where the trains are handled is nothing very special. It is a rather gloomy, low-roofed shed, with no more than two platforms, flanking a number of carriage sidings. Many English stations were built on similar lines, but whilst these have gradually removed the sidings and replaced them with platforms, it is a measure of how expectations have remained unfulfilled on the GS&W that Kingsbridge can still handle practically all its traffic with the two original platforms. There is actually a third, a bay let into the departure side known as the military platform, but it is little used by ordinary passengers, its principal function being to serve troop trains running between Dublin and the Curragh camp.

Beyond the station are extensive goods yards. On one side there are the Guinness sidings, where there will probably be an 0-4-0ST preparing to work some wagons over the street railway to the brewery, whilst on the other are the GS&W's own sidings. In charge of the shunting there will be some 0-6-0Ts, a modern-looking 0-6-2T, and a 4-8-0T, this last quite the largest locomotive that we shall see in Ireland. Completed at Inchicore in the previous year, she is numbered 900, and with her Belpaire boiler which exceeds 5ft in diameter she completely dwarfs all the minions around her.

On the passenger side we shall not find anything larger than a 4–4–0, although we might have heard something of the four-cylinder 4–6–0 which Mr Watson is said to be building at Inchicore. For many years, until succeeding to the post of Chief Mechanical Engineer of the GS&WR, Watson worked at Swindon, and there is great speculation about the possibility of his producing an improved Star. For the present the most powerful passenger locomotive we are likely to see at Kingsbridge is No. 341, the solitary new design produced by R. E. L. Maunsell during his two-year reign at Inchicore. Most unusually for a GS&W engine it bears a name, that of the chairman of the company, *Sir William Goulding*. Although obviously related to its somewhat underpowered predecessors it is a fairly hefty looking machine, and by all accounts has put in good work on the Cork Mails since its introduction three years earlier, but as yet no further of its type have been constructed.

A 20-minute walk, or a five minute journey in a cab, takes us across the Liffey and around one edge of the Phoenix Park to the MGWR's Broadstone terminus. Although not as elegant as Kingsbridge it is impressive enough and more than adequate for the not over-demanding needs of the Midland and Western counties of Ireland. The MGW comes third in the list of the country's railways both in mileage and receipts. If you have shares in it you are not going to make a fortune: as with most of the companies 1913 was its most profitable year, when it paid 3 per cent to the ordinary stockholders.

The MGW's main line, to Galway, 126½ miles long, is somewhat shorter than the GS&W's, although it does work through trains over greater distances, to Sligo, which is 134 miles from Dublin, and to Westport, 161 miles. 4–4–0s are again in the ascendancy on passenger trains, assisted by a number of 2–4–0s. Examples of both types are adorned with peculiarly-shaped cab roofs which tip up at the back, but there are other, more conventional-looking engines, the Celtic class 4–4–0s of 1902, and some very useful 5ft 8in 2–4–0s with superheater boilers, the most powerful examples of that wheel arrangement in the British Isles. Nearly all the MGW engines, including the 0–6–0T shunters, are named, and although their basic livery is black, their lining out in red and red-and-gold nameplates give them a certain sparkle. The MGW owns quite a lot of comfortable bogie carriages, but six-wheelers are still a common sight, particularly on the infrequent trains which work the Kingscourt and Cavan branches. Apart from being the MGW's headquarters Broadstone is also the site of the company's locomotive and carriage works, and of a large engine shed which lies just beyond the station.

If we now turn eastwards, past the flower and vegetable market, over Sackville Street, Dublin's principal thoroughfare, we shall, after some 30 minutes' brisk walking, come to Amiens Street. This is really two stations, the smaller one belonging to the D&SER, and the larger to the GNR. The latter company is Ireland's most prosperous railway, paying 6 per cent in 1913; much of its business originates in Belfast. In size it comes second to the GS&W, possessing a route mileage roughly half that of the larger company, but serving the fairly populous East Coast the amount of traffic it carries, both passenger and goods, is almost as great.

One might well, from the look of it, assume that this is the Irish branch of the English Great Northern, just as the NCC is the Midland's. The carriages are not painted but varnished, as on the English line, although their hue is somewhat redder; they are lined in gold with gold numbering and lettering, shaded blue. The livery of the express engines is almost identical with that found on the English GNR, although some are coming out from Dundalk Works in wartime black; goods engines and the smaller passenger classes are already so painted. None of the Irish engines are as impressive-looking as Ivatt's Atlantics, but the 4–4–2 is a wheel arrangement quite unknown in Ireland, although there are some recently built 4–4–2Ts. These, and the 4–4–0s and 0–6–0s which make up the bulk of the GNR(I) locomotive stock, would not look at all out-of-place on the East Coast main line, although their cabs are rather more curvaceous than the Ivatt design.

As it happens the only connection the Irish GNR has with its English namesake is James Park. He was at one time District Locomotive Superintendent at Peterborough, giving up this post to become Chief Mechanical Engineer at Dundalk in 1880, and although he has been dead for over 20 years much of the reverence he obviously felt for his one-time employers in England still remains. He even built a couple of 4–2–2s, the only examples of this wheel arrangement to run in Ireland, although they differed in a number of important respects from the Stirling engines, having inside cylinders and 6ft 7in driving wheels. They worked the Mail trains between Dublin and Belfast for some ten years until 1895 and were then retired to locals in the Dublin area, which they handled until their demise in 1904.

Bogie coaches, on both long-distance and local trains, are much more in evidence at Amiens Street than the other Dublin termini, and there are three return restaurant car workings on the main line, the midday one out of Dublin having just been introduced, along with two brand new cars to work it. These are Nos 401 and 402, elliptical-roofed vehicles, unlike their predecessors which are all clerestories, each seating 15 first and 19 second-class passengers; as yet it is not thought likely that any third-class passenger will care to eat or drink while travelling.

In all there are some half-dozen through trains in each direction over the 112½-mile main line, and a number of stopping trains to Drogheda and Dundalk, as well as the intensive suburban service over the Howth branch, connecting with the Hill of Howth trams. Trains connect at various points at the main line with lines branching off to the east and, beyond Dundalk, to the west; in summer there are through coaches to the Donegal resort of Bundoran, where the GNR owns a hotel, and, by way of the NCC, to Portrush. Goods traffic to and from the North Wall is fairly intensive, although nothing like that generated at the northernmost end of the system by the industries and dockyards of Belfast.

The D&SER suburban trains which run into Amiens Street have their own platforms alongside the GNR ones, although the two companies each have separate entrances. The D&SER station has no overall roof, unlike the GNR one, but is none the worse for this. Like Kingsbridge, the terminal section of Amiens Street possesses but two platforms, with a number of sidings in between them, and one bay, this latter for the use of the Howth trains. The roof, covering nothing like the area of its larger English counterparts, is rather low and might as well have no glass in it for all the light which manages to penetrate the smoke-blackened panes. At the outer end of the bay platform is the principal signal-box, controlling both D&SER and GNR movements, there being a connection between the two systems between it and another, smaller box, just by the bridge over the Royal Canal. Further out still is a third box, East Wall Junction, controlling the line from North Wall and the docks, which trails in by way of a steep incline and provides a connection with the GS&WR and the MGWR, and with the LNWR yard and warehouses. Immediately north of East Wall Junction is a further bridge, spanning the Tolka, a rather polluted river which flows through the northern suburbs and enters Dublin Bay almost beneath the railway.

On the eastern side of the passenger station at Amiens Street are extensive warehouses and sidings and, almost backing on to the Royal Canal, the engine shed. The latter is well within view of the end of the platforms, providing there are no lines of carriages or wagons shunting in between, and there are always some half-dozen or so engines in steam standing outside. On the opposite side the D&SER has a small depot with a couple of 2–4–2Ts in residence.

This then was the railway scene in Dublin in the early spring of 1916. As yet the war had had little visible effect and services were much as they had been two years earlier. Generally speaking the Dubliner was well served by his public transport, although a large percentage of the population seldom used it; most workmen lived within walking distance of their places of employment, and a ride on a train or a tram was a luxury that few in any case could afford. Once or twice a year a great splash might be made and the whole family taken out on the steam tram to Blessington, where they could get a rare breath of fresh air up in the hills, or else a tram or a train might transport them for a day by the sea at Howth or Bray, but otherwise a railway train was a rather middle-class conveyance; so too was the tram though somewhat less exclusively so. There were motors, but very many fewer proportionately than in England, and lumbering horse-drawn drays were the standard form of goods transport in the streets of Dublin. The Dublin United Tramways Company was much too well-run a concern for the motor-bus to have any significant effect upon its takings, and rail-borne transport, for both short and long-distance travel, reigned very nearly supreme.

CHAPTER THREE

Easter Week, 1916

WHILST OUR TERMS of reference are to relate the history of the railways in Ireland since 1916 we must at times widen our horizons and look at events which, although not specifically concerned with the railways, are of such magnitude that they affect every aspect of life, the railways included. Easter Week, 1916, falls very clearly within this category; indeed it is by general consent the most momentous week in Irish history, ancient or modern, and we may therefore consider ourselves justified in taking a look at the political and social conditions that led up to it, before we go on to survey the particular role played by the railways.

For as long as Ireland had been occupied a great many of her citizens had been in rebellion, often openly, against government from Westminster. Although many Irishmen had come to live and work in England and sometimes had achieved great eminence, they had never as a nation come to accept their position as part of Great Britain as had their fellow Celts in Scotland and Wales. It would be a bold Englishman who today would not admit that Ireland and the Irish were shamefully exploited and discriminated against for centuries, and whether this was because of differences in religion, on economic grounds or simply because Ireland refused to do what England wanted need not concern us now. The potato famine in 1845–6, when railways were in their infancy, in 1916 was still within the memories of many Irishmen. The population had been decimated through death by starvation, while England took no action, preferring to devote her energies to Empire-building further afield, and although Gladstone in 1886 made a brave attempt to give Ireland home rule his government was defeated over the issue and the matter was put aside until another Liberal administration, Asquith's, took it up again and actually succeeded in getting a similar bill through Parliament in 1914. The outbreak of World War I prevented its implementation and it was held in abeyance while hostilities lasted.

Having had the prize for which they had striven so long whipped away when within inches of their grasp, the Irish Nationalists were understandably infuriated. Meanwhile another section of the community was becoming equally hot under the collar precisely because Home Rule, even if not yet a reality, was now only a measurable distance away.

For a number of historical reasons the north-east corner of the country, around Belfast, had long been predominantly Protestant and fiercely loyal to Britain. It had no wish whatsoever to be separated from it and ruled by Dublin, and rather than see this happen the Protestants began to arm themselves in order to fight the British Army should the latter be obliged to force them out of the United Kingdom. It was a farcical situation, but one that could easily turn into something desperately serious. In the event the authorities largely turned a blind eye to the gun-running, and at the Curragh there was actually almost a mutiny amongst some Army officers at the suggestion they might be called upon to fight the Unionists. This in turn lead to alarm amongst the ranks of the Home Rulers, who began to realise that there was a very fair chance that the Home Rule Bill might never become law, and they too took to arms, although with considerably more difficulty, for the authorities were far more diligent in preventing weapons reaching the South. A number of organisations were united in the demand for independence, and prepared to fight for it, but such was the fear of infiltration by Government informers that very few knew that a decision had been taken in the early months of 1916 to promote an uprising in Dublin at Easter. This worked both ways, for while the authorities were certainly taken by surprise when the rebellion began on the morning of the Monday of Easter Week, most of the Anti-Unionists outside the capital were equally unprepared and disorganised.

If the rebels were to stand much chance of success it was essential that Dublin be cut off from the outside world, and the main line stations and other railway installations therefore figured prominently among their objectives. The most vital line of all was that connecting Dublin with the port of Kingstown, and shortly after noon Westland Row and Harcourt Street were both occupied. A suburban train approaching Westland Row was held up at Ringsend, the passengers were forced to get out on to the track, and all but one were led to a small side exit near the station and let go. The exception was a young army cadet, G. F. Mackay. He was blindfolded and taken to Boland's Mill, close by the railway and the Grand Canal, and kept there as a prisoner. The D&SER Works at Grand Canal Street were also taken, and track near Kingstown was ripped up and used as a barricade.

The other three main line termini were attacked but the rebels had a by no means unlimited supply of either men or arms, and although they succeeded in gaining control of Broadstone they failed to take Amiens Street or Kingsbridge. The latter in fact was guarded by a company of soldiers larger than the entire rebel force active in Dublin. As soon as news reached the authorities that the General Post Office had been captured and set up as the rebel headquarters all ordinary trains in and out of Kingsbridge were halted, and commandeered by the military to bring in troops from the Curragh. Within hours thousands had arrived in Dublin while others were assisting the Royal Irish Constabulary in various parts of the South.

Further attempts were made to put Amiens Street out of action. The line at Fairview, $\frac{3}{4}$ mile from the terminus, where the diesel railcar sheds now stand, was blown up, as was a bridge between Donabate and Lusk, but in each case only the down line was affected. Plans had been made to blow up a bridge at Malahide, but the army got wind of the attempt, and the rebels, finding themselves outnumbered by a strongly entrenched force, retired.

There does not seem to have been much effort made to disrupt Great Southern & Western traffic, for no doubt the military were too numerous here too, but on the Midland Great Western, apart from occupying Broadstone, rebels blew up the track at Blanchardstown, four miles to the West, and derailed a cattle train. At Liffey Junction also, where the Broadstone and North Wall lines divided, a light engine was sent off driverless but soon derailed itself without causing any damage.

Whether the track was actually put out of action or not the rebels achieved their object in that by the evening all trains in and out of Dublin stopped running, as did the trams. Initially the civil and military authorities were caught unawares; many army officers and a large section of Dublin society, the Anglo-Irish West Britons, were at Ferryhouse races well outside the city, so that the rebels established a firm grip on the capital. They were lead by Padraic Pearse, a schoolmaster, poet and idealist, and James Connolly. Certainly neither were military men, and they can have had little real hope of defeating the might of the British Army once it had been mobilised against them.

For several days little news of the rebellion reached, or was allowed to reach, the newspapers and the outside world. Practically all the fighting was confined to Dublin but there were limited outbreaks elsewhere. Galway was captured and the line to Dublin "smashed up and all the wires cut". At Clonadadoran in Queens County, 60 yards of the GS&WR Kingsbridge–Waterford line were torn up and the engine and bogie brake of a passenger train derailed. The Dublin & South Eastern Company appears to have suffered the most, for in addition to the attacks on its property in the Dublin area, Wexford also was captured. A workman's train conveying 300 passengers was held up at Enniscorthy, the engine was detached and the occupants of the train had to walk the 13 miles back to Wexford. The signal wires were cut and instruments in the signal-box destroyed. Meanwhile a troop train had arrived at Camolin, ten miles away, the soldiers unaware of the rising.

Exactly what happened next is unclear. According to a contemporary newspaper report a full scale battle developed, complete with an armoured train, *The Enniscorthy Emily*, manned by a "Stout Hibernian", which shelled the rebels after they had unsuccessfully tried to blow up a bridge, and had retired to a hill outside the town. One of the rebels interviewed some time later said that in reality there had been no shelling and no serious fighting as the small company of Sinn Fein rebels had soon realised that they were no match for 300 well-armed soldiers and had quickly retired. The so-called armoured train was no more than an abortive attempt to place a few iron sheets around a locomotive, and the entire affair seems to have been a minor skirmish embroidered into something considerably grander by the flights of fancy of a local newspaperman.

In Dublin the rebels soon gave up their hold on Broadstone and Harcourt Street and for a short while a full service of trains to and from the latter station was resumed, but was then prohibited by the military. Otherwise Dublin remained without trains and trams for as long as the rising continued. Reinforcements for the British Army were hastily summoned from England and as Easter Week wore on the rebels were forced back on the defensive. Without a general uprising they could have no hope of success. Things might have been different if a shipload of arms from Germany had been landed on the coast of Kerry as intended. The ship, the *Aud*, arrived on time and a group of men from Dingle had set off by train for Tralee where they were to receive them, but a series of misfortunes, one of them the sudden appearance of Sir Roger Casement, a former British civil servant and a leader of the rebels, who came ashore from a German submarine and was almost immediately arrested, ensured that the British got the arms first. So the Dingle men returned by the morning train next day empty-handed.

The fighting all over Dublin was fierce, but at the same time a sense of chivalry prevailed, well illustrated by the experiences of five carters employed by the LNWR at North Wall. On Easter Monday they were driving a convoy of ammunition wagons to a barracks on the other side of the city when they and their military escort were attacked. The newspaper report of the incident gives only the bare facts which are that although the attack was repulsed the convoy was under siege until the Thursday and that a number of soldiers were either killed or wounded.

It is recorded that the five carters remained unscathed, that they were relieved by five others, volunteers, at noon on the Tuesday, and that these in turn were relieved by five more at noon on the Wednesday. Eventually more soldiers got through to the convoy and it was able to reach its destination. It seems to be rather more than good fortune that not only should none of the carters have received any injury, but that they should also twice have been relieved, while the soldiers among them were being shot at and hit without any military assistance being able to get through to them for three days. The ordeal of the carters was not over when the convoy gained the barracks, for while walking home they were arrested by other soldiers and held at Dublin Castle until they could establish their identity. Finally back at the docks they were approached by Sinn Feiners and asked to join in the fight, but the carters said they were "not fighting men" and they were allowed to go.

The attitude generally of the working people in Dublin at the time was that the rebellion was a great inconvenience; it meant a week's loss of wages for which it was no compensation to be told that the rising was all for their ultimate benefit and that of future generations, particularly as it was obvious that the rebels had no hope of winning. To them it made little difference whether their employer was English or Irish, and although there were some trade unionists, supporters of Connolly, who either took part or were sympathetic to the struggle, the majority wanted no part of it. At the time James Larkin was in the USA raising funds for the Trade Union movement and for the Irish Republicans and the Citizen Army, but had become so embroiled in the American labour movement that eventually he got himself jailed as a "criminal anarchist", and did not return to Ireland until 1923. In England the rising was seen as a stab in the back, and to a nation where most families had members fighting and dying in France and Flanders it must have seemed particularly cruel that others should be shot down in the streets of a city they had always considered to be part of the United Kingdom by men they regarded as fellow Britishers.

On Sunday, April 30, with all hope of help from outside gone and many of their number dead or wounded, Connolly amongst the latter, the rebels surrendered. The young cadet who had been captured within a few minutes of the start of the rising was released. In his account of his captivity in Boland's Mill he recorded that he had been well treated by the rebels, six of whom had been killed. The man in command of the Mill was a lecturer born in America, Eamonn DeValera, and cadet Mackay remembered his words as he surrendered, "Shoot me if you want but look after my men".

Apart from the brief resumption of services at Harcourt Street no trains had run in Dublin for a week and the city was in severe straits. Food was low and drastic action had to be taken to get life back to normal. On the day before the capitulation an officer had managed to get through by road to Belfast, which had remained peaceful, if tense, and special vans containing 10,000 loaves of bread were hastily attached to the 7.30am passenger train from Belfast to Drogheda. At Drogheda the vans, together with others containing further provisions for the beleagured city, were made up into a special train and taken on to Clontarf, as near as the GNR could get to Amiens Street, and from there the food was distributed throughout Dublin.

Gradually services were restored. The day after the rebellion ended, May 1st, the Cork Mail trains again ran to and from Kingsbridge, and from the 8th all services on the GS&WR were gradually restored. The total loss suffered by the company was estimated at £21,000. The GNR, which lost a similar sum in receipts, also restarted normal services on May 8. The MGWR got its day and night mail trains, with their connections, running on the 8th but it was a little while longer before the full timetable at Broadstone was back to normal. The Dublin tramways had suffered severe dislocation and a certain amount of track, overhead wiring and one or two cars had been damaged, particularly at the principal city terminus outside the GPO. In the later stages of the fighting the GPO, at which the declaration of independence had been read by Pearse, and many of the surrounding buildings, had been heavily shelled and the whole area presented a scene of considerable devastation. Nevertheless trams began to run again on Wednesday, May 4, and by the 8th a full service once more was in operation.

The Dublin & South Eastern took rather longer to get back to normal. The Loop line bridge across the Liffey had been damaged by shells fired at the rebels in the Custom House from a ship, the SS *Helga*, anchored in the river, and although the 9am and 3pm Westland Row to Wexford trains recommenced running on May 3, the military remained in strict control of the line for a number of days afterwards. Passengers to and from Kingstown were required to carry permits and as late as May 10 four people were removed at Kingstown from a Dublin to Wexford train and told that it was not sufficient just to have tickets and they had only themselves to blame for their predicament.

Meanwhile the leaders of the rebellion had been tried by court martial and and sentenced to death, while the men who served under them were imprisoned, principally in England. Many prominent people on both sides of the Irish Sea, politicians, churchmen and writers, protested at the death sentences but the Government took the line that the rebels were not patriots fighting for their country's freedom but citizens of the United Kingdom and therefore traitors. De Valera escaped the death sentence possibly by virtue of his American birth, but at intervals during May, and amidst mounting resentment from the ordinary Irish people who until now had felt little involvement with the rebel leaders' cause, the rest of them were executed by firing squads. The appeals for reprieve were particularly strong in Connolly's case, on account of the wound he had suffered in his leg during the fighting and which rendered him incapable of standing, but they were of no avail.

In the long run it may be said that James Connolly did not die in vain, for independence was achieved and the working class has gradually edged nearer to an acceptable standard of living. Yet one feels a resentment that his life should have been cut short. There is no clear answer to the question why this Trades Union leader, who was something of an intellectual, should have found himself at the head of a rebel army, but the consensus of opinion seems to be that he had grown so frustrated at his apparent lack of success in improving the lot of the working class that he could see no other solution. What would have happened if there had been no rising or no executions is a matter of conjecture, but Connolly was sorely missed during the troubled years from 1916 to the end of the Civil War. It is just possible that with his deep concern and involvement for the Belfast workers, Roman Catholic and Protestant, he might have kept Ireland united, had the British had the sense to give him the chance to try. Very likely they would not, for Carson and the Unionists had a great deal of support on the right in Britain. Yet Belfast finished up with the one thing it had pledged never to accept, its own Parliament separate to a degree from Westminster.

Connolly is as greatly revered today as he ever was, although the Church is still a little wary of his left wing brand of Socialism. His book *Labour in Irish History*, first published in 1910, has been reprinted many times and for anyone interested in the union movement in Ireland, and other fields touching on it, up to the beginning of the 20th century, it is required reading.

Claims for compensation for damage suffered during Easter Week were filed by a number of the railway companies. The GS&WR for instance, told Maryborough Quarter Sessions that the Clonadadoran derailment had resulted in the tearing up of twelve 30ft rails, 66 sleepers and 208 bolts, apart from the severe shaking up suffered by the train. It was decided to award the GS&WR in all £5,500, the MGWR £5,000 and the D&SER £3,000, these sums being for damage sustained as a result of military action; but they probably contained an element of compensation for lost traffic receipts, for the D&SER estimated that the damage to its property by the Sinn Fein and the military amounted to no more than £2,000.

CHAPTER FOUR

From 1916 Onwards

WHILST THE WAR in Europe continued Ireland settled back to a sort of peace, but in the waters of the Irish Sea and the Atlantic it was a different story. German submarines were everywhere and sometimes came so close in that they could be seen by watchers at coastguard stations and elsewhere around the coast. Much the most notorious of the U-Boat sinkings was that of the *Lusitania* off Kinsale, in 1915, and a memorial to the victims stands close by the railway station at Cobh where many of the bodies were brought and from which the Cunard liners used to sail, but there were two other much less well-known disasters at this time. Both involved cross-channel steamers, one the result of bad weather, the other of German submarine action.

On the night of November 3, 1916, the LNWR steamer TSS *Connemara* had just set out from Greenore bound for Holyhead and was heading into a south-westerly gale when she was struck amidships by the collier *Retriever*, sailing from Garston to Newry. The *Retriever* was showing no lights as no one had dared venture on deck to rekindle them after the wind had blown them out, and the force of the collision was such that both ships sank almost at once. All but one of the *Retriever*'s crew perished, and every soul on board the *Connemara*, 51 passengers, four railwaymen and 31 crew, were drowned. The only survivors, apart from the solitary member of the *Retriever*'s crew, were a number of cattle, penned on the deck of the *Connemara*, who struggled free as the ship went down and managed to swim three miles to the shore.

The worst disaster ever to befall an Irish cross-channel ship overtook the City of Dublin mail steamer *Leinster* on Friday, October 11, 1918. She was one of the boats regularly employed on the Holyhead–Kingstown run and had already been attacked by enemy vessels and aircraft, the most recent occasion being the previous Monday. She sailed as usual on the early morning run from Kingstown on a fine, clear day, though the sea was fairly rough, the storm of the previous day having not quite abated. A short distance out she passed her sister ship, the *Ulster*, inward bound from Holyhead, and less than 15 minutes later the *Leinster* was struck amidships by a torpedo. Some of those on deck claimed to have seen the wake of an earlier one which had missed, but if there were two the second followed in such rapid succession that the captain had no time to change course.

The *Leinster* began to settle by the head and it was immediately obvious that she was going to sink. Hardly had the order to abandon ship been given and the first lifeboats reached the water when a second torpedo hit the *Leinster* and, in the words of one survivor, "The ship was shattered like matchwood". Her funnels were blown into the air, she heeled over, and still within the sight of the *Ulster*, she sank.

There seems to have been little panic aboard the *Leinster* in her last moments, probably because events overtook the passengers so quickly that there was little time for any sort of action. A number of boats managed to get clear of the ship, but many of these were overloaded and were swamped by the heavy seas and overturned. The radio operator had just time to send out an SOS which was picked up by ships and shore stations in the vicinity, and in less than an hour survivors were being pulled out of the water. Some 200 were brought back to Kingstown, whilst a few were taken to Holyhead.

Once it had been determined that there was no one left alive in the water the rescuers set about collecting the dead, and eventually these totalled over 500, amongst them being the captain, who had actually survived the sinking but had been very badly injured and had slipped from the grasp of a sailor on one of the rescue ships just as he was being pulled from the water. Others who died were the father of George Wild, CME of the D&SER, and all but one of 21 Post Office sorters employed on the *Leinster*, one of the torpedoes exploding in the sorting room and instantly killing most of the occupants. One sorter left a widow and ten children, and there were so many tragic stories, of newly married husbands searching for their brides amongst the rows of bodies laid out along the pier at Kingstown, children drowning whilst one or other of their parents survived, and similar tragedies that reading the accounts of the sinking, even though it all happened over 50 years ago, is still harrowing.

Within a month the war was over, and although more than one Irish Sea steamer was sunk during World War II and over 100 people died in the *Princess Victoria* in 1953, there has never been a disaster to equal that which befell the *Leinster* in 1918.

It is rather difficult to imagine a world where prices remain stable year after year, yet such was the case throughout most of the 19th century and the first decade and a half of the 20th. The war ended this and by late 1916 the cost of living was beginning to rise significantly. In November of that year the National Union of Railwaymen put in for a "War Bonus" of 10s per week. Figures do not convey much on their own and one may best demonstrate the standard of living a railwayman enjoyed (or suffered) by quoting from a pamphlet issued in 1913 by the Railway Clerks' Association. At that time an experienced clerk earned around 35s per week. The RCA was pressing for a scale giving up to £150 per annum and if it had been granted at the time a married man with three children would have had no money for beer or cigarettes, no joining a club, no going to football matches or to dances, the cinema, or the music hall with his wife, no sweets for the children, not even at Christmas or birthdays; just enough for the rent, food, clothes, the bare necessities. That was how he would have lived if he had got the rise; but he didn't.

The GS&WR recognised that the men had a case but said it did not feel that it could offer more than 2s. To this the men replied that if the companies had not got the money then the Government must provide it, and if it was not prepared to do so they would strike. The *Irish Times*, a paper not normally very sympathetic towards organised labour, this time was firmly on the railwaymen's side. "In normal times their wages are low enough", it said, "the position of the majority of Irish railwaymen is now much worse," and it went on to declare that the State should take over the railways as had already happened in England. The men's demands were widely supported throughout the country and in December 1916, the Irish Railways were placed in the charge of a Railway Executive Committee. This committee consisted of six members, the Under-Secretary of State for Ireland, and one representative from each of the five largest railway companies. The Board of Trade presided over the wage negotiations and, a few days before Christmas, the men found themselves with a very welcome bonus of 7s, not as much as they had asked for but considerably more than the companies had been prepared to give.

This was only the first of a long series of rises which by 1919 totalled 33s for every railwayman over the age of 18. So most of them had more than doubled their wages in five years, but as the cost of living had gone up by 125 per cent in the same period they had simply been running at great speed in order to remain in the same place. Neither did the companies derive any benefit from this situation. The Railway Executive Committee pegged passenger fares and goods rates at an artificially low level with the consequence that the GS&WR, for example, which in 1913 had a wage bill of £549,235 and a net income of £682,803, was faced in 1919 with a wage bill three times that of 1913 and a net loss of £407,266. Overall the Irish railways suffered a deficit in 1919 in excess of £1m. The Edwardian days of comfortable prosperity were gone for good.

In August 1919, Westminster set up the Ministry of Transport, and the following month a senior official from that Ministry, H. G. Burgess, was appointed Director-General of Transport for Ireland. He was given absolute control of the railways and while there was no mention of lower rates and fares, he was given liberty to raise both as he saw fit. Burgess also had authority to compensate the companies for the losses they had incurred while under Government control.

Simultaneously the Government proposed that a joint negotiating board, consisting of five general managers from the companies, three representatives of the National Union of Railwaymen, and two of the Associated Society of Locomotive Engineers and Firemen, should be established and be responsible for negotiating all conditions of employment as well as wages and hours. When one considers the attitude of the authorities to the Trades Unions a mere six years earlier during the Dublin Tramways strike, one realises just how much the sufferings of the men and their families in those years had achieved in so short a time. J. H. Thomas of the NUR, a Welshman and a Westminster MP, who was prominent in Ireland at this time, declared that the Government's offer was the first real step towards giving the men a say in the running of the railways. At the same time he scotched the suggestion that legislation should be introduced to outlaw strikes. Such a bill, he said, would be the best way of ensuring that a national strike would take place immediately.

There was now a slight but definite improvement in the living standards of

GSWR single No 36 (built 1848) which is now preserved at
Kent station, Cork, seen at the Stockton & Darlington
centenary celebrations in 1925.   [*Sport & General*]

MGWR Atock 2-4-0 with "fly-away" cab roof in the heart of
Connemara on the Galway-Clifden line.
                          [*Locomotive Publishing Co*]

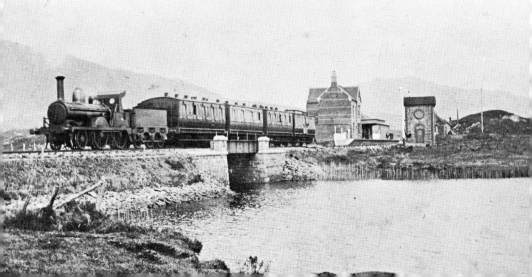

GSWR McDonnell 4-4-0 No 10 of 1880 at the turn of the
century.   [LPC

GSWR rail-motor 0-6-4T No 92 of 1881 at Inchicore.   [LPC

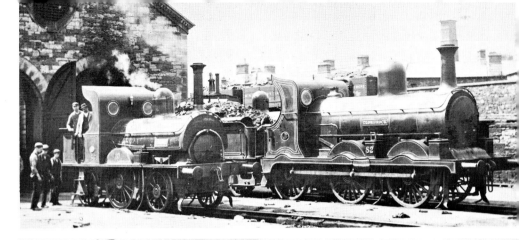

Top: Atock 0-6-0 No 82 *Clonbrock* (1892–1963) and an old
2-2-2T at MGWR Broadstone shed. *[LPC*

Above: GNR 4-4-0T No 7 (1885–1920), one of the first
engines built at Dundalk, with a push-and-pull train around
1910. *[LPC*

Below: Listowel & Ballybunion monorail Kitson locomotive
at Ballybunion station. *[LPC*

Dublin & Blessington steam tram No 6. *[LPC*

A GNR Hill of Howth tram at Howth station on March 21, 1954. *[N. W. Sprinks*

Giants Causeway terminus with open electric car on the
left and closed one with trailers on the right. *[H. C. Casserley*

The GNR Fintona horse tram seen leaving Fintona Junction.
[H. C. Casserley

Above: Cork & Muskerry Light Railway 4-4-0T No 7 *Peake* (1898–1935) threading the outskirts of Cork.   *[LPC*

Below: Clogher Valley Railway 0-4-2T No 3 *Blackwater* (1887–1942) at Aughnacloy.   *[H.C. Casserley*

Foot: Schull & Skibereen 4-4-0T No 4 *Erin* (1888–1954) in GSR days.   *[P. Ransome-Wallis*

Former Cork, Blackrock & Passage 2-4-2T of 1899 working
on the Cavan & Leitrim section in CIE days.
[P. Ransome-Wallis

County Donegal Railway scene at Castlefinn.

[P. B. Whitehouse

NCC narrow-gauge 2-4-2T No 43 (1920–54) at Ballycastle
with two corridor coaches.
[H. C. Casserley

railwaymen, particularly amongst the lower paid, who were getting 240 per cent more than in 1914. The wages bill for the railways had gone up by a staggering amount between 1913 and 1920, from just over £1½m to not far short of £6m. Despite this the GS&WR managed to pay a dividend of 5 per cent, but only because the Government granted it compensation amounting to £1,043,000, enabling the company to convert a loss of around £400,000 into a net profit equal to that achieved in 1913. It was obvious, however, that the railways would have to raise their charges very considerably and in August 1920, passenger fares went up by 33½ per cent, and on September 1 goods rates were advanced by 120 per cent.

At this point we must leave the railways for a while and consider what was happening in the country at large. The Armistice in November 1918, served only to increase tension in Ireland. Sinn Fein, which in 1916 commanded the support of hardly more than a handful of idealists and fanatics, had so gained in popularity following the uprising and the execution of its leaders that in the December 1918, elections it captured 73 of the 105 Irish seats. These 73 refused to go to Westminster and set up their own Parliament in Dublin, Dail Eireann, with DeValera as Prime Minister or Taoiseach. It need hardly be said that this Parliament was not recognised by Britain, and many of its members were either arrested or forced into hiding. DeValera himself was sent to Lincoln Jail but a daring rescue attempt, organised by two of his supporters, Harry Boland and Michael Collins, succeeded and he got away to the United States. There, among the Americans of Irish descent and many others, he found considerable sympathy for the cause and was able to raise 5½m dollars to finance the fight for Irish independence.

The nation-wide rebellion which Pearse and Connolly had been hoping for in 1916 was now raging. To put it down the British Government recruited, from dubious sources, a volunteer force which it dressed in a make-shift uniform of black trousers and khaki tunics and sent over to Ireland. A great many savage acts were committed by this force, the Black-and-Tans, against the civilian population on the pretext that it was in league with the rebels, and inevitably there were retaliations.

The Irish population was now almost to a man united in the struggle for independence and the railwaymen played their part. On May 25, 1920, a group of LNWR employees at North Wall, Dublin, refused to unload munitions. They were supported by railwaymen all over the country and a ban was placed on trains carrying British troops. Thousands were suspended from work but the ban continued. On October 15 the Government announced that the railway companies would be held to their agreement to give Government traffic priority. If they did not comply with this order the lines would be closed and motors would be used instead. At the end of December the railwaymen met and reluctantly agreed to lift their ban.

Although there was some Sinn Fein support in Belfast, the north-east of the country was predominantly Unionist and was as determined to remain within Great Britain as the rest of Ireland was to get out. It was alleged that employers in the North refused to take on men who were known to be either members of or sympathetic to Sinn Fein (in effect most Roman Catholics),

I.R.—C

and in retaliation Sinn Fein called for a boycott of Belfast. The GNR bore the brunt of this and lost a great deal of goods traffic; in the riots and disorders then occurring in and around Belfast a number of goods wagons belonging to the GNR were either damaged or destroyed.

All over the country the population was actively opposed to British rule. There were frequent disturbances in the streets, police stations and army barracks were attacked, and Black-and-Tan patrols ambushed. If the attackers were not either killed or captured on the spot it was virtually impossible for the authorities to trace them, for almost any able-bodied male member of the population might have been responsible. The few Irishmen in the South who were content with British rule did well to keep their opinions to themselves. When the parcels office at Clonmel station was raided by the IRA the stationmaster telephoned the police barracks and within five minutes the station was surrounded by a large force of Black-and-Tans. The raiders, however, slipped away, and some months after the signing of the Treaty between Britain and Ireland the unfortunate stationmaster was called before an IRA court-martial and asked to account for his action. He was known to be a keen "company man" and was able to prove that he was motivated solely by his concern for the property of the GS&WR rather than by any political feelings. He was let off with the advice that he would do well in the future to contain his zeal, and could consider himself a lucky man, for the penalty imposed by the IRA for "assisting the enemy" was death and in a number of instances it was carried out.

In an attempt to restrict the movements of the population an evening curfew was imposed throughout the country at the beginning of 1921, and consequently suburban rail traffic in Dublin, Belfast and Cork was severely limited. For train crews it meant considerable hardship; if they arrived at their destination after the curfew had begun they were not allowed home but had to sleep on railway premises, either at a station or, in the case of footplate crews, inside the engine shed. Nevertheless they were expected to put in a full day's work the next day.

By the middle of 1921 it was obvious that if Ireland was to be subdued by force virtually every man, woman and child would have to be detained indefinitely. On June 22 King George V, on a visit to Belfast, declined to read the speech which had been prepared for him, and with the help of General Smuts, the South African Premier, who had once fought against Britain for his country's independence and had sympathy for the Irish cause, he composed a new one appealing for peace. Nineteen days later the British Prime Minister, Lloyd George, invited DeValera to London for discussions.

At first there was little progress and DeValera returned to Dublin, but towards the end of 1921 a further attempt was made, and on December 5 the Irish representatives signed a Peace Treaty. Under its terms Ireland was to have its own Parliament whilst remaining within the Commonwealth, and as the Unionists in the North absolutely refused to be ruled from Dublin, the Six Counties of Down, Antrim, Londonderry, Tyrone, Fermanagh and Armagh would for the time being remain part of Great Britain, with a provincial capital in Belfast.

Among a great many other complications the setting up of a border meant that five railways, the Great Northern, the County Donegal, the Londonderry, Lough Swilly & Letterkenny, the Sligo, Leitrim & Northern Counties, and the Dundalk, Newry & Greenore would be operating in two countries, so that customs and immigration facilities would have to be set up where the lines crossed the border. In all this occurred at 18 frontier points, 14 of them on the GNR. There were places where the GNR crossed from Northern Ireland to the South and back again within a very short distance, and the Clones to Cavan branch found itself in a farcical predicament for it passed from Southern to Northern Ireland, then back to the South, returned to the North, then finally back to the South, all within some five miles. At each crossing passengers had to submit to customs examinations and would have probably found it quicker to walk.

The idea of dividing the country was *anathema* to most Irishmen, and the delegation which had signed the Treaty returned to Dublin from the London talks with the firm impression that such a solution was only a temporary one, and would shortly be reviewed. Just what was in Lloyd George's mind has been hotly debated ever since. He has been accused of saying one thing to the Southern Irish and another to the Northerners, allowing the former to assume that the country would eventually be united, and the latter that the Protestant North would never in fact be handed over to the Roman Catholics in Dublin. Lloyd George was himself in a dilemma. His administration was a coalition, and whilst the Liberals in it were by tradition and inclination in favour of Home Rule, the Conservatives sided with the Unionists. Lloyd George took the only way really open to him, hoping, as politicians so often have to, that time would provide a solution.

Government control of the railways ended on August 15, 1921. Negotiations had been going on for some months over the amount of compensation to be awarded and on August 9 the Government said that unless agreement was reached quickly the compensation bill would be dropped. The Great Northern Railway held out the longest, but eventually settled for £670,799. The GS&WR got £878,458, and the Dublin & South Eastern, the Midland Great Western, the Northern Counties, the Cork, Bandon & South Coast, and the Belfast & County Down, £950,743 between them. The remaining 26 minor railways shared £500,000.

At the end of August a tribunal met in Dublin and put forward a number of proposals to improve working conditions on the railways. The most important were that no one should work more than eight hours a day and that those eight hours should be continuous. Any overtime must be paid at a rate of not less than 25 per cent over the normal. Until then there had been no uniform wage scale or conditions of employment on the railways, although the unions had been negotiating towards this end. Now a porter was to receive between 43s and 60s per week, a guard up to 65s, and an engine driver up to 90s. All of these worked a 48hr week.

Ireland at last had gained its independence, but the rejoicing in Dublin was by no means universal. DeValera, who had not gone to London for the second series of talks, denounced the Treaty on the grounds that the oath of allegiance to the Crown remained, and that the country was now divided and part of it remained under British rule. He forced a division in the Dail, and although the Treaty conditions were accepted nearly half the TDs (MPs) 57 to 64, voted against them. The Anti-Treaty faction refused to recognise the peace settlement and the IRA split into two, one-half becoming the army of the new Government, and the other, led by DeValera, an outlaw organisation opposing it. The Anti-Treaty forces occupied the Four Courts beside the Liffey in Dublin, and on May 28, 1922, the first shots in the Irish Civil War were fired.

CHAPTER FIVE

Civil War

ONE MIGHT ASK why Irishmen, having fought the British for so long, now needed to fight each other. They had not gained everything but they had achieved a great deal. Perhaps this was precisely the reason. Eamonn DeValera was 40 years old; for the last ten years he had schemed and fought for a free Ireland; he had seen his closest friends executed in 1916 and had himself barely escaped a similar fate; he had been imprisoned by the British Government and then accepted by it as leader of the Irish people and invited to negotiate for their independence. Yet in the end not all the Irish people were free of British rule and each of them had still to swear allegiance to an alien monarch. It must have seemed to DeValera that the Irish cause had once again been betrayed, and not this time by the British, but by the Irishmen who had been content to accept less than total independence. Both factions were composed of decent, sincere men who felt that their cause was the right one, and this, if anything, made their determination to achieve power the stronger.

The railways had suffered relatively little disruption and damage during 1916 and the Black-and-Tan period, but now they found themselves in the thick of the fighting. The Anti-Treaty forces were well aware that by cutting communications they would make it virtually impossible for the Government to retain effective control of the country, and in this they were no doubt influenced by the events of the Russian Civil War, which was at that time just coming to an end. The vast wastes of Eastern Russia may have appeared totally unlike the compact green countryside of Ireland, yet there existed in both countries a dependence on rail communications linking sparsely populated rural areas, and the severance of these was one of the primary objectives in both campaigns.

While few of the companies went completely unscathed, the largest, the

GS&WR, came off the worst, the majority of the actions taking place within its territory. Between June 28, 1922, and January 5, 1923, its permanent way was damaged on 375 occasions, roughly two incidents per day, and in addition bridges, signal-boxes, various other installations and buildings, and a considerable amount of rolling stock, were put out of action. The very much smaller D&SER fared scarcely better, the locomotive department being particularly hard hit; nearly a third of its complement of 60 locomotives suffered damage of varying severity. At the best of times the D&SER had hardly been in the front rank as far as adequate motive power was concerned, and by the beginning of 1923 it had sunk to a parlous state. The worst was yet to come, the most crippling blow descending upon it during the last few weeks of hostilities, when it was already clear that the Anti-Treaty cause was a lost one.

At 10 o'clock on the morning of January 20, 1923, a large force attacked the station at Palace East in County Wexford. Although the junction for the Bagenalstown, Waterford and Macmine lines, Palace East was normally a sleepy sort of place, the arrival and departure of a train being something of an event. The raiders, however, had chosen their time well, for the station was occupied by two goods trains, the 6.30am from Waterford in charge of an 0-6-0, No 51, and a cattle special from Macmine with 4-4-0 No 68 *Rathcoole* at the head. The latter, with her sister No 67 *Rathmore*, was the company's most modern express engine, having been built by Beyer Peacock in 1905. They were accustomed to much grander duties than cattle specials, but because of the emergency and the disruption to normal workings locomotives found themselves performing a variety of unlikely tasks, and it was sheer bad luck for the D&SER that *Rathcoole* should be pressed into duty on the cattle special that day.

The raiders warned the railway staff to keep well out of the way and then set about the task of destruction. They first uncoupled the cattle trucks from No 51's train, leaving the engine attached to the remaining goods wagons; then they uncoupled *Rathcoole* and ran her back in the direction of Macmine. The regulators of the two engines were opened wide and each engine was set off along the single track towards the other. They met at a combined speed of 40mph with an almighty crash; clouds of steam erupted but, remarkably, both held the rails. They were however, considerably damaged, particularly about the frames and motion, and had to be towed away by the breakdown gangs which reached them many hours later.

There was nothing which could be done while the emergency continued, and the 0-6-0 was sent to Dublin and *Rathcoole* to Macmine, where she languished for some nine months. Later she was moved to Bray where she was inspected and her fate deliberated over. The possibility of having her repaired by the GNR at Dundalk was mooted, but it was eventually decided that the damage to both engines was so extensive that it would be cheaper to replace them with new ones, and although *Rathcoole* was still intact when the D&SER was absorbed by the GSR both she and No 51 were never steamed again. *Rathcoole's* sister, No 67, had a long life and as CIE No 454 was the last D&SER passenger tender engine at work until her withdrawal in 1949.

A considerable number of Anglo-Irish landowners had settled in Counties Wexford and Waterford over the years but despite, or perhaps because of, this, the area had always been a centre of dissent. Any uprising had seen Wexford and Waterford men in the thick of it and 1922–3 was no exception. One railway bridge, No 367, which crossed the Enniscorthy–New Ross road near Palace East, was destroyed 13 times during the Civil War, being blown up once and burnt on the other occasions.

A rather remarkable incident and the last major one on the railways took place on February 23, 1923. The afternoon Mail from Waterford to Dublin had just crossed the much-abused bridge, No 367, when it was held up. The passengers were got out, with their luggage, two 30ft rails were removed from the track some distance behind the train, and it was then set back. In most cases the men who carried out the raids on the railways knew exactly what they were doing and there is not much doubt that they numbered railwaymen or ex-railwaymen amongst their ranks. But on this occasion they miscalculated. The rear carriage, a six-wheeler, was the first to reach the gap, but such was its speed that it jumped across and landed safely on the rails beyond. Its fellows, also six-wheelers, followed suit, then the tender, and finally the engine. This was an 0–6–0, No 50, and without the encumbrance of a bogie and given the athletic prowess of its train might have been expected to follow the latter's example. It very nearly did; the rear, and then the middle driving wheels came down safely on the rails but the leading ones just missed, and such was the speed at which the train was now travelling that it ran on for a mile before stopping. None of the vehicles came to any harm, but the two derailed engine wheels caused as much damage to the track as the derailing of the entire train would have done, the rails being completely ripped up behind them.

The Waterford to Macmine Junction line was under almost continual assault during the latter part of the emergency despite the fact that it was of no particular strategic importance, there being alternative routes between Waterford and Wexford and Waterford and Dublin. The probable explanation of its popularity with the wreckers was that Anti-Treaty forces happened to be particularly thick on the ground in this part of the world.

One of the redeeming features of the campaign against the railways was the almost total absence of loss of life amongst passengers and railway staff. Although many trains were derailed the rebels made it a rule that they were first stopped and emptied of all their occupants and only then sent on to their destruction. Usually one of the raiders was able to set the locomotive in motion and then jump off and it was only rarely that the crew were forced to assist. Occasionally something would go wrong and there were instances of trains being wrecked without prior warning. One such occurred at Castlebellingham on the GNR main line, 47 miles north of Dublin.

The chain of events leading up to it began soon after seven o'clock on the night of December 20, 1922 with the halting of the 5.30pm mail train from Belfast, due at Amiens Street at 7.55pm. The newspaper account of the incident states that the "points" were set against the train but one assumes this meant the signals. The passengers, post office sorters, and the railway staff were taken off the train and it was then reversed on to the down line, derailed, sprinkled with petrol and set alight. At this point a heavy goods train of 68 wagons approached on the down line and collided with the burning express. Fortunately the latter was travelling very slowly and neither the footplate crew, the guard, nor the eleven soldiers guarding military stores in some of the rear wagons were hurt. The raiders by now had disappeared, and the soldiers, assisted by reinforcements from Ardee and Dundalk, set about extinguishing the fire. Just how much damage was done is difficult to estimate. The newspaper account claimed that it was so extensive that it could not be estimated, but the reporters of the time were never averse to adding a few embellishments to a good story. It was stated, for example, that a practically new dining coach costing over £2,000 was destroyed, but the newest dining car running on the GNR at the time was six years old, and there is no record in the GNR books of it or any others disappearing from service in 1922.

A couple of weeks later another incident on the GNR main line, in a cutting at Raheny on the outskirts of Dublin early on the morning of January 6, 1923, resulted in slight injuries to seven passengers, and although these were, strictly speaking, unintentional, the wreckers did nothing to prevent them. They had held up and derailed a goods engine, and on being told by its driver that a passenger train was due, said that he might take a red lamp and signal to it. Hardly had he done so when the passenger train, a local from Howth hauled by one of the then new T2 4–4–2Ts, rounded a bend and struck the derailed engine. The passenger train kept the rails and must have been travelling fairly slowly as the driver was able to pull it up within 50 yards. There was a certain amount of damage to the offside of the engine and considerably more to the three bogie coaches, their sides being stove in and the panelling shattered.

In the half light of the January dawn the nearby residents who, hearing the crash, had dashed down into the cutting, must have thought that some of the passengers had suffered frightful injuries, for there were two small children, at least one woman and a number of men covered in blood struggling to get out of the wreckage. In fact the injuries looked much worse than they were, being mostly superficial cuts caused by flying glass, and no one had to be detained in hospital for very long. Naturally this affair did the rebel cause no good at all, and the probable explanation for the failure to prevent it lies in the state the campaign had reached; the Government forces had established control virtually throughout the country and the Anti-Treaty faction was all but defeated.

The Raheny incident was not quite the only one in which rail passengers found themselves in some peril. On the MGWR a month earlier there had been one which produced a statement by the Government and produced considerable dramatic licence in the press. The evening mail train from the west was brought to a halt at Liffey Junction, a fairly routine occurrence, but instead of shortly getting the right-away the driver and firemen found themselves looking down the barrels of a number of pistols held by masked men. They were forced off the footplate and the front coaches of the train were sprinkled with petrol, the passengers having first been invited to alight and get into the rear coach. The guard was instructed to uncouple this but before he could do so the train, by some misunderstanding, began to move.

Naturally the passengers were alarmed and made haste to jump out of the the rear coach before it cleared the platform. This they mostly managed to do, no one coming to any harm apart from a lady who had some front teeth broken and a gentleman from Ballina who was "severely shaken". Three or four lady passengers remained in the train however, the front coaches of which were by now "blazing fiercely". Fortunately help was at hand as the driver, who had slipped off the footplate on the side away from the platform, sprinted along beside the engine unobserved by the raiders, leapt back aboard and brought the train to a halt outside Broadstone station. A Government Minister in a statement made the following day said that but for the driver's prompt action the passengers would all have been burnt to death, which was not strictly true, as the fire in fact had failed to gain a hold. Damage was confined to two compartments of the leading coach, and the fire had practic- ally gone out of its own accord by the time the train stopped. None of which detracts from the driver's resourcefulness, for whatever the severity of the fire the consequences of the train careering down the steep incline into Broad- stone might have been most unpleasant.

I have mentioned earlier that there were a number of railwaymen in the ranks of the Anti-Treaty forces. Some of them took an active part in opera- tions against the Government and there was at least one occasion when it was known that they paid with their lives. Three young employees of the GS&WR, a goods clerk and two engine cleaners from Inchicore, did so one night on the outskirts of Dublin. They were carrying a mine, intending to set up an ambush on the Naas road, when it exploded; two of them were literally blown to pieces, and the third died almost immediately. He was still alive when found, but apparently the only comfort anyone could offer was to ask him which hospital he preferred to be taken to.

The penalty imposed on anyone convicted of actions against the railways, whilst always severe, varied considerably. A man who held up a train near Nenagh was given 12 years penal servitude, whilst elsewhere on the GS&WR seven men belonging to a column which had been responsible for derailing two engines from Kildare Shed at Cherryville, in an attempt to disrupt the entire system, were tried, found guilty, and summarily shot.

The last attack of any significance against railway property was on March 23, 1923, and on April 30 a cease fire was agreed. An election followed and the Anti-Treaty party secured 44 seats. This time the Government were taking no chances and once again DeValera found himself in jail. Now there was no one to get him out. Michael Collins, in many people's eyes the most romantic figure of the Black-and-Tan and Civil War period, had become commander of the Government forces opposing DeValera and had been killed in an ambush during the early part of the war.

The question arises as to how effective the campaign against the railways was. Its purpose, to prevent troop movements and communications, was quite clear. There seems to have been no overall detailed plan but rather a hope that the cumulative effect of the actions in various areas would achieve the desired end. As has already been suggested the raiders were generally well disciplined and tried to avoid causing injury to passengers and railway employees. No doubt this attitude stemmed partly from humanitarian considerations, but there was also an element of public relations. The Anti-Treaty faction was always in the minority and needed all the public support it could muster; derailing and blowing up trains with the passengers still in them would hardly have helped in this direction. Unfortunately in any war situation the maladjusted and lunatic fringe appears more reasonable than it does in normal conditions, and as the war dragged on there were occasions when this element seemed to be gaining the ascendancy. Towards the end one cannot escape the conclusion that sometimes trains were derailed for no better reason than the satisfying of someone's destructive urge. Some railwaymen lost their lives and there were instances of unnecessary shootings by both sides.

The closest the Anti-Treaty forces came to achieving their objective was on the GS&WR. By November, 1922, a third of its mileage was closed down owing to war damage. There was widespread redundancy amongst railwaymen due to the lack of traffic and matters came to a head when the NUR called a strike in the middle of October. The union said that all workers should be paid for a six-day week, but the GS&WR claimed that there was not sufficient work for everyone and that it was up to the company to decide how many men were needed. The strike mostly affected the Dublin area, virtually cutting off the capital from the South, and by early November had spread to Naas and Sallins. It ended on November 13, after the NUR had agreed to offers by the company to provide full work for everyone for the time being, and to re-employ those men who had been declared redundant.

In an effort to provide some sort of protection for railway property a number of armoured trains were fitted out and used by the Railway Defence and Maintenance Corps under the command of Major John Russell in the south-western part of the country, but their presence seemed to goad the rebel forces into greater, rather than lesser, activity. A variety of locomotives powered the trains, amongst them being a former Webb 2–4–2T which the D&SER had bought from the LNWR in 1902. It was sent down to Kerry where it received the name *Fag-a-ballagh*, ("Get out of the way"). Its armour-plating was removed when the emergency was over and it continued in ordinary service until 1936. Another engine whose armoured, tank-like, appearance earned it a nickname was MGWR 0–6–0T No 102, which had previously born the prosaic name of *Pilot*, but now went under the far grander title *King Tutankamen*, although quite what its connection was with the ancient Egyptian I am unable to say. There were at least four other armoured locomotives, all of them tank engines, two from the GNR and probably two from the CB&SCR. Curiously, although the armoured trains mostly worked on GS&WR metals none of that company's engines seem to have been used on them.

In addition to these trains the Defence Corps used some petrol-driven Lancia armoured cars, one, known as the *Grey Ghost*, featuring in one of the most widely reported actions of the Civil War. Whilst patrolling the Thurles–Clonmel line it was ambushed by an IRA force which ripped up the track ahead of it and blew up a bridge in its rear. After a fierce battle its crew were forced to surrender, more through shortage of ammunition than because of damage to the car. They were later released and the line was quickly restored by the Corps.

The railway companies were now running at a combined annual deficit of over £1m; on the Dublin Stock Market the value of GS&WR ordinary shares steadily dropped, and by January 1923, had sunk to £35, a loss of £9 in six months. The effect which the collapse of the GS&WR, now spoken about as a possibility, would have had on the Country's economy was spelled out by a Dublin stockbroker, who said "Scarcely an investor in the South of Ireland is without stocks in the GS&WR". Wage cuts were suggested, the MGW, the GN and the D&SE proposing a flat rate reduction of 3s 6d per week, whilst the GS&WR, with a deficit of £400,000, wanted a much larger one. A conference on December 28 could reach no agreement and it was feared that a number of companies might cease operation in the New Year.

Then on January 3, three days before the NUR men on the GS&WR were due to strike, the Minister made a move that took almost everyone by surprise. He announced that the Government would run any services which the GS&WR Board of Directors felt unable to maintain and would pay the difference between receipts and expenditure but no interest. This was not at all to the Board's liking and they decided that they would carry on themselves as best they could.

At the beginning of January two broad gauge railways, the Cork, Bandon & South Coast and the Cork & Macroom, with three narrow gauge lines, the Cork, Blackrock & Passage, the Schull & Skibbereen, and the Tralee & Dingle, were at a complete standstill as a result of the attentions of Anti-Treaty forces. Many areas in Cork and Kerry were cut off for months at a time whilst Tralee, the most important town in Kerry, had been completely isolated since the summer of 1922. Newspapers had become a precious commodity and most of the townspeople had only the haziest notion of what was happening in the outside world. The blowing up of bridges on all the rail and road routes leading to and from the town had ensured that only those travelling on foot were able to get in or out, and even then it was a hazardous journey with troops of armed men roaming the countryside and liable to shoot first and ask questions afterwards. Postal services had ceased, and when the town was relieved on January 8 the first train in, the 8.30am from Killarney, carried 80 bags of mail.

In the end, because its forces were heavily outnumbered, and because the population, weary of war, was willing to settle for something less than total independence and tolerate for the time being a divided country, the Anti-Treaty side admitted defeat. The railways, not very soundly placed before the war, had suffered much damage and were considerably weaker. A great deal of money would have to be spent on restoration, and as the companies themselves were plainly incapable of providing it there was no alternative to the Government once again stepping in.

CHAPTER SIX

Unification

FOR AS LONG as there had been railways in Ireland there had been talk of Government control. It had come, temporarily, during World War I, and although this had ended in 1921 there were who few could foresee the Government steering clear of railway entanglements for long. In the spring of 1922 following the refusal of the railway workers to accept the recommendations of the Corrigan Tribunal (which had been looking into the position of the railways and rates of pay and salaries, and had got nowhere in talks with the Six Counties), the newly-formed Provisional Government of the Irish Free State set up a Railway Commission. This reported rather more speedily than such bodies usually do, and came to the conclusion that the railways had not been badly managed in the past, but that the stockholders' position had deteriorated during the period of Government control. It made the point that dividends had been maintained at a satisfactory level before the war only by underpaying the employees, and it recommended that the railways be nationalized. A minority report suggested unification as an alternative.

By this time the Civil War was in progress, despite which the Government found time to consider the Report, and on January 3, 1923, the Minister for Industry and Commerce made a long statement in the Dail. Apart from his proposal to take over the GS&WR immediately if its Board felt unable to maintain services, he had a great deal to say about the long term situation. The Minister expressed it as his eminently praiseworthy intention to see that the companies brought their services "to the highest attainable degree of efficiency and economy", and he felt that this would be achieved only if the 45 separate railway undertakings were amalgamated under one management. Purchase by the State was out, which was not surprising, for the Irish Free State was hardly born with a silver spoon in its mouth. The railways had been told of the Government's plans in December, the larger ones responding by suggesting grouping rather than the formation of a single undertaking. The Government was prepared to consider such a scheme, but if none was produced which it could approve within three months then it would bring in legislation to unify the railways within a further six months.

The companies agreed to put off any wage cuts for the time being, thus relieving themselves of union pressure, but they failed to present a united front to the Government over the grouping proposals, the chief stumbling block being the adamant refusal of the D&SER to go in with the GS&WR. The D&SER was quite happy to carry on by itself, which was a brave but not very practical attitude to take; its locomotives were old-fashioned and under-powered and its once lucrative suburban traffic between Dublin and

Bray had taken a hammering from the tramways. If it had to merge with somebody it wanted to go in with the Great Northern. This at one time would have been a possibility, and through services between the Northern and Southern suburbs of Dublin might have come decades before they did, but since the partition of Ireland the GNR was working within two countries and therefore had to be left out of any unification schemes.

So it was that the Railways Act, 1924, was presented to, and approved by the Dail. The only lines within the Free State not included in the amalgamation scheme were those which also worked in the Six Counties and the Listowel & Ballybunion monorail. Many of the railway companies would have preferred to merge into two or three groups rather than one, but hardly any could deny the impossibility of continuing in their present form. Wages and salaries had increased three fold since 1914, and with numbers of former Army lorries and motor buses and cars appearing on the roads the old monopoly had gone. Amalgamation was no guarantee that many of the country branch lines, particularly the narrow gauge ones, would survive, but no amalgamation would have made it certain that they would not do so. The Listowel & Ballybunion was omitted from the Act for the very good reason that it had closed down by the time it came into force.

It was really rather remarkable that this most curious concern lasted as long as it did. Opened in February 1888, it connected the small market town of Listowel in North-East Kerry with Ballybunion, a seaside resort some nine miles distant, close to the mouth of the Shannon. The track was built in the form of a trestle, the single running rail being positioned along the top of the trestle approximately three feet from the ground, there being a guide rail on each side of the trestle a few inches high. This arrangement necessitated some of the queerest-looking rolling stock ever seen. The locomotives each had two boilers, side by side, with the cylinders, motion and driving wheels between them. There were two sets of chimneys, domes, and safety valves, and one large cab. The carriages looked like contemporary four wheelers which had been sliced down the middle, turned inside out so that the two sections of the roof sloped towards each other, and the original outsides, instead of now facing in, had been removed and stuck on the outsides. Each section was quite self-contained, and if one wished to move from one side to the other one had to get out, climb across the track by means of a set of steps marshalled in the centre of the train, and get in from the far side. Nearly all the trains were mixed, the line depending more on the cattle trade for its livelihood than on passenger traffic.

Curious though it was, the Listowel & Ballybunion was not quite unique; its inventor, Charles Lartigue, had built another line at Tours in France, some horse-and-mule worked ones in Algeria and Tunis, and a further steam-operated one in the Argentine. He had also demonstrated the system at Tothill fields in North London in 1886, but the Irish line far outlived the others; although nearly 50 years have now elapsed since its demise many people in that part of Kerry still remember the "Lartigue". Some of the tales have no doubt been embellished with the passing of time, but there is no reason to doubt that they are based on the truth.

Apparently the rolling stock was rather finely balanced, and if there was too much weight on one side of the train it would heel over. Therefore it was part of the guard's duties to walk around the train before it started and if he found too many large ladies in the starboard half he would request that some of them transfer to port, thus restoring the equilibrium. The Lartigue locomotives were noted neither for their speed potentialities nor their hauling powers, and it is said that the unofficial motto of the railway was "First-Class keep their seats, Second-Class get out and walk, Third-

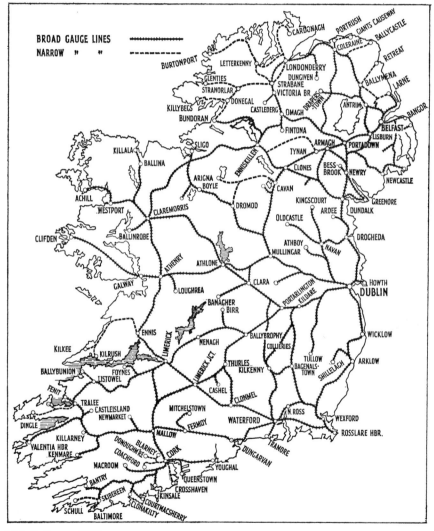

Irish Railways, 1920

Class get out and push". As there was no Second-Class on the line, however, it is possible that this was in fact said of the West Clare, on the other side of the Shannon, and that the Kerrymen have appropriated it and added it to the legends of the Listowel & Ballybunion. It is true that any gradients taxed the engines severely, and my father-in-law and his brothers, who lived close by the railway when they were boys, often used to race the train on their bicycles up the hill out of Listowel, beating the little panting engine by a fair margin.

This lack of speed made the railway a sitting duck for the motorcar, and it was further hampered by the system used for crossing roads and tracks. A drawbridge was provided in the trestle, and it would sometimes happen that farmers neglected to replace it in position after using it, so that the next train which came along had to pull up whilst the driver or the guard alighted and replaced it. A few relics of the line survive in Listowel and in Ballybunion, and Mr Cecil Fry has a working model of one of the trains on his famous layout at his home in Dublin.

The Listowel and Ballybunion wasn't quite the first line of any significance in Ireland to shut down. This not very enviable distinction went to the $10\frac{1}{4}$-mile branch of the GNR from Castleblaney, on the Dundalk–Clones line, to Keady, which gave up the ghost on August 10, 1924, a month and three days before the Listowel & Ballybunion. There had been various diversions and closures during the 19th century, but none of these amounted to much, and they certainly were not the consequence of any competition from the roads.

In all, 26 railways merged to form the Great Southern Railways, most very small concerns. Many possessed no rolling stock of their own, their services being worked by one of the larger companies, usually the one which had provided most of the original capital. The Great Southern was much the largest railway company in Ireland, though hardly gigantic by British standards; indeed, the Southern, the smallest of Britain's Big Four, possessed 2,260 locomotives against the Great Southern's 563. Of that number 311 came from one railway, the G&SWR, and in many ways the GSR was no more than the GS&WR much expanded. Of the Great Southern's original 16 directors 13 were GS&WR men, the other three coming from the D&SE and the LMS. One might wonder what the latter company was doing with a seat on the Board; it did after all control two other Irish railways, the NCC and the DN&G, but poking a finger in the Great Southern's pie might have been considered overdoing it a bit. Actually, one of the predecessors of the LMS, the LNWR, had had a seat on the D&SE Board since 1902. This had come about when the English company had subscribed a loan of £1m towards the construction of the New Ross and Waterford Extension Railway, the line by which the D&SE acquired access to the latter city.

Around the turn of the century several English companies had suddenly become very interested in Ireland, the Midland, as we have seen, buying up the Belfast & Northern Counties, while the GWR promoted, with the GS&WR, the Fishguard & Rosslare Harbour Company. The latter was a serious threat to the traditional route to Cork and the South, which had always been via the LNWR to Holyhead, and no doubt the gentlemen at Euston saw the projected D&SE route as a possible way of regaining some of this traffic. It was rather a forlorn hope, for the Fishguard–Rosslare crossing enabled a passenger to reach Waterford several hours earlier than going via Dublin; nevertheless the LNWR purchased £87,000 out of the New Ross & Waterford's £100,000 guaranteed stock. The Holyhead–Kingstown route remained the most popular for passengers to Dublin, the Midlands and the West, and the LNWR, which took over the Holyhead–Kingstown mail boat service from the City of Dublin Steam Packet Company in 1918, agreed to pay the D&SE a percentage of the receipts, some £20,000 per annum. The successor to the LNWR, the LMS, said that if the loan for the Waterford line was repaid in full it would be quite happy to give up its seat on the Board, but the Great Southern was in no position to do this, and thus acquired an English director along with the D&SE's other assets.

Kingsbridge became the GSR's headquarters, just as it had been that of the GS&WR, and Inchicore became its principal locomotive and carriage works. Broadstone Works continued to play an important role; indeed, it was just about to introduce the prototype of what was to become the principal mixed traffic class of steam locomotive on the Great Southern, but the third of the Dublin locomotive works, that of the D&SE at Grand Canal Street, closed almost immediately the Amalgamation came into effect. This caused no one any surprise, for Grand Canal Street could have put in a well-supported claim to be the most inconvenient and archaic engine-building establishment in existence. Nevertheless it had had a long history and occupied a prominent place in the story of locomotive development, for on April 4, 1841, a 2–2–2T named *Princess* was completed there, and was the first locomotive in the world to be built by a railway company at its own works. This was no consolation however, to the men who were having to make do in the third decade of the 20th century with buildings so inadequate and so cramped that the larger locomotives would not fit inside, but had to be dealt with in the running shed opposite, so necessitating a continual procession of people carrying materials and tools across the main line which divided the works from the shed. It says much for the men of Grand Canal Street that down the years they had managed to construct 41 locomotives in their tiny little shops, the last of them, 4–4–2T No 20 *King George*, appearing as late as 1911. *King George* became the Great Southern's C2 Class No 455, and was scrapped by CIE in the last days of steam in 1959. Two sister engines were built in the very last year of the D&SE's separate existence, but like all the company's locomotives subsequent to 1911, they came from the Manchester Works of Beyer Peacock. The buildings housing the Grand Canal Street Works were sold off by the GSR and are still occupied, having changed hands more than once since 1925, though altering but little externally.

The Amalgamation added a new dimension to the Kingsbridge empire, one it could well have done without. This was the narrow gauge. Much has been written about the 3ft railways of Ireland, a disproportionate amount perhaps in relation to their size and importance. They were marvellously diverse and in many ways unique, and were therefore almost impossible for the GSR to run efficiently. Laid out mostly in the 1880s in areas where the traffic could not support a full-sized line, these narrow gauge lines were a boon to the small farmers, and although they did not offer a particularly speedy means of travel, they nevertheless were a great advance on what had gone before.

But in 1925 the motorcar had penetrated even the remotest areas of Ireland, and it was very much quicker, for example, to carry a dozen sheep from Annascaul to Farranfore on the back of a lorry rather than load them first into a Tralee and Dingle train bound for Tralee, and there transfer them into a 5ft 3in gauge wagon and take them on to Farranfore. Similarly a small 12 or 15 seater bus was almost as fast as a train, of sufficient capacity for most purposes, and much cheaper to run. It was also considerably more convenient for it would pick you up much nearer your home and drop you nearer your destination than would the train. As yet the possibilities of the motor were only beginning to be explored, but the implications of it for the narrow gauge, and many 5ft 3in gauge branch lines, were clear for those who cared to see them.

The railways which worked wholly within the Six Counties were no concern of the Free State Government, and the Amalgamation passed them by. Similarly those companies which possessed mileage on both sides of the Border, the Great Northern, the Dundalk, Newry & Greenore, the Sligo, Leitrim & Northern Counties, and the 3ft gauge Londonderry & Lough Swilly and the County Donegal Railways Joint Committee, retained their independence.

The County Donegal was the largest of all the 3ft gauge lines. It had started out as a 5ft 3in line from Strabane to Stranorlar in 1863, and had expanded and amalgamated with other lines until it attained its greatest extent in 1909, by which time the whole of its 110 miles were of the 3ft gauge. In 1906, finding itself smitten with that well-known light railway disease "financial difficulties", it was taken over by a joint committee of the GNR and the NCC, each of which supplied half the members for the six-man Board of Directors. One consequence of this take-over was that the Midland Railway's western frontier was extended to Killybegs on the Atlantic coast of Donegal; unfortunately three different gauges and the Irish Sea prevented the running of through carriages to St Pancras! The section of the County Donegal within the Six Counties, from Derry to Strabane, was actually the sole property of the NCC, but was always worked by County Donegal locomotives and stock.

The second biggest of the Irish narrow-gauge systems, the Londonderry & Lough Swilly, was almost as large as the County Donegal; it owned 99 route miles, and whilst it chiefly served the northern part of Donegal it overlapped to an extent with the CDRJC, both companies working between Londonderry and Letterkenny. The Lough Swilly's chief claim to fame was its four largest engines. Nos 11 and 12 were 4-8-0s, built by Hudswell Clarke in 1905, and the only narrow gauge tender engines in Ireland; Nos 5 and 6 were tank engine versions of these, 4-8-4Ts built in 1912. They were the most powerful 3ft gauge locomotives in the country, and with the two GSR 4-8-0Ts were

Top: GSR former GSWR Aspinall 4-4-0 No 57 (1888–1957)
at Achill with a Dublin train. *[H. C. Casserley*

Above: CIE class K1A Woolwich 2-6-0 No 397 approaching
Killarney with an excursion from Tralee in June 1954.
[N. Fields

Below: GNR 4-4-2T No 188 heading an up local train near
Rush in July 1951. *[J. Macartney Robbins*

GNR SG3 class No 49 0-6-0 (1921–65) on the Belfast Central
line with an Easter Monday excursion from Portadown to
Bangor on April 19, 1965.   *J Goss*

Above : NCC former Malcolm compound 4-4-0 No 50
Jubilee at York Road, Belfast. This locomotive was built
in 1895, rebuilt as a simple in 1926 and scrapped in 1946.

Below : SLNCR 0-6-4T *Sir Henry* (1904–57) near
Manorhamilton.   *[P. Ransome-Wallis*

Foot : Greenore station (DN&GR) with GNR PG 0-6-0,
JT 2-4-2T and DN&G Ramsbottom 0-6-0STs and former
LMS cargo boat.   *[British Railways*

GSWR Ivatt 4-4-0 No 58 (1888–1953) leaves Kingsbridge
with a Cork express at the turn of the century.　　*[LPC*

CIE rebuilt two-cylinder 4-6-0 No 409 (1923–58) about to
leave Kingsbridge with the "Cork Mail".　　*[Seaton Phillips*

CIE No 800 *Maeve* (built 1939) at Mallow with a
Dublin–Cork express. This locomotive is now preserved
in Belfast Transport Museum.   [P. Ward

GNR S class 4-4-0 No 173 *Galtee Moré* (1913–64) pulling out
of Amiens Street with the "Bundoran Express".
                                        [Noel A. Machell

UTA former GNR U class 4-4-0 No 66 (formerly 201,
1948–65) *Meath*, at Strabane with the 10.15am Derry–Belfast
train. Behind are former County Donegal 2-6-4Ts Nos 5
and 4 and carriages.
                                    [Noel A. Machell]

UTA former GNR VS 3-cylinder simple 4-4-0 No 58
(formerly 208) *Lagan*, still in GNR blue pulling out of Amiens
Street on a September evening in 1959 with a Belfast
express.   *[Michael H. C. Baker]*

Brand new GNR compound 4-4-0 No 86 *Peregrine*
(1932–61) in lined black livery leaving Amiens Street for
Belfast on the first day of the accelerated timings, June 6,
1932.   *[H. C. Casserley*

The brand new NIR "Enterprise" made up of seven
modified BR Mark 11B carriages with Hunslet 1,350hp
Bo-Bo No 101 *Eagle* at the head and 102 *Falcon* at the rear.
The train is seen passing Fairview in the Dublin suburbs
in the summer of 1970.   *[Michael H. C. Baker*

Above: GSWR steam rail-motor of 1905 at Inchicore alongside Coey 4-4-2T No 317 (1901–55). *[LPC*

Left: A group of Irish Railway Record Society members standing around GNR railbus No 3 during a tour at Navan Junction. *[J. Macartney Robbins*

Below: The original GSR Drumm battery train.

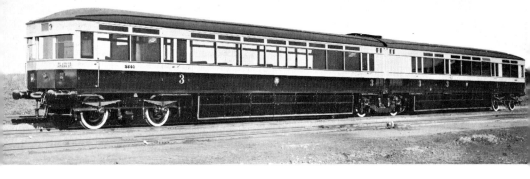

the only eight-coupled steam locomotives ever to run in Ireland. This stupendous effort quite seemed to exhaust the L&LS, and it was forever in debt. In 1925, despite receiving compensation of £1,700 and a grant of £5,250 from the Northern Ireland Government it lost £2,309 4s 3d. By contrast the County Donegal did vastly better, and made a net profit of £16,026.

The L&LS had the most carriages, 52 against 46, and the most wagons, 283 against 263, but the County Donegal had more engines, 21 against 17, which in a year travelled slightly farther, 304,365 miles against 296,497; the CDRJC locomotives also pulled rather more merchandise, 71,088 tons against 63,701, and cows, sheep, pigs and other four-legged passengers, 38,024 against 25,062, but quite a lot fewer two-legged ones, 236,586 against 395,715. Some 202 of the L&LS passengers travelled on season tickets, but only 67 County Donegal ones did. The L&LS owned three steamships which sailed about Lough Swilly, and one horse and cart, which didn't. Unless it was the latter which ate up all the profits one can only assume that the great difference in the financial results of the two companies came about through the much more efficient operating methods of the County Donegal, backed up by the resources of its wealthy godparents, the GNR and the NCC.

The Sligo, Leitrim & Northern Counties had a very impressive name, but like many such companies fooled no-one who knew it. It possessed but one line, 43 miles long from just east of Sligo to Enniskillen. At one extremity it connected with the Great Southern and at the other with the Great Northern. Its passenger traffic never amounted to much; it owned 11 engines and only four more carriages, and what profit it made came chiefly from the cattle trade, a great deal of this being passed on to the GNR at Enniskillen. The SLNCR had a great fondness for the 0–6–4T type and eight of its locomotives were of this wheel arrangement, built by Beyer Peacock at intervals between 1882 and 1917. The odd men out were an 0–6–0T and two second-hand 4–4–0s, bought at knockdown prices from the Great Northern.

The two largest railways entirely within the Six Counties were both based on Belfast. Biggest of all, the NCC, by 1925 was showing signs of its Midland ownership, although plenty of evidence of the former *régime* remained. At the time the Midland took over the Belfast & Northern Counties (as the NCC then was known) it was almost entirely controlled by two men, Cotton, the General Manager, and Bowman Malcolm, the Locomotive Superintendent. The latter had assumed office in 1876 at the age of 22, comfortably lowering Gooch's record on the Great Western (a parallel might well be drawn between Brunel and Gooch and Cotton and Malcolm), and he retired 46 years later in 1922. Not surprisingly Malcolm had some original ideas which he lost no time in trying out, and rather more surprisingly they proved perfectly practical, with the consequence that all his engines were still running in 1925, most of them in unaltered condition. The majority were two-cylinder compounds of the Worsdell-Von Borries type, primarily 2–4–0 and 4–4–0 passenger engines, although there were also two 0–6–0s and six narrow-gauge 2–4–2 tank engines. After Malcolm's retirement Derby assumed a rather tighter hold on York Road's activites, and began to rebuild the compound engines as simples, endowing them with a variety of typical

Midland features such as extended smokeboxes, Belpaire fireboxes and Derby cabs, so that they came quite closely to resemble Deeley or Fowler engines.

The NCC was primarily a passenger line linking Belfast with Antrim, Ballymena, Coleraine and Derry, and the resorts of the North Atlantic Coast. In 1925 it carried 3,213,849 passengers *plus* 2,619 season-ticket holders. It owned three hotels, in Belfast, Larne and Portrush, and did all in its power to popularise the Antrim Coast as a holiday area, running excursions at very low fares which were much appreciated by the tens of thousands who took advantage of them to get away for a few hours from the grimy terraces of Belfast. As far back as 1902 the BNCR had operated a motor-bus, the very first in the world to be owned by a railway company, and it was generally agreed that the NCC was one of the most enterprising and financially sound lines in Ireland.

Across the River Lagan from the NCC's York Road terminus stood Queen's Quay, home of the Belfast & County Down Railway. This was even more of a passenger line, carrying 3,694,349 persons in 1925, and some 4,195 season ticket-holders. Its mileage was less than a third that of the NCC's, but because its goods traffic was so meagre it had a net income of just under £50,000, which despite its superior passenger figures, compared unfavourably with the NCC's £72,301. Strictly speaking, the County Down's 12-mile line along the shores of Belfast Lough to Bangor was no more than a branch, but it was vastly busier than the main line proper to Newcastle, and more than offset the losses made on the latter and on the Donaghadee, Ballynahinch and Ardglass branches.

No one ever accused the County Down of being the most progressive of railways, although it had had its periods of prosperity. It had also known times of extreme penury, and in 1877 had seemed to be on the point of giving up altogether. No dividend had been paid since 1860, the value of £50 shares was down to £10, and the entire Board of Directors and the company's solicitors decided they had had enough and resigned. As things could get no worse they then began to get better, and from 1891 to 1920 the County Down was in the happy state of being able to pay a 6½ per cent dividend on its ordinary shares. But with the end of World War I the company's fortunes began to slip back. It was particularly vulnerable to competition, being in the unfortunate position of providing a longer route between practically any two points on its system than did the road. By 1924 it could pay no more than 4½ per cent, and in 1925 this had dropped still further to 2 per cent.

While there was probably little that the company could have done to avoid this sad decline, in one respect its policy in the first two decades of the 20th century had almost invited it. In 1896 it had built six bogie carriages, and the following year added seven more, including a Royal saloon, No 103. Then for reasons best known to itself it reverted to six-wheelers. For the next 26 years, while everyone else was busy turning out eight and twelve-wheel bogie coaches the BCDR blithely went its own way, building antique little rigid-wheelbase boxes on wheels, and even having the nerve in 1922 to purchase eight very second-hand ones from the GNR. Thus in 1925, out of a total carriage stock of 214 vehicles, a mere 13 of them were of bogie types, and even these were nearly 30 years old. Perhaps the Board were convinced that such carriages, like the motor car, were only a passing fancy and the world one day would revert to the Presbyterian virtues of the hard-backed, hard-riding six-wheeler. Unfortunately the decadent 20th century had planted in the mind of the third class passenger the insidious notion that he was entitled to the same consideration as his betters, and if the railway company was not prepared to see it that way then Henry Ford and William Austin were.

In locomotive matters the County Down was rather more up-to-date. Like many Irish lines it favoured the products of Beyer Peacock, and between 1901 and 1925 put 15 4–4–2Ts of that firm's manufacture into service. Being mainly a suburban system the BCDR had little use for tender engines, and when it became possible to purchase new locomotives after World War I the company decided to go in for some really large tank engines to cope with the heavy rush-hour loads on the Bangor line. At that time the 4–6–4T was very much in vogue, and so Beyer Peacock supplied four splendid-looking machines of this wheel arrangement. It was bad luck on the B&CDR that, like practically all the British Baltic tanks, they failed to live up to their appearance. They were too heavy for any part of the system but the Bangor line, and on that they proved no more powerful than the 4–4–2Ts, and rather less economical. So when another two engines were supplied by Beyer Peacock in 1924 they were once again of the well-tried 4–4–2 tank type, the only improvement on their predecessors being an increase in cylinder size and boiler pressure.

Down at the opposite extremity of the country there lived another group of Beyer Peacock tank engines, the 4–6–0Ts of the former Cork, Bandon & South Coast Railway. They had belonged to a company which in some respects was rather like the B&CDR, and in others markedly different. The CB&SC was even fonder of tank engines than the County Down, each one of its 20 locomotives being of this type. Its route mileage, just over 94, was similar, and it carried a certain amount of suburban traffic, although Cork was a much smaller city than Belfast and the traffic was nothing like as heavy. The CB&SC was much more of a goods line, and if it had never made the profits of the County Down, neither had it descended to such depths. Its terminus in Cork was down beside the docks at Albert Quay, whence ran a connection to the GS&WR station at Glanmire Road. Of the 20 CB&SC engines handed over to the Great Southern, eight were of the standard 4–6–0 tank type built between 1906 and 1920, and their six predecessors were originally 4–4–0Ts. One of these had been converted to a 4–6–0T in 1906, becoming the prototype for the later standard engines, and three more were rebuilt as 4–4–2 tanks. There were also five saddle tanks, and the twentieth engine was a little 2–4–0T, which, rather curiously, carried the same type of boiler as the original 4–6–0T.

Cork, the second city of the Irish Free State, was well endowed with railways, there being one other 5ft 3in gauge line in addition to the GS&W and and the CB&SC, and two narrow-gauge lines, all with stations within the city boundaries. The broad gauge concern was the Cork & Macroom Direct, which ran to the latter town, 24 miles due west of Cork, and owned five engines, all tanks. The two narrow-gauge lines were the Cork & Muskerry and the Cork, Blackrock & Passage. The latter at one time had been a 5ft 3in gauge concern, but had been converted to 3ft at the turn of the century. It ran along the western shore of Cork Harbour, opposite Queenstown, down to the small town of Crosshaven, a journey of 16 miles, although in a direct line it was little more than half this distance. The company owned four 2–4–2 tank engines, all built by Neilson Reid in 1899. Particularly vulnerable to road competition, owing to its indirect route and the slow speed of its narrow gauge trains, the CB&P was in a bad way when absorbed into the Great Southern.

The Cork & Muskerry served the area lying to the north-west of Cork, with lines running to Coachford, Donoughmore and Blarney, a total route mileage of 26. Blarney sports a famous castle and an even more famous stone, but all the eloquence in the world could not persuade visitors to patronise the Cork & Muskerry route in preference to the rival GS&W one or a jaunting car, and this tourist attraction within its territory was not the benefit to the company that it might have been. There was little chance that the other small towns and villages it served would ever generate sufficient traffic to make its fortune, and by 1925 the C&MLR had become one more small railway struggling for survival.

South-west of Cork City, in a remote corner of County Cork, the West Carberry Tramways and Light Railway Company eked out a precarious existence. Better known as the Schull & Skibbereen, it had got off to a inauspicious start in 1886, for its three tram engines proved so unreliable that the line had to close down almost as soon as it opened. The locomotives then were heavily rebuilt, and although even then they were not capable of raising much more steam than was necessary to keep themselves on the move, the company managed to provide some sort of service until 1888, when it was reclassified as a light railway and was able to purchase something rather more substantial in the way of motive power. By 1925 practically all the traffic on the Schull & Skibbereen's 14¾-mile route around Roaring Water Bay was in the charge of three 4–4–0Ts, aided, in theory if not in practice, by one of the original tram engines. The Great Southern's opinion of the latter may be gauged by the fact that as soon as a representative from Inchicore struggled through to the Wild West and clapped eyes upon it, it was scrapped.

The Schull & Skibbereen, despite its 40-odd staff working a twelve-hour day for very low wages, could usually be relied upon to make a steady loss, and in 1922 its working deficit, *plus* interest payments since 1888, totalled £152,755. The timetable provided for two trains a day in each direction, usually mixed, and a third one for the tourists on Sundays. In its last years of independence it suffered various interruptions, a locomotive being derailed and overturned during the Civil War, while services were totally suspended for some months during 1922. Although the Schull & Skibbereen connected with the Cork, Bandon & South Coast Railway at Skibbereen it was many years before through tickets were issued between the two companies. The S&S

existed solely for the benefit of the local people, and when these found road transport more convenient there was little point in its carrying on.

North of this area, but further to the west, was the Tralee & Dingle Light Railway. Opened about the same time as the Schull & Skibbereen, it served a part of Ireland which was, if anything, even more remote than West Cork. Tralee, the largest town in Kerry, was a substantial sort of place, but beyond lay the Dingle Peninsula, which even today is populated by no more than a few thousand small farmers and their families. The only town in the Peninsula is Dingle, and it was from there to Tralee that the railway ran, with a branch to Castlegregory, on the western shore of Tralee Bay. The Dingle Peninsula, with its bare, high hills, and dramatic bays and cliffs, is one of the most beautiful parts of Ireland. Because of its remoteness the Irish language survived there when it had disappeared from most other parts of the country, and among the locals there were those who saw the railway as an unwelcome intruder in this last outpost of Irish nationalism. In fact the only change it brought was an increase in trade to the port of Dingle, and the opportunity to ride down to Tralee and from there take a GS&W train to view the sights of Dublin. There was little traffic in the opposite direction, and in 1925 life in the Peninsula carried on much as it had before the railway came. The most westerly tip of the peninsula is the nearest point in Europe to America, and in a curious way London was more remote than New York. Many Dingle men migrated to the USA, and it was almost an everyday occurrence to see a crowd of relations and friends gathered at the station to say their goodbyes to a young farmer's son as he set off for Queenstown and the liner which would take him to Boston or New York. Such scenes still take place today, although not on a railway station, and the farewells nowadays are seldom final. Last summer we met a middle-aged man in Dingle who told us that he had emigrated to the USA 20 years earlier, but flew home each August to keep in touch with his relations and practise his Irish; his ambition was to retire and come home for good.

For a short while, during World War I, there was a regular sailing of a ship from Dingle to America with fish caught locally, but in normal times this trade was hardly profitable, and most fishermen were also farmers. The station at Dingle was on a hill above the town, and a line continued from it down to the harbour; it was used principally to carry fish, and also coal which came into Dingle in colliers from South Wales. At Tralee the T&D had its own terminus some way from the GSWR one, a 3ft gauge line connecting the two.

The Tralee & Dingle locomotives, like those of the Schull & Skibereen, were equipped with large cowcatchers and acetylene headlamps on account of the many ungated crossings and unfenced stretches of track running alongside roads, and they consequently presented quite a transatlantic appearance. The first three, 2–6–0Ts, came from the Hunslet works in Leeds, in time for the line's opening in 1889; a year later they were joined by a small 0–4–2T for the Castlegregory branch, then came a 2–6–2T, three more 2–6–0Ts, (two of them from Kerr Stuart) and finally in 1910 a last Hunslet 2–6–0T. The carriages and wagons were all bogie vehicles, there being 21 of the former and 77 of the latter, and the cattle trucks were much in demand on fair days. The basic passenger service, unaltered over the years, consisted of a morning and evening train in each direction between Tralee and Dingle, one with a portion for Castlegregory, and there was in addition a separate train from Castlegregory to Tralee and back. The 31¼-mile journey between Tralee and Dingle took around 2½hr, the actual time depending upon how many stops were made; there were 13 altogether but most of these were conditional. No one had ever expected the Tralee & Dingle to make a profit; baronial guarantees had to be given to raise the capital to build it, and for most of its independent life it was under the control of a Committee of Management appointed by the Grand Jury of the County of Kerry, which made good the annual deficit.

Heading north again, past the remains of the Listowel & Ballybunion, and across the Shannon, we come to Kilrush and the West Clare, perhaps the most celebrated, or infamous, of all the Irish narrow gauge railways. It owed its notoriety chiefly to Percy French, the entertainer, who composed a song "Are You Right There Michael, Are You Right?", which was all about the eccentric ways of the West Clare, and the remote possibility of any of its trains ever arriving on time. The management of the West Clare got very hot under the collar about this and unwisely took Percy to court. The story goes that he arrived very late for the hearing, and when rebuked by the judge explained that he had come by the train; the case was promptly dismissed.

The line was opened in 1887 from Ennis, the principal town in County Clare, to Miltown Milbay, 27 miles away on the coast, and was later extended southwards to Kilkee, with a branch to Kilrush. The extension was constructed by a separate company, the South Clare, but it never owned any rolling stock and was always worked by the West Clare. The total length of the two systems came to 53 miles.

A particular hazard the West Clare had to face, apart from the ever-present financial one, was high winds. Much of the coastline along which it operated was bare and exposed and took the full brunt of storms from the Atlantic. There was always the possibility of a train being blown off the tracks, and to prevent this, slabs of concrete ballast were placed on the floors of goods and passenger vehicles. In addition, an anemometer was installed at Quilty station, right beside the sea, to measure the velocity of the wind; when it reached 60mph the stationmaster would send out a message instructing that all unballasted vehicles must be taken out of service, and if 80mph was reached then trains had to cease running altogether. It was the duty of other stationmasters along the coast to ring up Quilty and confirm that trains might proceed; if no answer was received they were to assume that the telephone wires were down and trains must therefore be halted.

The West Clare's first four engines were all very small 0-6-0Ts, and were replaced around the turn of the century by three very much larger 0-6-2Ts. These became the best-known of the West Clare engines, chiefly on account of the diameter of their trailing wheels which was equal to that of the drivers; the reason for this curiosity was easy interchangability and therefore economy. There followed four 2-6-2Ts and five 4-6-0Ts, the last two of these coming out in 1922; they were the newest narrow-gauge locomotives in the Great Southern's possession. Carriages were all six-wheelers, firsts, thirds and composites, there being no second-class.

In its earliest years the West Clare deserved all that Percy French said about it. The scheduled 3hr journey from Ennis to Kilkee frequently took twice as long owing to engine breakdowns, and altercations with cattle and their indignant owners were common; the latter sometimes resorted to placing stones on the track or, when unusually sorely tried, to tossing them through carriage windows. Eventually the West Clare pulled itself together and developed into quite an efficient and busy concern. Inevitably rising costs and road competition after World War I took their toll. The distance from Limerick to Kilkee was 15 miles less by road than by rail, and as the rail traveller was further impeded by having to change from the standard to the narrow gauge at Ennis, the West Clare was at some disadvantage. One drastic remedy bandied around from time to time was conversion to the 5ft 3in gauge, but this would have been a costly business and would have done nothing to solve the problem of the extra distance covered by the trains.

Finally there was the Cavan & Leitrim, situated in the middle of the country, just below the Six Counties border. The Cavan & Leitrim's particular peculiarity was the fuel burned by its engines. This was coal mined locally, at the western end of the company's territory. Ireland is a country poor in mineral deposits, practically all its coal being imported from Great Britain. It has plentiful supplies of turf, but this is useless for most industrial purposes, as it burns very quickly and leaves very large deposits of dust. There was an area up in the Arigna Valley in County Leitrim, however, where coal was found in sufficient quantity to make mining it worthwhile, at a rough estimate some 15m tons. It was reached by way of tunnels driven in horizontally from the valley sides, most of the mines being privately owned, and rather haphazardly worked. There was not sufficient coal to have any significant effects on the economy of the country, but the Cavan & Leitrim used it, its engines having larger than normal fireboxes to cope with its soft quality.

Horse-worked tramways had existed in the mines from the earliest times, but the first steam railway to penetrate the area was the Ballinamore to Arigna branch of the Cavan & Leitrim, built in the late 1880s. The main line of the company ran from Belturbet, a small town of 1,000 inhabitants right up in the north of County Cavan, by way of Ballinamore to Dromod, an even smaller town in South Leitrim. At its northern end it connected with the GNR branch which ran from Ballyhaise on the Cavan to Clones line, and at the other with the main MGWR Dublin to Sligo line. Ballinamore was the hub of the system, and the sheds and workshops were situated there, but it was a place of little importance other than to those who lived in and around it, and one wonders how such a sleepy, out-of-the-way part of the country could ever have been expected to provide a railway with sufficient traffic to pay its way.

In locomotive matters the Cavan & Leitrim was much more standardised than most narrow gauge railways. All but one of its nine engines were identical 4-4-0Ts, built by Robert Stephensons in 1887. The ninth was an 0-6-4T, purchased in 1904 from the same manufacturer but little used. The carriages were distinctive affairs with clerestory roofs and open-ended verandas, and looked as if they might well have come from America.

In 1920 a 4¼-mile extension from Arigna up to Aughabehy was opened by the Government in order to give better access to the mines. The Ministry of Transport hired two former NCC 0-4-2STs which had been used on the Ballymena, Cushendall & Red Bay Railway, but the extension was worked from its opening by the Cavan & Leitrim and the saddle-tanks worked all over the system. Needless to say the extension failed to pay and the Government had to grant the Cavan & Leitrim an annual subsidy to work it.

There remain to be described a number of narrow-gauge lines which never seemed to be quite sure whether they were proper railways or merely tramways. One such was the Clogher Valley, which opened for business in 1883 as a tramway and became a railway 11 years later. It ran from Tynan, on the GNR Armagh–Clones line, through Counties Armagh, Tyrone and Fermanagh to Maguiresbridge on the GNR Clones–Enniskillen line. It made a net profit of £6,337 in 1916, but by 1925 was in much weaker health. The Clogher Valley owned six Sharp Stewart 0-4-2Ts, built for the line's opening, and a somewhat larger 0-4-4T, built by Hudswell Clarke in 1910. As the line ran for much of its length alongside public roads the engines had their nether portions enclosed in typical tram-engine fashion. The headquarters of the company were at Aughnacloy, 9½ miles from Tynan, and if for some curious reason one chose to travel the entire length of the line rather than go by the much quicker GNR route, the 37-mile journey took ten minutes short of four hours.

Due north of the Clogher Valley but still in County Tyrone was the Castlederg & Victoria Bridge Tramway Company, another 3ft gauge line connecting with the GNR, this time the Derry–Omagh main line, Victoria Bridge being a few miles south of Strabane. It too first saw the light of day in the early 1880s, and although a very small concern it served the local community faithfully, and quite profitably, at least until the end of World War I. Its 7-mile line ran alongside the county road and the inevitable happened; a bus service started up, and within a couple of years or so the railway found itself in the red, but it did not give in easily. The company's engineer, Mr Pollard, enlisted the aid of a local carpenter and a blacksmith and between them they designed and built a railcar. As there was virtually no money to spare for such a project it was built mostly out of scrap materials, the engine coming from a Fordson tractor which the ingenious Mr Pollard converted to run on paraffin. At first it was rather underpowered so the three set to work again, and the next time they came up with a 24-seat vehicle, weighing 10 tons, with the drive transmitted by way of chains to the leading wheels which were in turn centrally coupled to the driving wheels. With this arrangement the car managed to exceed 30mph, fully loaded, and turned in a fuel consumption of 8–10mpg. It was a roaring success and took over virtually all the passenger workings, drastically reducing the company's running costs. Two steam engines remained on the books, a 2-6-0 tank and an 0-4-4 tank, both built by Hudswell Clarke in the early years of the present century, the three original engines having all been withdrawn by 1912, although one, an 0–4–0T, was still in existence in 1916. There were some twenty-odd goods wagons and these continued to give the steam engines something to do after the railcar appeared on the scene.

Most northern of all the Irish narrow gauge lines was the Giants Causeway Tramway. This had another distinction, which was that it was the first electric railway in the country. Yet another line to be opened in 1883, it was naturally a great novelty and there was a sizeable section of the local populace who approached with trepidation the idea of a live rail carrying 250V and exposed to all and sundry. This lead to a quite different sort of exposure for the engineer, a truly Victorian eccentric, removed his trousers in front of the Ministry of Transport inspectors and sat on the live rail, thereby proving beyond all dispute that this newfangled form of traction threatened no danger to any part of the human anatomy. At least we must assume this was proved, for although the engineer apparently suffered no ill effects it was not categorically stated that all his powers remained unimpaired.

Despite this spectacular opening ceremony the line was worked chiefly by steam until 1899, during which year the third rail was replaced by an overhead wire. By 1916 steam haulage of passenger trains had entirely ceased, although a couple of vertical-boiler engines were retained and were still in existence in 1925. Normally annual reports of railway companies stick strictly to statistics, but the 1917 one for the Giant's Causeway, Portrush & Bush Valley Tramway, to give it its full title, is a poignant exception. It records that of its staff of 28 at the beginning of 1916, all but six had since joined the Army and many were now dead, four being killed on the same day during the Battle of the Somme. The Giant's Causeway was a holiday line and something of a curiosity, so that it suffered less than most from motor competition. It was still doing quite well in 1925, its open cars proving one of its greatest attractions, and on warm summer days they hummed up and down the 7-mile line between Portrush and the Causeway filled to capacity with passengers drinking in draughts of Atlantic ozone.

Close by was another tramway, the dimunitive Portstewart one, only $1\frac{1}{2}$ miles long and connecting Portstewart main line station with the town. It was entirely steam-operated, with three Kitson tram engines, and three cars, two of them open-top bogies and one single deck toastrack; there was a a four-wheel van for luggage. Owned by the NCC the line was rather antiquated, and on the point of expiring, which it did at the end of 1925, being replaced by a privately-operated motor bus.

One of the best known Irish tramlines was the Bessbrook & Newry. A traveller between Belfast and Dublin could hardly avoid noticing it for it ran beneath the high Craigmore Viaduct over which the GNR main line passed. The Bessbrook & Newry was one of the very few Irish lines which owed its origin to the needs of industry. It opened in 1885 and was constructed primarily to carry coal and flax from the docks at Newry to the spinning mills at Bessbrook, and to bring the manufactured goods back again. Some of the employees of the mill company lived in a model village close by, but most travelled each day to and from Newry and the tramway also served to transport them. Although the Bessbrook & Newry opened after the Giant's Causeway line it had some claim to the title of pioneer electric line in the country, for it employed no other form of traction right from the start. One of the original 1885 cars, No 2, a 24-seat single-decker with an Ashbury body and Hopkinson motor, was still at work in 1925, and there were two others, 32 and 40-seat cars, almost new, which were delivered by Hurst Nelsons in 1921, with three trailers.

The goods side of the business was carried on by 27 rather special vehicles, wagons so designed that their flangeless wheels could run on both the railway by means of a second rail placed immediately alongside and a little lower than the usual one, and also through the streets of Newry, where they were hauled by either horses or tractors. Although open to the public the line depended almost entirely on the Bessbrook mills for its traffic, and so long as these continued to conduct their trade by rail it had nothing to fear from road competition. As with the Giant's Causeway line, hydro-electric generators supplied the power. The Camlough stream, beside which the line ran, has a fall of 29½ft, and this energy was harnessed at a power-house not far from Craigmore Viaduct. The current was carried in a centre third rail, apart from a 50yd section where the line crossed the Bessbrook–Newry road, it then transferred to an overhead wire, the trams being fitted with bow collectors in addition to the pick-up shoes on the motor bogies.

This just about completes the survey of narrow gauge lines, apart from a few small industrial ones, the best-known of these being that serving the Guinness works in Dublin. There were also some purely street tramways, though not narrow gauge. Dublin, Belfast and Cork all had tramway systems, the two former being particularly extensive; there was one which ran from close by Kingsbridge station to Lucan, later taken over by the main Dublin system, and finally a steam tramway on the other side of Dublin, out to the illage of Blessington.

CHAPTER SEVEN

The Late 1920s

ACTING ON THE adage "if you can't beat them, join them", the Great Southern began to consider the possibility of operating its own road services. At the time of the Great Southern's formation the railways were prevented by law from doing this and it was generally admitted that this really was rather unfair. The law had always kept a close watch on the railways, as was only to be expected when one considers how implicitly the public trusts the rail-

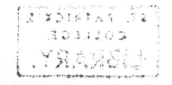

ways to see that no harm comes to it or its possessions whilst in their care. Consequently over the years a great many acts had been passed in Parliament carefully regulating all aspects of railway operation in Great Britain and Ireland. The situation on the roads was rather different.

At first the authorities seem to have acted under the assumption that a mechanically-propelled vehicle rumbling along the public highway would cause the collapse of every building and old lady for miles around, and therefore forbade any machine to move faster than a man could walk. Around the turn of the century someone took a deep breath and removed this restriction, and from then on the law remained fairly aloof, almost literally allowing private and commercial vehicle operators the freedom of the road. In 1925 there were no legislative or administrative restrictions governing the routes road operators might work, or how much they should charge, a very different situation from that which obtained on the railways.

In 1927 the Dail decided to take steps to remedy this state of affairs and passed the Railways (Road Motor Services) Act. This enabled railway companies to operate road motor services, subject to certain controls imposed by the Ministry for Industry and Commerce, and the Great Southern immediately took advantage of the changed circumstances. Many of the buses and lorries competing with the branch lines belonged to one-man concerns, and there was nothing which could be done about them for the time being, but at the other end of the scale there was the Irish Omnibus Company with routes covering most of the Free State. The Great Southern entered into an agreement with the company for it to operate road passenger services on the GSR's behalf, and four years later, in 1931, a controlling interest was acquired by the GSR in the largest of the road haulage firms, John Wallis & Sons Ltd. The GNR followed suit, buying up a number of road passenger concerns and simultaneously starting an extensive road goods service based on its principal railway stations. Up in the north-west of the Free State the narrow gauge Londonderry & Lough Swilly Railway, grasping at the chance of cutting its ever increasing losses, began in 1931 to operate a fleet of single-deck buses, at the same time reducing its rail passenger services.

The GSR benefited little from its new acquisitions. It was as if it felt that it was not quite proper for a respectable railway company to be seen dabbling with internal-combustion engines, and it allowed its road services to go pretty much their own way, with the consequence that road and rail continued to compete, to the advantage of neither. Losses on the railways continued to mount and by 1931 the gross receipts of the GSR were £770,519 down on the 1925 figure of £4,430,519, not withstanding wage reductions all round of between 4s and 5s 9d which were put into effect between June 1926, and January 1927. For the first six years of its existence the GSR paid a dividend of 1 per cent, in 1931 this fell to $\frac{1}{2}$ per cent, and the next year there was no dividend.

Again the Government stepped in and passed the Road Passenger Act (1932), placing a number of restrictions on road passenger operators. These were not entirely designed to assist the railways, but were equally an attempt to improve the standards of the bus companies and to bring some order into the highly individualistic, not to say chaotic, road passenger business. The

1932 Act repealed the 1927 one, but gave railway, tramway, and canal companies further powers to enter the road motor business, though these powers were not taken up to any great extent.

At the same time an Act was passed which, on paper, appeared to open up the possibility of momentous changes, but which in fact lead to very few, at least during the rest of the decade. The Railways (Miscellaneous) Act, 1932, gave the railways power to abandon or reduce train services on lines which had been constructed or operated with the assistance of money from public sources. In other words, the railway companies could, if they chose, cease operation over a considerable part of the system within the 32 Counties.

One might wonder why this had not been made possible earlier, and why, indeed, road transport was not allowed to blossom unhindered in free-for-all competition, letting passenger carriers and merchandise hauliers go wherever trade offered, and fixing rates and fares according to what their customers were prepared to pay. After all, Ireland had fought for so long for freedom and now she had it why should it not apply in every sphere of the nation's life? In a highly industrialised country such as the United States or Great Britain there might be arguments in favour of this charmingly uncomplicated notion, but it happens to embrace within its ethos the notion of the survival of the fittest, and it might well have happened that the fittest would have been a handful of operators who would refuse to operate except where they were assured of a handsome profit. In a largely rural country like Ireland this could have resulted in a sizeable percentage of the population waking up one morning and finding itself with no trains, buses or road hauliers of any kind other than its own tractor and donkey-powered transport.

But this was not the Irish way. The people certainly had fought for freedom, but they had also fought for independence from rule by a tiny, privileged minority, and whichever party had been in power since 1922 the Government had always been strongly in favour of public ownership. There was not sufficient money in the national purse to buy the railways outright, but the Dail kept a close watch on the whole field of transport within the Free State.

DeValera dominated politics in Ireland to an even greater extent than did Churchill in Britain. Released in 1924 after spending a year in prison following his activities during the Civil War, he might have been thought to have ended his political career. Yet within two years he had formed a new party, Fianna Fail (Warriors of Ireland) and a year later he came within an ace of winning a general election. DeValera resumed his seat in the Dail, having first to take the Oath of Allegiance, which he neatly got around by saying that he was merely putting his signature to a piece of paper, and it was no business of his what the writing above it said. In 1932, after winning the February election, Fianna Fail came to power and DeValera once again had become Taioseach (Prime Minister). He immediately abolished the Oath, which annoyed various people in and out of power in Britain, but otherwise had little effect apart from giving a lot of Irishmen a great deal of satisfaction. DeValera's next important act was of much greater material significance.

Ever since 1922 Ireland had been paying a considerable sum each year to the dispossessed British owners of land in Ireland. DeValera argued that they had no right to the money as the land had been taken by force from its original owners, and said they would get no more. Two members of the British Cabinet, Lord Hailsham (father of the present holder of the title) and J. H. Thomas, came scurrying over from Westminster and put it to DeValera that he had acted unconstitutionally, and as Ireland was a member of the Common-wealth the matter should be handled by the Commonwealth Office. DeValera replied that Ireland belonged to no such thing and on those terms refused to negotiate. It was ironical that Thomas should have been one of the delegation sent on such an errand. In his days as a leader of the National Union of Railwaymen he had been firmly on the side of the Irish workers and people in their struggle for independence, claiming that English rule in Ireland had failed. "Every form of Government had been tried except liberty" were his exact words, yet now as a member of the Coalition Government, formed after the Labour one, of which also he had been a member, he was doing his best to prevent Ireland gaining complete political and economic freedom. The upshot of DeValera's refusal to pay up was an economic war, with the imposition of penal tariffs on Irish imports into Britain, and, in retaliation, similar Irish ones on British goods. It was not a state of affairs calculated to improve the lot of the Great Southern.

Despite the worsening financial position the GSR's network had managed to remain intact throughout the 1920s, although in 1929 it was decided that the main line from Dublin to the West should be converted from double to

Ex-MGWR G2 2–4–0 No 653 negotiating a single track section near Galway

single track working. Even in MGWR days not quite all of it had been double, two sections near the Galway end, totalling 23½ miles, remaining single, but after the GSR conversion, carried out on the grounds of economy, only the seven miles from Dublin out to Clonsilla were still double. The conversion had little effect on the timetable, as there were only four principal trains a day in each direction, between Broadstone and Galway, Sligo and Westport, plus goods trains and the odd Navan and Cavan branch services. To reduce to a minimum any delays which might result double-way signalling was installed at the crossing loop stations so that fast trains could run through in either direction at speed, although neither the MGWR nor its successor had gone in for much of this.

The sum of £25,000 was set aside for signalling improvements on the MGWR section. The Webb–Thompson Electric Train staff was adopted and installed at all the signal-boxes at either end of and along the single line sections, extra apparatus being put in at Clonsilla, Enfield, Mullingar and Athlone, so that much longer block sections could be used on Sundays when there was little traffic. Advanced starting signals were done away with, and calling-on arms were installed on each home signal. The purpose of these was to allow a train to be admitted to a platform whilst another train was approaching the other platform from the opposite direction. Concrete posts were provided at the ends of each section to accommodate the tablet exchange apparatus. This was not entirely foolproof; if the tender of the locomotive was swaying excessively or the rail height had altered consequent to the ballast being repacked the exchange might not take place, and it was known for the staff to go flying off and disappear. On one such occasion it was found long afterwards in tall grass a couple of hundred yards away and on another it had hidden itself in the net of a Travelling Post Office attached to the train. When a mishap like this occurred and the staff could not be found immediately pilotmen had to be provided to ride on the footplates.

There was a limited amount of locomotive construction after 1925, but nothing like sufficient to replace all the worn-out curiosities the GSR had inherited. As J. R. Bazin, the Great Southern's first CME put it on surveying his charges, "I like historic locomotives but I wish I had less of them in day-to-day traffic". The MGWR was the best off out of the 5ft 3in gauge companies, having only just completed building 23 very powerful mixed traffic 0–6–0s with 5ft 8in wheels as well as being in process of bringing its largest 4–4–0s up to date with new boilers, superheaters and piston-valves. The most useful legacy the MGWR passed on to the Great Southern was a brand new class of mixed traffic engine, the first of which was not completed until April 9, 1925, after the MGWR had ceased to exist. This was No 49 and was not a Broadstone design but a 2–6–0 constructed from a "do-it-yourself" kit supplied by Woolwich Arsenal. One hundred of these kits had been built, partly to give employment to redundant munition workers, and partly with an eye too on the possibility of nationalisation coming to Britain's railways and the need for a standard mixed traffic engine. This 2–6–0 was, in fact, a Maunsell design, a continuation of the SE&CR N Class, and it was a curious twist of fate that the GSR should acquire an engine of his from such an unlikely source to go with his Inchicore-built *Sir William Goulding*.

Although No 49 was the only one to appear in MGWR livery, and almost before the paint was dry it had been covered over by GSR grey, the MGWR had another eleven sets of parts waiting to be assembled. These were each purchased at the knock-down price of £2,000. On inspecting No 49, or No 372 as she soon became (she also bore the number 410 for a very short time) the GSR authorities, who were probably considering building more Bazin 500 class 4–6–0s, decided that the Maunsell engines were such a bargain that they ordered another 15 sets of parts from Woolwich. The original eleven were put together at Broadstone, the last of them, No 383, being the very last engine built there. The others came out from Inchicore between 1927 and 1930, one set of parts being kept as spares, and the last six completed engines had 6ft instead of 5ft 6in driving wheels. These latter engines were at first used exclusively on the GSWR section, even working the Cork Mails on occasions, but the rest were mostly to be found on the Midland, where they were put in charge of the principal passenger and goods turns.

Apart from the alterations necesssry to convert them from the 4ft 8½in to the 5ft 3in gauge they looked identical with the Southern Railway engines, although they never acquired the smoke-deflectors with which the English ones were later fitted. Like them they were not entirely successful as express locomotives, although they had a fair turn of speed; the 5ft 6in engines were capable of 75mph, and the 6ft engines of slightly more. Their chief fault was their riding qualities, which have been described as just about the worst of any GSR type, and this naturally did not endear them to enginemen. This unsteadiness very likely resulted from the weakening of their frames caused by the removal of some of the stays in order to effect weight reduction when they were modified for the 5ft 3in gauge. Nevertheless they were a great bargain and were of considerable value to the Great Southern through the difficult years of the 1930s and 1940s.

The state of the D&SER locomotive department was quite the opposite of that of the Midland. True, there were two excellent new 2–6–0s, quite the equal of the Maunsell engines, but the MGWR had nothing to match certain poor old things on the D&SER, whose crews, it was rumoured, on occasions had been observed tieing down safety-valves in order to get themselves and their trains up the banks around Bray and Killiney. Grand Canal Street did wonders in keeping its ailing charges going at all, but what was needed were brand new locomotives, not patched-up old ones. The GSR scrapped a number of the most decrepit of the D&SE locomotives and replaced them with a variety of pre-1925 types from other sections, but these were no great improvement.

In October 1928, Inchicore unveiled a spanking new suburban tank engine, the P1 class 2–6–2T No 850. It is likely that her coupled wheels and one of the pony trucks came from the spare set of Woolwich 2–6–0 parts, and she looked rather like a cross between a Maunsell River 2–6–4T and a GWR 5100. She was a handsome engine, but like the Inchicore 4–8–0Ts did not really come off, and no more of the class were built. It is difficult to pinpoint just what was wrong with her, but she spent a great part of her career in the works. In between she put in some good work on the coast road as far as Bray, and at least one driver considered her "a wonderful machine"; he said that she took the banks as though they didn't exist, and declared her to be the best engine he had ever worked on.

The carriage department at Inchicore carried on as if there had been no change at all in ownership, and continued to produce wooden-bodied carriages of pure GSWR design down to 1928, including three sets of non-corridor coaches for the D&SE section. Some of these were given under-frames built in Belgium which had been bought by the MGWR and never used. The most interesting development in the carriage field during the early years of the Great Southern was the introduction in 1926 of Pullman cars. Four, Nos 100–3, were built by the Birmingham Carriage & Wagon Company, of design virtually identical with those which were then going into service in Britain, These were put to work between Dublin, Cork, Limerick and Sligo. They were third class cars, accommodating 46 passengers, and were painted in traditional Pullman chocolate-and-cream livery. No more carriages entered service on the Great Southern after the 1928 batch had been completed until the mid-1930s, with the important exception of dining cars Nos 2400/1, which came out in 1931. These were designed to work together, one containing a centre kitchen and seating for 30, and the other being an open 48-seat trailer. Their rather striking interiors were decorated with Celtic *motifs*, but possibly these proved to be no aids to digestion for within five years the cars were renovated in a much simpler style.

Not much was attempted in the way of improvement to buildings; most of the stations taken over by the Great Southern had been substantially built affairs, capable of many more years' service. Indeed, some of the more remote ones were much superior to the cottages of the country people living round them. The one noticeable change which gradually took place was the provision of name-boards in Irish to supplement the English ones; the policy of the Government was to encourage the use of the native language wherever possible, including its teaching in all schools.

CHAPTER EIGHT

The 1930s

THE RECESSION OF 1929, while not affecting Ireland quite as severely as some more heavily industrialised countries, certainly did it no good. Irishmen who had been working in England and Scotland found themselves unemployed and came home, knowing that there would be no work for them there either, but at least it was better to be on the dole among friends and relations than among strangers. The economic war, brought about by DeValera's refusal to continue paying land annuities to Britain, caused further hardship, particularly to farmers, whose chief source of income, the British market, was now denied them. A host of small industries sprang up in Ireland in an attempt to cash in on the high cost of British manufactured goods which had had tariffs placed on them as a retaliatory measure against the British embargo, but unfortunately the inexperienced Irish produced goods of inferior quality and the population preferred to buy British, whatever the cost. This inevitably pushed up the cost of living, and the members of the Government took a cut in salary in the hope that this would set an example and reverse the trend. The railway workers in the 26 Counties reluctantly accepted the necessity for wage reductions, but when the Northern Ireland Government announced its intention to pass a similar measure, the railwaymen in the Six Counties refused to co-operate.

They had been having a bad time, wages having already been cut by between $3\frac{3}{4}$ and $4\frac{3}{8}$ per cent in May 1931, and the additional 15 per cent cut proposed in August 1932, was the last straw. The NCC had bought up a number of competing bus services, and it had continued to operate these while reducing rail services, thus putting a number of railwaymen out of work; the construction of the Greenisland Loop line admittedly had provided a number of additional jobs, but only on a temporary basis, for the completion of the project saw the termination of employment for most of the men engaged on it. While road operators were allowed to compete unrestrictedly there was little the railway companies could do except to cut their own costs wherever possible, and if this meant fewer jobs and lower wages for railway workers it was unfortunate but inevitable. The NCC Directors followed the example of the members of the Dublin Government and took a 5 per cent cut in salary. As a gesture this failed to impress the employees, for 5 per cent off their wages brought them rather nearer the bread line than did 5 per cent off the directors' fees; so a strike was called for early 1933. Malcolm Speir, the Manager of the NCC, sent a circular to all his staff, pointing out how much the railways would suffer from a prolonged stoppage, but the men's patience had been tried once too often, and at noon on January 31, all union members (other than those of the Railway Clerks Association and on the B&CDR) went on strike.

A few services continued to run, operated by clerical staff, apprentices, non-union men and, on the NCC, LMS men brought in from Scotland. The importation of the latter caused particular resentment among the strikers and they determined to stay out as long as possible. But their cause was a lost one, for jobs were hard to come by in the North at the best of times, and there were precious few ways a striker could supplement his meagre strike pay. There was little likelihood that the managements would withdraw the wage cuts in the immediate future, and by early April the strike was broken.

A most unpleasant consequence on the NCC was the singling out of the strike leaders for dismissal. It was understandable that Speir should feel aggrieved as he stood helplessly by and watched bus and lorry operators cashing in on the situation, but they were only speeding up an inevitable process which the Government was apparently determined should in any case come about sooner or later. To victimise men who, either through desperation or political awareness, had felt impelled to stand up for a maintenance, not an extension, of their rights, strikes one as a rather vindictive act. It was also out of character, for although Speir was something of an autocrat, he did much work amongst the under-privileged and for the youth service, taking a particular interest in the rehabilitation of released prisoners.

Undoubtedly the strike had a detrimental effect on the already shaky financial position of the Northern Irish companies, but it was hardly the death blow freely predicted. The only services on the NCC to close as an immediate consequence of the strike were two narrow-gauge ones, passenger trains on the 24-mile Ballymena–Larne section, and goods trains on the 5¾-mile Ballymena–Doagh branch. One really could not make much of a song and dance about these, for the Doagh branch had already lost its passenger service, in 1930, and the Larne Town–Larne Harbour branch had gone in 1932, leaving the future of the remainder of the Larne line uncertain. On the Great Northern the Goraghwood–Armagh, Dungannon–Cookstown and Scarva–Banbridge branches all lost their passenger services, although they remained open for goods, and the poor little 7-mile Castlederg & Victoria Bridge narrow-gauge line failed to reopen after the strike. This not very extensive list of closures hardly matched the dire forebodings that the managements had made prior to, and during the strike; it might be claimed that the position of the railways had been further weakened and that subsequent closures were a result of the 1933 stoppage, but this, to say the least, is arguable, particularly when one considers how far down the slippery slope towards penury the railway companies had already descended by 1933.

The Castleblaney–Keady branch of the GNR went as early as 1924, while passenger trains on another GNR line, from Keady to Armagh, ceased running at the beginning of 1932. On the NCC the Draperstown passenger service and the narrow-gauge Ballymena–Parkmore one both ended in 1930; the latter line reached the highest point of any Irish line, 1,250ft, a record it retained for some while longer because its goods service continued to operate. The Limavady Junction–Dungiven passenger service ended in December

1932, and the Portstewart Steam Tramway had closed down and been dismantled in 1926.

Despite the fact that the 26 Counties were unaffected by the strike, their lines had begun to shut down too. The first narrow-gauge one to go was the Cork, Blackrock & Passage; with it went the only double-track section of narrow gauge in Ireland, the two miles from Albert Street station, Cork, to Blackrock. The line had been dying for years and had twice gone into comas before being revived by the GSR in 1925. The Haulbowline dockyard, situated on an island opposite Queenstown, had closed down in 1922, bringing to an end the railway's steamer services, while trams had gradually taken away most of the traffic between Cork and Blackrock, and buses that between Cork and Crosshaven, the terminus of the line. The railway did well enough in the summer, when it found plenty of customers willing to be transported out for a day at the sea, but for eight months of the year it might as well have not been there. It was therefore no surprise when the GSR called "enough" and put the line out of its misery on September 19, 1932. Shortly afterwards Cork's other narrow-gauge line, the Cork & Muskerry, went too, its traffic having "nearly reached vanishing point", to quote a contemporary account of its demise at the end of 1934, for the anticipated suburban traffic along the Blarney line had failed to develop. One of the Cork & Muskerry and all four of the Cork, Blackrock & Passage engines were transferred to other narrow-gauge sections of the Great Southern for further work.

In between these two closures came another, that of a tramway, which possessed sufficient railway-like features to warrant inclusion within these pages. This was the Dublin & Blessington, a 15½-mile, 5ft 3in gauge line which ran from Terenure in the south-western suburbs of Dublin out to the village of Blessington, at the foot of the mountains. There was an extension, the Blessington & Poulaphouca Steam Tramway Company, not very much longer than its title, and worked by the larger company. The Dublin & Blessington had two particular claims to fame, one for introducing the forerunner of the modern diesel electric railcar, the other for deciding that there was no future in the notion and becoming the last steam tramway to remain in operation in the British Isles.

The pioneer railcars were actually petrol-electrics, rather than diesels, but the principle was the same. Two were put into service in 1916 at a time when the company found itself short of coal. Designed by J. P. Tierney, the consulting electrical engineer, their bodies were built in Dublin and the electrical components came from Westinghouse. They were 68-seat double-deckers, with two powered bodies, each bogie driven by a 500V, 65bhp motor, but apparently they were not very reliable and rather underpowered, and when coal supplies improved their services were dispensed with. The company had no money to spend on experimenting with such a new and untried method of propulsion, and steam saw out the line's last days. A number of the trailers finished their careers as tea-rooms halfway up Bray Head, dispensing refreshments to energetic Dubliners who had clambered up from the beach below; a bar in Tallaght, on the Blessington Road, has recently decorated one of its walls with a large photograph of one of the steam trams in action. Being classed a tramline the Dublin & Blessington was not included in the 1925 amalgamation; it connected with the DUTC trams at Terenure, but there was never any through running between the concerns, apart from a limited goods service which did not last long.

The broad gauge mileage of the Great Southern also began to contract around this time. The former GSWR branch connecting the Wexford–Waterford line at Palace East with the Waterford–Kilkenny–Carlow–Dublin line at Muine Bheag (formerly Bagenalstown) lost its passenger service early in 1931. The nearby Castlecomer branch passenger service went around the same time, as did that on the short branch from Birdhill to Killaloe on the shores of Lough Derg, and the former MGW Nesbitt Junction–Edenderry one. All these lines continued to be served by goods trains. Finally in 1931 the Kinsale branch of the old CB&SCR was closed to all traffic.

One gets the impression that the Dail at this time was mostly occupying itself discussing transport. Following the Road Transport and the Railways (Miscellaneous) Acts of 1932, it passed two more the next year. One was a Road Transport Act, setting up a licensing system which placed further restrictions on operators, confining them to certain areas, classes of merchandise and weights of vehicle, and giving statutory transport companies powers, compulsory if necessary, to buy up other passenger and merchandise transport operators. The second Act of 1933, the Railways Act, provided formal recognition of the parlous state of the Great Southern, writing off over half its capital, and bringing it down from the 1925 figure of £26m to the much more realistic one of £12.3m. The Act also gave the Minister for Industry and Commerce powers to permit railway companies to end or reduce railway services, provided that adequate road ones were substituted.

It hardly needs to be said that these powers were frequently used. The remote regions of the West suffered particularly. First the $7\frac{3}{4}$-mile branch from Ballina to Killala closed in July 1934, then, on April 27, 1935, the 49-mile line from Galway City to Clifden went, and finally the $26\frac{1}{4}$-mile Westport Junction to Achill Sound branch went out of business in September 1937. One of these lines, particularly the Clifden one, which ran through the heart of Connemara, traversed a beautiful part of Ireland, an area of bare mountains and deep lakes, but it was also a remote one and sparsely populated. Both the Midland Great Western and the Great Southern had run through coaches between Dublin and Clifden in an effort to popularise the area, but the general public refused to desert Killarney, and eventually the line shut in early spring, before the holiday season had even got under way. Well over 30 years since the last train steamed out of Clifden it is still possible to trace much of the track bed, and the station buildings, platform, and even the awning, at Clifden are still intact, the station house being used as a tweed storeroom.

A curious and rather terrible story relates to the beginning and the end of the Achill line. In 1893, the year of its opening, a sailing ship left Achill bound for Westport with 120 local men, who were on their way to take the steamer for Scotland, where they hoped to find employment helping with the harvest. As the boat was entering Westport harbour the men crowded to the side, causing a sudden list which so unbalanced the boat that it capsized, throwing the men into the water and trapping some in the upturned hull; 38 of them died. The railway line was at that time not yet open although it was all but ready. The finishing touches were hurriedly completed so that the bodies of the drowned Achill men could be brought home for burial. At the mass funeral a local man, known for his predictions, declared that the first, and the last, train to Achill would carry corpses. In September, 1937, the month the line was due to close, another group of Achill men who had gone to work in the mines in Scotland were caught in a fire at Kirkintilloch and ten were killed. On September 19, eleven days short of the time predicted, an ex-MGW 4–4–0, No 534, pulled into Achill station with a train of two bogie carriages and three six-wheel vans, the latter containing the coffins of the dead men. The inhabitants of the far West have a fatalistic affinity with the supernatural and have long fascinated writers, J. M. Synge in particular; very possibly the tragic events of 1893 and 1937 were linked by mere coincidence, but it must be allowed that it was rather a singular one.

Two further passenger services ceased during the 1930s. One was the Patrickswell to Charleville line, linking the Dublin–Cork main line with that from Limerick to Tralee, and the other was the Tralee & Dingle. Both lines retained their goods services, the former for another 30 years, during which it continued to see the occasional special passenger train, while the principal *raison d'être* of the Tralee & Dingle, the cattle trade, kept it in existence for some while longer.

A bus service had been running through the Dingle peninsula for some years prior to 1939, although it had not been very well patronised, but the time eventually came when the authorities felt they could go on subsidising the trains no longer. The buses knocked 50 minutes off the overall run between Tralee and Dingle, and if they were rather less comfortable than the trains and lacked their character, they were certainly more convenient and economical and so the decision was taken to end the rail passenger service on April 16, 1939. The locomotives in charge of the final runs to and from Dingle, and on the Castlegregory branch, were 2–6–2T No 5 and 2–6–0Ts Nos 6 and 8. There were seven locomotives in active service and all continued to be put in steam after the passenger trains ceased to run in order to work the daily goods on the main line and the cattle specials. One of the former Cork & Muskerry engines, No 6K, worked on the Tralee & Dingle Section in 1935–6 before moving onto the Schull & Skibbereen.

In October 1935, one of the most northerly sections of railway in Ireland, the 18¼-mile Buncrana to Carndonagh line of the LLSR, which served the peninsula between Lough Swilly and Lough Foyle, closed down completely and was replaced by lorries and buses belonging to the railway company. It was a move that immediately paid off, and although the company still made a loss that year it was the smallest since 1923.

Apart from closures of lines the railway companies, and particularly the Great Southern, were continually casting around for ways of cutting costs. The introduction of railcars, variously powered by steam, electricity, and diesel and petrol engines, was probably the most significant measure and is dealt with elsewhere. A more retrograde one was wage reductions. The employees naturally objected forcibly and although only one serious strike resulted there were other minor ones from time to time. One, in March 1935, confined to Dublin, affected, among other people, Sir Harry Lauder and his company, who were then touring Ireland.

There were times when wage reductions were not sufficient to ease the company's position and then it had to resort to dismissals. No one's job was really safe, and to quote just one example, in December 1928 a chief draughts-man, eight assistants, and two apprentices were sacked out of the CME's department at Inchicore. It must have been rather like the purges in Russia, and when one talks to the survivors, now senior officials of CIE, one gets the impression that throughout the period everybody went about in daily expectation of losing his job.

At the end of 1933 the Great Southern offered to restore $2\frac{1}{2}$ per cent of the $7\frac{1}{2}$ per cent cut, and although the men were pressing for more they reluc-tantly agreed to accept it, at a conference held early in the new year. Further restorations were made later in 1936 and again in 1937. A union spokesman claimed that the GSR was now doing better, and as the cost of living was rising he was justified in continuing to press for an increase, but W. H. Morton, the General Manager, denied the accuracy of the first part of the statement and said that in reality traffic was declining alarmingly. Even the road services were doing badly and between Christmas 1936, and June 1937, over 300 men at Broadstone, the principal road department works, had been laid off.

Broadstone's role had gradually been changing since its take-over by the GSR. The last locomotive to be built there had come out in 1927 and by then rumours of the impending closure of the works were in the air. Improve-ments were being put in hand at Inchicore and it was obviously to the Great Southern's advantage if all locomotive building and heavy repair work could be concentrated there. Unlike Grand Canal Street Broadstone was well laid out, with plenty of room for expansion, and so it was decided that it should be retained and developed as a maintenance centre for the road fleet, railway activity gradually being phased out. Broadstone passenger station had its disadvantages, of which the principal was its distance from the city centre. The least busy of the Dublin terminals, there was no reason why, with a bit of ingenuity, its services could not be diverted to Westland Row or Amiens Street, to the advantage of practically everyone, for the only people likely to be worse off were inhabitants who lived in the station's immediate vicinity, in North Dublin. Virtually no commuter business was involved so the inconvenience was hardly unbearable.

The Cavan and Meath branch line trains began to run to and from Amiens Street in 1929, but it was some years before the long-distance services linking Dublin with the Midlands and the West followed suit. A connection between the former MGW line to North Wall and Amiens Street already existed, by way of Newcomen Junction, but this was rather inconvenient and it was decided to resuscitate Glasnevin Junction, which had been out of use for a number of years. There had been stations at Glasnevin and further along the line at Drumcondra, $1\frac{1}{2}$ miles from North Wall, and these had been served by the steam rail-motor service from Kingsbridge during the early 1900s, but the route was a roundabout one and could not really compete with the much more direct trams.

In July 1935, work started on an £18,000 rebuilding scheme at Glasnevin, remodelling the junction so that it faced the opposite direction. When complete this would enable trains from the MGWR line to run via Liffey Junction through Glasnevin and Drumcondra to North Strand Junction and thus gain the GSR platforms at Amiens Street. By the beginning of the following summer the new route was ready for use, although trains continued to run into Broadstone until the end of that year.

At midnight on January 16/17, 1937, the Night Mail from the west ran into Broadstone for the last time, all but 90 years after the station had opened. The following afternoon a special left with buyers for the Athlone and Edgeworthstown fairs, but from that day onwards railway trains no longer graced Broadstone's interior. Externally it remained much the same and one did not have to make much of a journey to come upon signs of railway activity, for the shed remained open and continued to provide motive power for the Midland Section services. The engines ran up the bank to Liffey Junction and either picked up their trains there, or reversed around to Westland Row. For a while the largest ex-MGWR classes were not allowed over the bridge across the Liffey between Westland Row and Amiens Street, so that the Woolwich Moguls, which already were the mainstay of the services, found themselves even busier.

In MGWR days it was as well for those addicted to the bottle to keep well clear of Broadstone after a night spent indulging their hobby for they might well have heard fairy music. Or thought they had, for the sound was actually that of steam engines gently whistling to themselves. This hardly makes the matter any clearer so I had best explain that it was the practice of the steam-raiser to slightly open the whistle-valve of each locomotive so that he could detect by the gently increasing note how the fire was building up and the steam rising. The varying pitches of all the whistles, soft rather than strident, must have produced a distinctive and rather haunting sound.

The Great Southern did what it could to modernise, but its financial position so restricted its efforts that they appeared less than wholehearted, and there were times when customers hardly got value for their money. Holiday periods always put a severe strain on the system and passengers from England, mostly Irish people returning home, often received such rough treatment that it was a wonder that they had the courage to commit themselves to the Great Southern's tender mercies for the journey back again. There were still far more six-wheel than bogie coaches in service, even on many long-distance trains at peak periods, and even more non-corridor vehicles. The staff on the D&SE section between Dun Laoghaire Pier and Dublin were said to be "extraordinarily ignorant of their duties and will volunteer no information to a harassed passenger". On occasions local services had to be cancelled to provide stock for boat trains and this achieved the distinction of alienating two groups of customers at one go, the regular commuters who found themselves with no trains at all, and the boat passengers who found themselves with a non-corridor commuters' train and didn't think much of it.

During Christmas Week, 1937, the boat from Holyhead failed to make the rail connection at Dun Laoghaire each morning, with the consequence that passengers to the West had to kick around Dublin until 2.30 in the afternoon. Their plight was sometimes hardly improved once aboard the train; on one occasion only three of the twelve densely packed coaches of a Sligo train possessed corridors, and on another passengers were expected to spend 6½hr in a train bound for the west without a single lavatory between them. Again, porters had to be called to sweep water from the corridors and compartments of a relief train which presumably had been standing around on a siding for weeks without any attention.

The position down at Rosslare was hardly any better. At least a thousand people used to arrive from Fishguard each Saturday morning in summer, and they would have but one restaurant car, capable of seating 30 passengers, if they were going to Cork, and none at all on the Limerick and relief Cork trains when these ran. Mind you, harsh words were also said about the connecting services on the other side of the Irish Sea. Carriages were said to be too crowded and dirty, the food in the restaurant cars was "scrappy", and time-keeping was poor, the attitude being that the Fishguard–Rosslare route was primarily a mail and freight one and that passengers only got in the way. One always thinks of the late 1930s as being the culmination of a hundred years of glorious progress on the Great Western, but it would seem that not everything in the Empire had managed to attain perfection.

Cars were beginning to form a significant feature on this route and in 1936 over a thousand were carried. Unloading at Rosslare was a slow business, each car having to be swung out of the hold of the ship on to a railway flat truck, then hauled by a locomotive along the pier and deposited at the far end. Passengers had been forbidden to ride in the cars while they were aboard the train, since one had gone over the edge and put itself and its occupants in the sea. A marginal improvement was brought about in time for the 1936 season, with the replacement of the original trucks by two cut-down former MGWR six-wheel carriages, each capable of carrying two vehicles, a doubling of the train's capacity.

The boat trains between Rosslare and Cork were a tough proposition, usually heavily loaded and worked over a route which, west of Waterford, abounded in gradients. Much of the original 1906–7 rolling stock was still in use, including some 66ft carriages, unique in Ireland. Even so the ten compartments in the thirds hardly allowed much leg-room, the GWR deeming it necessary to provide another 4ft in the 70ft vehicles they employed on the Paddington–Fishgard run. For a long period up until the late 1920s Coey 5ft 8½in 4–4–0s provided the motive power on the Irish side, but although five similar engines were built in 1936, Woolwich Moguls took over the trains around 1930 and maintained a monopoly until the end of steam.

Not that the overall schedule was anything very startling. In 1906 it took 13hr to reach Cork from London, whilst in 1939, with the advent of customs delays, it had gone up to 14hr 8min in one direction and 15¼hr in the other. Nevertheless the 2–6–0s found themselves hard pushed, and when running late were frequently known to exceed the speed restriction around the curve at Rosslare Strand. The signalman there declared, "One night she'll go over and that'll learn 'em to go slower". Fortunately this dire prediction was not fulfilled.

The five 1936 4–4–0s were the only passenger tender engines, other than the 800s, built by the Great Southern during the 1930s. Of tank engines there were also five, designed, like the lone 2–6–2T of 1928, to work the suburban services out of Harcourt Street and Westland Row. Officially classified 13, but better known as the 670s, it was stated at the time that they were basically the tank engine version of the 710 class 0–6–0s. This was about as damning as you could get, although Inchicore was sufficiently confident of their chances to turn out all five simultaneously. They had larger driving wheels than the 710s and proved to be a more popular engine (a not very difficult feat), but were not really any better than other types already working the Dublin suburban services, particularly the ex-Bandon 4–6–0T, and no more were built.

Various people concerned with both types of engine expressed various opinions about them, the Bray locomotive foreman declaring that the 670s possessed excellent starting and hauling powers, while one of his drivers swore that they were sluggish and always in trouble. The same foreman did not like the Bandon tanks, yet there were drivers who were much enamoured of them and were able to produce some startling feats of acceleration with them when working the Dun Laoghaire boat trains. All of which reinforces the contention that the steam locomotive is a very subtle box of mechanical contrivances capable of much variation in performance. There was, however, little argument about the 670's predecessor, No 850, being a very temperamental performer, for except for a four-month period in 1938 she was continuously in the shops between October 1937, and April 1939. The only other steam engines put into service by the GSR were two Sentinel shunters, rather like those used on the Somerset & Dorset line, and purchased at the same time as the Sentinel railcars.

Not many locomotives were withdrawn during this period but among those that were was a notable machine, a well-tank of the former Waterford & Tramore Railway. This locomotive was built by Fairbairns in 1855, and her uniqueness lay in the fact that she had the 2–2–2 wheel arrangement, the last single-driver in normal service in the British Isles. Numbered 483 by the Great Southern, her end was sad and rather unexpected. She had had a complete overhaul in 1931 and was regularly employed hauling converted rail-motors between Waterford and Tramore, a job she performed with great efficiency, burning only 16lb of coal per mile. She was said to be cheaper to run than a bus and might have gone on indefinitely had she not derailed on September 17, 1935, running off the line in a cutting, injuring her driver and fireman and causing considerable damage to herself. For a time it was hoped that she might be repaired, but it was found that her injuries were too extensive and some time in 1936 "the most photographed engine in Ireland" passed away.

One realm in which considerable economies were made was the Carriage Department. The last few coaches of GS&WR design, turned out in 1927–8, were of lighter and less elaborate construction, thereby saving £300 per vehicle, a skimping which was noticeable in the low seat backs and generally sparse interiors, and building then ceased altogether for some years.

A programme was then devised enabling 100 vehicles to be withdrawn over a four-year period without reducing the total number of seats available. This was done by converting first-class vehicles and seconds into thirds, for the numbers of first-class passengers were declining steadily each year. At the same time it was admitted that an extensive programme of reupholstering was needed and it was hoped to deal with one-tenth of the carriage fleet each year. This figure was never reached, however, and by the end of the 1930s the interiors of most Great Southern carriages were rather shabby, although the standards of cleanliness, both inside and out, had improved and it was common to see porters at the Dublin termini filling in their spare moments by polishing door and grab handles.

In August 1929, the GSR possessed twelve dining cars, four of which had not been used since the beginning of World War I, and all of them were in urgent need of overhaul. Apart from these there were four Pullmans, not owned by the Great Southern, and being only recently introduced were presumably in rather better condition. Two dining cars were built in 1930, at a cost of £3,420 each, and were a welcome addition, enabling some older catering vehicles to be withdrawn, but the situation was far from satisfactory and various temporary measures had to be resorted to. Four bogie vans were fitted with counters for use as bars, and they were put into excursion trains and run on sports specials, the line of thinking presumably being that the customers would get sufficiently drunk not to object to confinement in a windowless wooden box. Later, in 1938, another variation on the theme was tried out, two six-wheel saloons of 1896 being similarly adapted. These were used on Mystery Excursions, the real mystery being how anyone managed to keep his beer in his glass whilst being tossed about a bucking, 40-year-old six-wheeler.

In 1934 carriage construction was resumed at Inchicore, and the vehicles which emerged were very much more up-to-date than those turned out from 1925 to 1928. They chiefly resembled contemporary LMS coaches, even to the extent that the livery was a close replica of Midland red. The possibility of all-steel ones had been considered but rejected, and Inchicore decided on wooden-framed, steel-panelled, 60ft long vehicles of both main line and suburban types. The suburban coaches were really rather ahead of their time in one respect, being open saloons without corridor connections, a layout then rarely found in locomotive-hauled stock. So popular were the new coaches that instructions had to be issued to railway employees not to travel in them if older stock was available. They were in service on most main line workings by 1939, but only on the Cork line were there sufficient to make up a complete train. Gradually all the Great Southern carriages were re-painted in the new livery, although it took a long time; some corridors never wore the chocolate and cream, and went straight from their pre-1925 colours to maroon.

By the late 1930s the Dublin suburban services presented a striking contrast between the most up-to-date and the antiquated. On the one hand there were a great many six-wheeled, flat-roofed, 19th century non-corridor coaches and a lot of equally ancient 2–4–0Ts and not very much younger 2–4–2Ts, while on the other hand there were the new steel-panelled saloons, the Drumm battery trains, and three-aspect colour light signals. The latter had been installed from 1934 onwards, from Amiens Street (GSR) along the Loop Line, through Westland Row and eventually out as far as Dun Laoghaire. These were the first such signals in Southern Ireland and much of the design work of the equipment was carried out by the Great Southern's own Signal and Telegraph Engineer. A mechanical lever-frame was devised to avoid the considerable cost of the use of a power frame would have entailed, and this also had the advantage of reducing the amount of maintenance and alterations which would otherwise have been necessary as the frame interlocked with the tappet-locking already used with mechanical operation. Points were electrically operated and automatic track diagrams were provided in the cabins.

In 1939, just before the outbreak of war, a similar scheme was completed at Kingsbridge, and the cabin there, with 76 levers, became the largest electrically-operated one on the Great Southern, and enabling a number of adjacent mechanically-operated ones to be closed.

A certain amount of criticism was voiced at the time of the signalling modernisation scheme in the Dublin area, that it was not really necessary and that the money might have been better spent elsewhere. Inevitably there were a few teething troubles, but once these were overcome the new arrangements worked very well, and with the steep rise in costs during and after the war the wisdom of the Great Southern in installing the scheme when it did came to be fully appreciated.

After a period of stability prices began to rise just before the outbreak of the war. The wage cuts were fully restored and on January 1, 1938, the Great Southern raised its passenger fares and merchandise rates by 5 per cent. In 1937 the British Government had agreed, on payment of a lump sum of £10m by Ireland, to give up any further claim to land annuities or other annual payments. DeValera and Chamberlain, who found much to respect in each other, signed the documents ending the economic war at a conference in London. Britain abandoned its naval bases at Cork, Berehaven and Lough Swilly, tariffs on British imports into Ireland were relaxed, and Irish cattle once again found a ready market in Britain. Relations between the two countries became more cordial than at any time since 1916, and it seemed that the Irish economy might well be in for a period of expansion. What effect this would have on the railways would have to be seen, whether it might mean more business or it might simply result in yet more transference of traffic to the roads.

CHAPTER NINE

The Northern Companies, 1933-9

DESPITE MANY FEARS the damage inflicted upon the northern railways by the 1933 Strike was not as extensive as it might have been and although passenger and freight receipts continued to decline, in some ways the last years of the 1930 decade saw the services of the GNR and the NCC at their peak.

The greatest stumbling block in the way of the NCC improving its main line schedules between Belfast and Derry was the necessity for all trains to reverse at Greenisland, 6¾ miles out of Belfast. As far back as 1872 powers had been obtained from Parliament to build a loop line, but they had not been taken up owing to insufficient funds. In the late 1920s the possibility of a loop was again raised, though not because the NCC was now particularly prosperous. Unemployment had always been high in Northern Ireland, and during the 1920s the Government had granted funds to the NCC to double the Larne line out as far as Whitehead, thereby providing some much-needed, if temporary, work for the unemployed of Belfast. With the successful completion of this, and the job situation worse rather than better, it was decided that now was the time to build the loop line, and in 1931 construction began. The scheme involved a new line, leaving the present main line at Whiteabbey, 4¼ miles from Belfast, to Mossley, 2½ miles distant, where it would rejoin the existing line and thus make possible through running between Belfast, Ballymena, the North Coast and Londonderry.

It was a large task involving cuttings, embankments, eight new road bridges and two large viaducts, and would certainly have not been possible without Government support. As a rule the Northern Ireland Government, from its setting up in 1921 down to the present day, has generally been less sympathetic to the railways than have successive Dublin ones, but the construction of the Greenisland Loop was one of the exceptions. The total cost of the works was £250,000, one-third coming from the Government, the rest from the LMS.

Although held up by the strike the work was completed on January 17, 1934, and a great beanfeast was held, reminiscent of Victorian times, attended by the Duke of Abercorn, the Governor of Northern Ireland. He and his party were conveyed in a special train of eight first-class carriages hauled by one of the new 2-6-0 engines, No 90, especially named after the noble Duke, which took the party on a grand tour of the new lines and then deposited them at the Northern Counties Hotel, Portrush, for lunch.

The loop line saved some 10–13 min running time, and in the summer timetables which came into operation on June 1 full advantage was taken of it. The fastest trains now ran non-stop between Belfast and Portrush in 80min, and a brand new express for commuters, the 8.10 ex-Portrush, was introduced. It arrived at York Road, Belfast, at 9.30am and left again at 5.15pm. This was the celebrated "North Atlantic Express", which was further speeded up in 1937 to complete the journey in 74 min; the 31-mile section from Ballymena to Belfast was then run at an average speed of 58.1mph, making this the fastest train in Ireland. The next summer the schedule was cut again, by one minute, which meant the Ballymena–Belfast run was now done in "even time".

The engines which worked the "North Atlantic Express", and were also taking over the other principal main line turns, were the W Class Moguls. Although designed by the NCC's Chief Mechanical Engineer, Stewart, they incorporated a number of standard LMS parts, for which Stanier's permission had to be obtained, and they looked rather like a Hughes/Fowler "Crab". It had been intended to name some of them after Irish chieftains, but as it was feared that this would "cause some resentment among certain sections of the Irish" they were given instead either local geographical names or those of British nobility and royalty. Presumably it did not matter if the latter offended other sections of the community. In Britain the 2–6–0 wheel arrangement

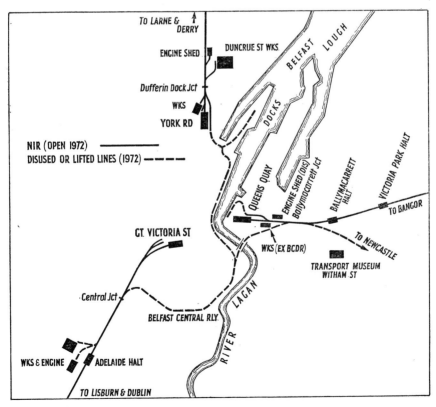

Belfast, 1972

has generally been for mixed traffic or freight service, but the Ws with their 6ft drivers were purely express engines and proved very popular, being well able to reach and exceed 80mph. Loads were not very heavy; the "North Atlantic Express" orginally consisted of no more than three coaches, later increased to five, and the relatively small 2–6–0s, assisted by the older 4–4–0s, served nearly all the NCC's needs.

The company by now had acquired a very LMS look. All its engines were painted Midland red with the LMS crest on the cab-side, although they had cast numberplates rather than painted numbers. Coaches were also obviously of Derby ancestry. Thirty bogie corridors of various types, very similar to their contemporaries on the LMS, had been built at Derby and delivered in 1924, and a further 21 carriages of the same design were constructed at York Road between 1925 and 1930. During this period four unique coaches, *plus* one new body on an old frame, were built for the narrow gauge. These were intended to work the boat trains between Ballymena and Larne, and were 3ft gauge replicas of the main line stock, complete with corridors and lavatories. Second-class was still popular in 1931 and four brake tri-composites were built in that year, a fifth coming along in 1934.

In 1932 the NCC put into service its first steel-sided, steel-roofed carriages, 12 non-corridors built at Wolverton for the Larne line. These were followed by more York Road corridors and then came the "North Atlantic Express" vehicles, over which York Road took particular pains, No 90, the buffet car, being a splendid example of the coach builder's craft. The carriage building programme went on right through the 1930s, closely following LMS practice, so that the later side and centre-corridor coaches looked like typical vehicles of the Stanier era with sliding ventilators in the wide windows and flush-panelled sides. By 1939 the NCC possessed a thoroughly modern carriage fleet, as up-to-date as any in Britain, and far superior to the Great Southern's, although that company could justifiably point out that if the NCC had not had the resources of the LMS to back it, the NCC might well have found itself in a state no better than that of the GSR.

Yet the Great Northern, which had no rich backer and was suffering from declining receipts, also managed to treat its passengers pretty well. It had built its first bogie coach in 1889, and from 1895 until 1932 at least one, and usually considerably more, bogie carriages were built each year. There were none in either 1933 or 1934, but Dundalk was obviously saving itself for something special, for in 1935 the first steel-panelled coaches, nine of them, arrived. Further such coaches followed up until 1939 when, rather curiously, hardboard was substituted for steel as the side panelling. This must have been for reasons of economy rather than shortage of materials, as the first of the coaches went into service before any embargo was placed on steel supplies. A number of these carriages are still at work, but the panelling is in a rather poor state, bulging and soft enough to allow inquisitive small boys and railway enthusiasts to push their fingers through in places.

The wooden-bodied GNR carriages in their varnished livery with blue shaded gold numbers had always borne a distinct resemblance to the English GNR, and later LNER, stock, but from 1935 onwards there came a marked change. For a short while the steel-panelled coaches were finished in imitation wood, rather like that of the post-war LNER Thompson vehicles, but this was soon changed to pale, flat mahogany colour. The old style of numbering remained and, indeed, persisted for long after World War II; as late as January 1969, a derelict brake second stood at Great Victoria Street, Belfast with a number in this style still clearly visible.

The late GNR carriages with their deep sliding ventilator windows, liberally interspersed with doors, and curved lower panels, were distinctive and elegant, typical of their period, but at the same time owing little to any other company's practice. As on the NCC second-class still persisted and as late as 1941 tri-composite coaches were being put into service.

Before leaving the subject of carriages, if I may revert to an earlier period for a moment, there was a piece of GNR enterprise which never really caught on, and this was the sleeping car. Distances in Ireland are not really of sufficient length to warrant the use of such vehicles, but for a while during World War I the GNR owned three. Two were run on the 8.20pm from Dublin, one going to Belfast, the other to Londonderry, while the third left Londonderry for Dublin at 9.30pm, passengers from Belfast joining it at Portadown. All three completed their journeys around midnight which was thought rather early for anyone to be turned out of bed, and the company considerately announced that the coaches would be "placed in a convenient place after arrival at the destination so that passengers can leave at any hour up to 8.0am." The vehicles were not proper sleepers, in the strict sense of the term, but a limited number of beds was made up at one end of specially adapted composite and tri-composite coaches. Hardly surprisingly the service wasn't very popular, and had vanished by 1920, since when nothing similar has been attempted in Ireland.

Like the NCC the GNR showed considerable interest in improving its main line services during the speed conscious 1930s. The fastest schedules on The Dublin–Belfast line were in force only for a short period during 1932–3. they were then slightly eased, but the best trains were still required to cover the 112.5 miles, with four stops, in 155min. In all there were eight weekday trains from Belfast to Dublin, and some of them might be loaded up to as many as eleven coaches. A number of trains carried through coaches to Londonderry, and there was also the "Bundoran Express". This was not a particularly fast train, for its circuitous route via Dundalk, Clones, Enniskillen and Pettigo precluded anything in the way of high speed, but its primary function was to encourage Dubliners to spend their holidays at the Donegal seaside resort of Bundoran where the Great Northern just happened to own an hotel.

The GNR's second main line, from Belfast to Londonderry, was in direct competition with that of the NCC, although each followed a quite different route. The GNR one was the more difficult to work, particularly after the NCC opened the Greenisland Loop, nevertheless the fastest GNR train, the 8.45am ex-Belfast, managed to get within 15min of the NCC's best, the 7.03am ex-Derry.

Both companies made the most of any additional and excursion traffic which came their way. In the Coronation year, 1937, there were great celebrations in the Six Counties, culminating with a visit from the newly crowned George VI and Queen Elizabeth at the end of July. A youth rally was attended by the King and Queen at the Balmoral Show Grounds in Belfast on July 28 and 21 specials conveying the children who took part in it were run by the GNR and the NCC, the latter company's engines being stabled at the GNR Adelaide shed while the rally was in progress.

Inevitably there were incidents connected with the visit. A mine exploded near Dundalk and there were some arrests, but apart from this everything passed off smoothly. It might be thought that the Southern Irish would not want to know, but this was far from the case. British Royalty seems to exercise almost as great a fascination for the Irish as it does for Americans. There are old ladies, who although they fully approved of Ireland gaining its independence, will nevertheless proudly recall being taken as children to see Queen Victoria when she visited the country in 1900. In 1937 no complete film of the Coronation was shown in Dublin and the Great Northern did a roaring trade, putting on duplicate trains for all the people who wanted to go up to the Newry and Belfast cinemas and view the great event.

All sorts of enterprising cheap fares were advertised by the NCC. A sixpenny excursion from York Road to the seaside was offered on Monday evenings for a time during the summer and proved so popular that on one occasion five trains had to run, straining the resources of the traffic department to their utmost. It was a strain that the NCC was quite happy to suffer, for despite the remarkably low fares it cleared a net profit of £500. Circular tours utilising seven-day tickets by road transport, a week at the Portrush Northern Counties Hotel with full board, and first-class return ticket from Belfast, all for £6, even in the high season, were some of the many bargains temptingly dangled before the public.

The Belfast & County Down, with nothing like the resources of the other two major northern companies, and its ageing band of locomotives and six-wheeled carriages, had far less to offer. Two new composite bogie carriages were added in 1937, but even these, with their low roofs and plethora of exterior panelling, while a great improvement on anything else the company possessed, nevertheless presented an out-of-date appearance. Traffic had been falling off for 20 years; the standard Bangor line train of eight six-wheelers had become four by the late 1930s, and on the main Newcastle line there was hardly any need for a train service at all outside peak periods. It was only these which kept the County Down in business, the Bangor line making quite a handsome profit and working to capacity with trains made up to 14 six-wheelers, packed with office and industrial workers who lived around the southern shores of Belfast Lough.

Not far away from the B&CDR, and with a good deal of its mileage actually within County Down, was another railway which was finding it hard to make ends meet. The Dundalk, Newry & Greenore, although owned by the LMS, had no physical connection with the NCC, and when Euston decided that it might be possible to cut its losses by integrating it with a larger concern it opened negotiations with the GNR, whose territory surrounded that of the DN&GR. The Great Northern was well aware that it was not exactly being offered a bargain and it was some five years before satisfactory terms could be agreed.

On July 1, 1933, the GNR took over the working and maintenance of the DN&GR, and by 1935 had managed to bring the losses below £10,000 for the first time since 1920. This was partly achieved by the transfer of two GNR railbuses to the DN&GR, which proved quite sufficient for most passenger journeys. Some steam passenger trains continued to run, many of them mixed, and the old six-wheel carriages, which had retained their LNWR livery under LMS ownership, continued to keep it, some of them having it renewed at Dundalk. One of the Ramsbottom saddle tanks was scrapped by the LMS in 1928, but the other five were all taken over by the GNR and used by them, despite bringing in their own engines, principally 2-4-2Ts.

Greenore still retained a certain importance as a port, mainly for the cattle trade, and in 1928 114,000 head of cattle passed through on their way to England. It had once done a fair amount of passenger business and had competed on more or less equal terms with the LNWR/LYR Fleetwood-Belfast and Midland Heysham-Belfast services. In 1920 one could leave Euston at 6.20pm, cross from Holyhead to Greenore in four hours, and arrive at Great Victoria Street, Belfast, at 9.55 next morning. The setting up of the Border put it at a disadvantage, the other two routes remaining entirely within Great Britain, and when the LMS took over the various LNWR, LYR, and Midland Irish Sea routes in 1923 and decided to rationalise them, the Holyhead-Greenore one was one of the first to go, sailings not being resumed after the 1926 General Strike.

Unlike the Dublin Government Stormont did little to regulate competition between road and rail until 1934, when it called in Sir Felix Pole, formerly General Manager of the GWR, and asked him to make a report on the position. Sir Felix recommended the setting up of a Northern Ireland Road Transport Board, combining the passenger and road freight services of the NCC, the BCDR and the GNR (within the Six Counties), and the rival road services. This was done, in 1936, but despite the pious hope, expressed in its statutes, that a single authority could better co-ordinate road and rail services, the opposite happened. An indifferent Government allowed the NIRTB to compete, rather than co-operate, with the railways, and the latter, having lost their profit-making road services, found themselves in even deeper trouble, and as there was not sufficient traffic for both road and rail the pooling arrangements optimistically set up to share out the expected profits soon fell into abeyance.

The Pole Report also recommended the absorption of the Belfast Corporation tram and bus services into the new Board, and the electrification of the County Down's Bangor line. Neither of these proposals were acted upon, although they were not entirely forgotten. Sir Felix felt that amalgamation of all the railways in Northern Ireland would be desirable, but the Border made this impossible and they were therefore left as they were.

The division of Ireland into two countries remained a bone of contention, the Southern Irish refusing to regard it as anything more than a temporary measure, while those in the Six Counties continually professed their loyalty to the Crown and the Parliament in Westminster. There were some who left such matters to politicians and made the most of the situation, while it lasted, by indulging in a profitable, if illegal spot of buying and selling and on several occasions crews of early morning trains running on lines close to the Border suddenly found themselves confronted by a herd of cows taking a short cut from Eire into the Six Counties. At McKinney's Bridge, between Strabane and Londonderry, where the GNR line crossed the River Foyle which marked the border, a goods train struck 16 cattle one morning in January, 1936, killing two, while the others avenged their fallen comrades by wrecking five wagons. Eventually the police arrived and took them in charge, but the men who had been escorting them had long since faded away among the fields.

There was a somewhat similar series of instances of cattle getting themselves into trouble on the railways, in Southern Ireland in 1934, although for rather different reasons. Farmers in County Waterford had beeh refusing to pay certain taxes, and the Government seized some of their cattle in lieu. The farmers decided it was not going to get away with this, so they removed a rail between Kilmeadon and Carrolls Cross on the Cork–Waterford main line, sawed through telegraph poles and cut down the wires in front of the train carrying the confiscated cattle. As an extra bonus the "Rosslare Express" was held up for 2¼ hours but the farmers did not get their cattle back, and with the end of the economic war the trouble petered out.

A further report on the Northern Ireland transport situation, the McClintock, was published in 1938, and had it been implemented might have proved of some benefit to the railways in their attempts to curb some of the NIRTB's excesses, but with the outbreak of the World War II the situation changed completely.

CHAPTER TEN

The Cork Mails and their Locomotives

THE BASIS OF the Great Southern & Western Railway's prosperity, such as it was, came from the monopoly that it enjoyed over the route between Southern Ireland's two principal cities, Dublin and Cork. For much of its length the line is free of excessive undulations and sharp curves and would seem to provide excellent operating conditions. Unfortunately this is far from the case, for trains starting out from both Cork and Dublin are faced with steep adverse gradients. That out of Dublin extends for a mile and a half at 1 in 117 steepening to 1 in 84 as far as Inchicore, after which it levels out briefly past the locomotive works and then continues mainly at 1 in 138 until milepost 4¼. The climb northwards out of Cork is even more daunting; ¾-mile at 1 in 78–64 through the tunnel immediately on leaving the station is followed by two miles at an even steeper 1 in 60, while the climbing is not finished until milepost 151½ is reached, 14 miles from the start. Add to this the fact that loads have always been heavier on this route than any other and it will be seen that the operating department is faced with considerable problems.

The principal service, the Up and Down Mail, was naturally required to maintain a fast schedule and stopping to detach pilot engines militated against this, apart from being uneconomic. Bankers could be provided, however, and in 1924 a second A class 4–8–0T was built and sent to Cork especially for this purpose, but obviously the ultimate solution was to produce locomotives capable of lifting their trains unaided out of both termini and of running at a fast speed in between.

The D1 4–4–0 No 341 *Sir William Goulding* was Maunsell's attempt to do this. It had two 19in by 26in inside cylinders, a large 5ft 2in diameter parallel boiler pressed to 175lb/sq in, Walschaerts valve-gear, 6ft 7in driving wheels and a tractive effort of 17,673lb. Maunsell left Inchicore in 1913 before *Sir William Goulding* was completed, and although it seems to have been capable of dealing with fairly substantial loads, it remained the only one of its type and was scrapped after a mere fifteen years' service. No 341 was certainly regarded as something rather special, for not only was it afforded the rare accolade of a name, but that name belonged to the Chairman of the Board of Directors; the engine was popular with enginemen, appears to have been a free-running machine, was not particularly heavy on coal, and was the most powerful passenger engine in Ireland at the time. One can only conclude that this 4–4–0 did not fit in with the plans which Maunsell's successor, E. A. Watson, had in mind, and that this inevitably dictated its early demise, for lone locomotives, particularly express passenger ones, seldom last long.

Watson was a Swindon man, and he lost no time in bringing out a four-cylinder 4–6–0 based to some extent upon the Great Western Stars. Watson's engine had similarly divided drive, almost identically sized cylinders, a slightly larger grate area, rather less evaporative heating surface, and driving wheels of 1½in less diameter. The superheater surface was much greater, despite the fact that both the G&SWR and the GWR used Welsh coal, but the boiler pressure was considerably lower 175lb/sq in against 225lb/sq in; the boiler, although fitted with a Belpaire firebox, was not tapered, and both the adhesion and the total weights of the Inchicore 4–6–0 were some five tons less than that of a Swindon Star.

The Watson engine, however, bore no great external resemblance to a Great Western product. Its appearance was quite within the tradition of the G&SWR, with a windowless cab very similar to that used by Maunsell on his SE&CR and Southern 4–4–0s and 2–6–0s, (no doubt he took the design with him to Ashford), a substantial dome and the usual Inchicore chimney. The 4–6–0 carried the G&SWR's standard dull grey livery lined out in red and white, and was numbered 400.

For a while it looked as if this engine also would, like Maunsell's 4–4–0, remain unique, but five years later, in 1921, another three were constructed at Inchicore, and a further six by Armstrong Whitworth in 1923. These later engines were all given stronger frames and motion, which brought their weight up to around 76 tons, virtually the same as that of a Star. Three of the Armstrong Whitworth engines moved another step nearer the Great Western 4–6–0s by having boilers pressed to 225lb/sq in. At first they were without superheaters, but these were soon added.

Hardly had the last of the 400s been delivered than a very different type of 4–6–0 was put into service. Numbered 500 it had two 19½in by 28in outside cylinders and 5ft 8½in driving wheels. It was obviously a mixed traffic engine, and as such might have seemed irrelevant to the problem of providing motive power for the Cork Mails. J. R. Bazin, No 500's designer (he had succeeded Watson in 1922) no doubt intended that it should be, but events forced him to have second thoughts. Very quickly he discovered that the one really significant difference between the Swindon and Inchicore four-cylinder 4–6–0s was their performance on the road. The 400s steamed badly and their complicated cylinder arrangement gave endless trouble. Drawings were sent to Maunsell, who was now CME of the Southern, in the hope that he could provide a solution, but the only one he felt he could give was that the whole class should be heavily rebuilt.

No 402 was therefore reconstructed in 1927 with two 500 class cylinders. She was also given the longer 28in stroke of the 500s, and this entailed new frames and driving wheel centres. In this form No 402 was an excellent locomotive, and one might have expected the rest of the class to be similarly dealt with straightaway. But one has to bear in mind the cost of all this. Each year the Great Southern was finding it harder to make ends meet, and it must have been heartbreaking for the Board of Directors to find that almost all its largest and most costly locomotives were liabilities rather than assets. The Maunsell 4–4–0 and one of the 4–8–0Ts were scrapped in 1928, the other 4–8–0T went in 1931 after less than seven years' service, the six Coey goods 4–6–0s of 1907 were withdrawn in 1928–31, and, perhaps saddest of all, No 400 went in 1929, followed by a further two, Nos 404–8, in 1930, which had lasted no longer than the second of the 4–8–0Ts.

Out of these catastrophes the Great Southern managed to salvage some-thing. In 1929 the Board approved the expenditure of £4,000 for the conversion of Nos 401–6 to a state similar to that of No 402; this was "in order to hasten the elimination of the former (400) type which has proved most costly in maintenance and in coal and oil consumption", as the minute book put it. At the same time £20,000 was authorised for five new 101 class 0–6–0s. The directors must have offered up thanks to the Almighty that if all else failed they could at least rely on the old McDonnell 0–6–0 design of 1866 to keep the system out of the bankruptcy courts. As it turned out, not even this apparently foolproof solution to some of the motive power department's problems worked out, for instead of exactly reproducing the superheated 101 design Watson made certain modifications, and the consequence was that the new engines, the 700s, were never as popular as the old ones. A further ten, the 710s, with a few more modifications, were turned out in 1934–5. These were supposed to combine the best features of Inchicore and Broadstone practice, but actually incorporated practically all the worst and were universally detested. With the exception of No 702, which went in 1955, all the 700s and 710s were scrapped within four years, 1959–63, leaving the old McDonnell engines to see out the last days of steam in Southern Ireland.

There was not sufficient money available to rebuild all the surviving four-cylinder 4–6–0s as 28in stroke, two-cylinder engines, and only one could be thus dealt with; the other three had to make do with a 2in shorter stroke, and so to keep their original driving wheels and also a fair proportion of their frames. The situation in 1938 then was that the principal Dublin to Cork trains were worked by the ten 6ft 7in and 5ft 8½in two-cylinder 4–6–0s, assisted by the nine old 321 class Coey 4–4–0s of 1904–6.

In 1926 Pullman cars had entered service on the Dublin–Cork route, and nine years later a set of new steel-panelled stock was built for the Mail. These innovations were a considerable advance in comfort but did nothing to ease the burdens of the operating department, the Pullmans, for example, each weighing close on 40 tons. In their rebuilt form the 400's were good engines, capable of plenty of hard work and quite speedy. No 402 hauled a special train of three bogies from Cork to Dublin in 1934 at an average speed of 67.3mph, and one of the later rebuilds did the journey with two stops in 163min running time, at 61.1mph average, with the new mail train. This latter run was something out of the ordinary, for although the 400s were certainly good they were not brilliant, and one would not have expected them to display this form as a matter of course.

Triple-heading was the rule out of Cork, and the Up Mail must have been a remarkable sight pounding up the 1 in 60 bank behind an 0–6–0, a 4–4–0 and a 4–6–0. The 0–6–0, a 101, would come off at Blarney, six miles out of Cork, while the 4–4–0 continued as far as Ballybrophy, almost two-thirds of the way to Dublin. Even this powerful combination does not seem to have produced anything startling; O. S. Nock recorded nothing higher than 24mph up the 1 in 60 during a trip in 1938.

Despite facing serious financial problems, the board decided to ask Inchicore to start from scratch again and produce a locomotive capable of solving for good the problem of the Cork Mails. By now A. W. Harty was Chief Mechanical Engineer, the sixth in 20 years, a perhaps not surprising turn-over when one considers the shoe-string budget on which the rolling stock department had been forced to manage since 1914. The new CME's salary was £800 pa plus £100 rent allowance, hardly a princely sum. It was against this background that the design of the new express engine was evolved, and it says much for the board that there appears to have been no pressure to skimp on it, a figure of around £12,000 being set aside for each locomotive. J. J. Johnston, who was later assistant CME, was intimately concerned with the work, and it is to him that I am indebted for much of what follows.

The board asked for a locomotive capable of hauling twelve, and if need be up to fourteen, bogie vehicles non-stop between Dublin and Cork at an average speed of 50mph. Three locomotives and one extra boiler were required and they were to be ready by July 1939. The maximum axle-load on the route was 18½ tons, and a four-cylinder locomotive conforming to this limit would hardly be big enough, but if a three-cylinder engine was used hammer-blow would be virtually eliminated and the axle-load could go up to around 21–22 tons. The Chief Permanent Way Engineer needed some persuading in this matter, but by using models the drawing office convinced him of the feasibility of their proposition.

The next question to be decided was the wheel arrangement. A 4–4–0 and a 2–6–0 were both considered before being rejected. One might ask why two such outdated arrangements should have even crossed anyone's mind when one looks at what was happening in Britain, let alone on the Continent at the time, but one must remember that this was Ireland, and that on the two other principal railways in that country these two types were in fact then current for express passenger haulage. But a 4–6–0 would be too small for the GSR, and a bissell truck was not ideal for high speeds (although they did not tell anyone as yet that the drawing office was thinking in terms of 100mph!) and so a 4–6–0 was the natural solution. I asked Mr Johnston why not a Pacific, and received the interesting answer that this would have been a lazy solution when it was perfectly possible to put sufficient power into a 4–6–0 chassis; also a 4–6–2 would have meant new, longer turntables at Cork and Dublin. Driving wheels were to be 6ft 7in diameter, as this was standard Inchicore practice, and at a rough calculation the total weight would be something over 80 tons, 63 tons being available for adhesion.

One gets the feeling that the Inchicore drawing office was more than a little excited, after years of having to make do, to get the opportunity to design an up-to-the-minute powerful express locomotive, and there was no shortage of new ideas waiting to be put into practice. The design staff were determined to use roller bearings wherever possible as they were much less trouble to maintain, but at that time they were in a relatively early stage of development and the manufacturers were loth to stick their necks out and commit themselves over performance figures. Hoffman appeared to be the most go-ahead of the firms concerned, and bearings of their design were used at the quadrant link trunnion and eccentric rod ends, on the return cranks, and on the axles of the engine bogies and those of the tender. Providing they were changed fairly frequently (which presented no problems as they were extremely cheap), the roller bearings gave no trouble at all throughout the life of the locomotives.

Inchicore was hoping to use poppet-valves because of their simplicity, but these again were a new feature, and in the end, mainly because the seatings were not very robust, the idea was reluctantly abandoned. To supply sufficient steam to the three 18in by 28in cylinders a nickel-steel parallel boiler, 6ft in diameter, with an evaporative heating surface of 1,870sq ft, and a super-heating surface of 468sq ft, was provided. The boiler actually appeared to be tapered but this effect was caused by lagging raised up and then brought down again over the firebox and put there merely for aesthetic appeal. Streamlining, then so much in vogue, was considered, but rejected because of its tendency to retain heat and cause the leading axleboxes to run hot.

Work progressed slowly on the new engines, and Irish railway circles were kept agog for any scraps of information which Inchicore cared to feed them. All sorts of rumours were abroad, one that there were to be ten engines altogether, and there was a particularly persistent one that No 407, the last unrebuilt four-cylinder 4-6-0, was to be given three cylinders and a boiler identical with those of the new engines so that she would in effect become the fourth member of the class.

At last, in April 1939, No 800, the first of the new 4-6-0s, emerged from Inchicore in works grey and went off to Sallins on her first trial run. All went well except for the left-hand trailing axlebox, which overheated. Fixing it ready for another run the next morning was an all-night job, but by the end of the day it was red-hot again. This happened three times in succession, and the consternation of E. C. Bredin (yet another CME, having taken over from Harty in 1937 whilst the designs of the new engines were in preparation) can be imagined. He was not the sort of man to mince his words and the atmosphere at Inchicore was becoming a trifle tense. Then Johnston discovered a polished spot on the axlebox which suggested that something was rubbing on it. What had happened was that the boiler had settled on to its mountings and moved back slightly. This was normal practice and should not have mattered but unfortunately, because of its great size, the boiler had had to be constructed in two sections rivetted together, very slightly askew as it turned out, which had resulted in the ashpan rubbing on the axlebox. Once discovered the problem was soon solved by cutting a pocket into the pan and no further bother was experienced. Everyone heaved a sigh of relief and the trials continued.

No 800 was worked down as far as Mallow on piloting duties and then towards the end of June was pronounced fit to take up regular work, and was brought into Inchicore for final painting. Her livery was quite different from the standard dull grey, being a light blue–green picked out with black and yellow lining. Further evidence of the importance the Great Southern attached to its new engines was the awarding to them of names, the last product so honoured having been Maunsell's *Sir William Goulding*. As if to emphasise the very different world into which the 800s had emerged they were named after legendary Queens of pre-Christian Ireland, *Maeve*, *Macha* and *Tailte*. These are the English translations, for the actual spelling on the nameplates was in Irish, a language which contains letters not used in the English alphabet. At either end of the nameplates were designs based on traditional Gaelic forms, these and the letters raised up in brass, on a blue background.

Maeve was immediately compared with an LMS Royal Scot although she looked rather more like one of the rebuilt versions of that class, none of which were then in existence or, failing that, a GWR King. She certainly presented a most impressive appearance, and if she was the equal of her proportions she might hope to prove as powerful as a King, let alone a "Scot". The question was whether she would, or whether, like her predecessors, she would fall short of expectations. A good part of the answer was provided on July 17 when she made her inaugural run on the down Mail.

With 300 tons behind her and driver Mark Foley and fireman Mat Ryan of Inchicore in charge *Maeve* pulled out of Kingsbridge at 7.15am. Working to the regular schedule she was ahead of time at practically every stop and was five minutes early into Cork. A celebration dinner, with Bredin presiding, was held at the Great Southern Hotel, and then *Maeve*, this time with a Cork crew, driver Broderick and fireman Sheehan, on the footplate, returned in triumph to Dublin. In the following months she logged many notable achievements. A top speed of 80mph, said to have been achieved only once previously on GSR metals, became commonplace, and *Maeve* showed herself capable of reaching even the magic 100mph, although as far as I know the highest actual recorded speed was 96mph, near Thurles. Even so, more important to the Great Southern than high speeds was economy, and in this department *Maeve* was eminently satisfactory. She was very light on coal, and once she had got her train on the move would run all day with the regulator no more than one-quarter open. At the foot of Ballybrophy bank, three miles at 1 in 128, the fireman would add some coal to the fire and up she would sail on a quarter regulator and breast the summit at a steady 50mph.

The late J. MacCartney Robbins recorded a typical run on August 26, 1939, on the down Mail. Driver Broderick was in charge, the load to Kildare was 300 tons, from there to Maryborough 270 tons, and from Maryborough to Mallow 255 tons. Scheduled to cover the 144.5 miles to Mallow in 166min running time, *Maeve* gained time all the way, averaging 59.9mph start to stop over the 37.5 miles from Limerick Junction to Mallow, which was reached in 158¼ minutes from Dublin, 7min 20sec early. The overall average speed from Dublin to Mallow was 54.8mph, nothing very exciting compared with what the Great Western and the LMS had been doing for years, and even less so against the speeds being achieved by Gresley's streamliners, but very much in advance of anything to which the Dublin–Cork main line had been used. The point really was that *Maeve* did all that the operating authorities demanded of her, economically, and with power to spare, and that surely is a near the ideal in a locomotive as one can expect. She was hardly ever really extended, but on the one occasion when she was it was fortunate that O. S. Nock happened to be on the footplate.

The train was the Up Mail and *Maeve* had her usual Inchicore crew, Foley and Ryan. A liner had called that day at Cobh, and the passengers from it, together with a great many holidaymakers, it was August 1939, so added to the usual load that *Maeve* found herself asked to cope with a 450-ton train. Up until a month or so previously it would have been considered necessary to provide three engines to get half that load up the initial climb, and pilot assistance was contemplated for *Maeve* also, but the authorities wanted to see just what she could do and she was left to cope with this heavy train unaided. Nock describes it as the stiffest job he had ever seen allocated to a 4-6-0. Up she went, blasting her way through the dripping wet Glanmire Road Tunnel and out into the light and the two miles of 1 in 60. With 50 per cent cut-off and almost full regulator she maintained a steady 23mph up the bank, and then at the summit a curious thing happened.

Maeve was still a very new engine, and just as some small fault often shows itself when an engine is fresh from shops, *Maeve's* regulator stuck wide open, and the combined efforts of the crew failed to shift it. The driver had to link right up, and the result was that *Maeve* was 3½min late into Mallow. The fault was soon corrected but now another problem arose. The coal supplied to engines in Ireland was often of rather poor quality and some of the stuff in *Maeve's* tender was pretty rough. So she had to be nursed over the 20 miles between Thurles and Ballybrophy until steam could be built up again. The final stop was at Maryborough and after that *Maeve*, now in perfect health, fairly shot away and the 50.9 miles to Dublin were run at a fraction better than even time, 50min 20sec: the top speed was 79mph at Newbridge. Despite the various troubles it had been a splendid run, and the initial climb out of Cork had created an Irish record.

Later in the year *Maeve* was jointed by *Macha* and the two sisters were then put in exclusive charge of the Mails, apart from Mondays, which was washing-out day. *Maeve* worked down to Cork on the 7.15am and returned at 4.05pm, whilst *Macha* left Cork at 7.45am and returned from Dublin at 6.30pm. The opportunity was taken to cut the schedule of the Mails, and the down train from now on covered the 165.5 miles, with six stops, in 215min running time. In reality this was seven stops, for although 23min were allowed for the 20.4 miles from Thurles to the notorious Limerick Junction, this included the time taken to come to a halt at the far end of the station and reverse back into the platform. This meant that the 20.4 miles was more often than not covered in even time or better. The load out of Dublin varied from 300 to 350 tons, one coach being dropped at Kildare, and another at Maryborough, but this was of little help to the engine, as it was the climb out of Kingsbridge which presented the hardest task of the journey.

The 37.6 miles from Limerick Junction to Mallow were scheduled to be run in 40min. This section was of undulating character with a nice ten miles of mainly falling gradients in the middle to counteract two miles of 1 in 153 at the start. The scheduled average speed of 56.4mph was the second fastest in Ireland, the GNR having a 57.7mph run between Dublin and Drogheda. The GSR assigment, considering the loads and the hard climb for the first four miles, was probably the tougher of the two, and as the War had by now taken its effect on timetables in Great Britain, it can fairly be claimed that at the beginning of 1940 the 800s were putting up faster times, day in and day out, than any other engines in the British Isles. On the start-to-stop down runs either side of Limerick Junction even time was frequently beaten, and it was not unusual to gain between 10 and 12min on the overall running time between Dublin and Cork.

The outbreak of World War II had no immediate effect on Southern Ireland, apart from reducing supplies of certain raw materials from Britain, and the 1939 timetables continued in operation through 1940. The construction of the third 800 class engine, No 802 *Tailte*, was held up for a while, but in June 1940 she started her trials, and on entering regular service she enabled *Maeve* to take a well-earned rest and check over. In July, 1941, the worsening coal situation forced the Great Southern to abandon its peacetime schedules, and by 1943 the Dublin–Cork route was reduced to one train daily in each direction. There were occasions when there were no trains at all and it was not until 1946 that the service was increased. The fastest of the three trains then running took 4hr 40min to cover the 165.5 miles, 1hr 7min longer than the best 1939 time. Schedules were very badly hit again by the 1947 coal shortage, and although a steady improvement took place from 1948, the full power of the 800s was never really needed again and they had their boiler pressures reduced to 180lb/sq in; also Nos 801 and 802 were rebuilt with single blastpipes. They were nevertheless still very much the pride of the Irish railways and *Maeve* was as much a household name to small boys and indeed the public as were the *Flying Scotsman* and the *Royal Scot* in Britain.

In 1950 the longest regular run in the Republic of Ireland, 106.9 miles between Limerick Junction and Kingsbridge, was instituted. The train was was the 12 noon from Cork, and although the schedule of 130min was child's play to the 800s it was a welcome step towards pre-war standards. A few months later the 800s were given another opportunity to shine when the "Enterprise" express from Belfast was extended from Dublin to Cork. Now the non-stop run was 110 miles, from Amiens Street to Limerick Junction. On this train the latest 6ft 7in 4–6–0 from works, whether it was an 800 or a 400, was put in charge. The "Enterprise" ceased running to and from Cork in 1953, and although the 800s continued to work the Mail trains for a few more years, the advent of the Park Royal diesel railcars in 1952 heralded a completely new form of motive power. These were not ideal for long-distance travel, but when they were new they worked on the Dublin to Cork line and proved very popular with passengers.

In July 1955 the first of the Metropolitan-Vickers 1,200hp diesel-electric locomotives went into service and within months steam had been swept away from all the principal passenger turns. By 1956 the fastest time was down to 3hr 28min. In 1961 the extremely efficient General Motors diesel-electrics began arriving from the United States, and gradually replaced the Metropolitan-Vickers diesels, although some of the latter, now re-engined by General Motors, have recently reappeared.

Notwithstanding heavy loadings times have been steadily reduced, and in 1967 a test train hauled by GM Nos B160 and 171 worked non-stop from Cork to Dublin in 144min at an average speed of 68.8mph. Scheduled speeds do not quite match this but it is now possible to travel between the Republic's principal cities at a start-to-stop average of a mile a minute. Recently I travelled from Heuston (as Kingsbridge has become) as far as Limerick Junction on the fastest train of the day, the 8.45 "Slainte". The train consisted of seven bogies and a four-wheel van, 210 tons, an unusually light load which was hardly likely to tax the combined 1,900hp of our two diesels, Nos B166 and 142. Their driver was William Shiels, an Inchicore man who had worked over the route as a fireman on the 800s back in the 1940s. He agreed that the latter were splendid engines, but now had no wish to exchange his vastly cleaner and more comfortable diesel cab for a steam footplate.

We pulled out on time and accelerated steadily up the bank to Clondalkin, 4.4 miles which was passed in exactly 7min. The precision expected of, and obtained from a diesel is astonishing. A graph showing the gradients and the exact speeds over the entire run is provided, and timetables are made out on the assumption that each train will exactly adhere to it. Gone are the days of rushing a bank in order to reach the top at a reasonable speed. The maximum scheduled speed is 68mph and Nos B166 and 142 maintained this mile after mile completely impervious to falling or rising gradients. Speed did drop to 50mph up Ballybrophy bank; this should have been 62mph, but it was because we were slightly ahead of schedule and Driver Shiels wanted to use up the 2min recovery time which we had not needed. We had also reduced speed around the curve at Portarlington, "so that the dining car passengers won't spill their coffee", he remarked, and there was a third scheduled slowing, to 60mph, through Thurles. Otherwise we hummed along at 68mph all the way and slid into Limerick Junction (there is no need for any undignified stopping and backing into the platform now that the layout had been altered) precisely at 10.30, 107 miles in 105min.

The return journey was rather more out of the ordinary for the train, the 11.30 from Cork, was heavier, 295 tons, and powered by a single diesel, albeit the most powerful then working on CIE, No A56R, one of the Metropolitan-Vickers Cos with a new General Motors engine which has been uprated to 1,500hp. Owing to the late arrival of a connecting train, we left the Junction 7min late, and I was interested to see what efforts the driver, John Horgan of Cork, would make to get us into Heuston on time. He did it quite simply by letting No A56R run at between 70 and 73mph instead of the prescribed 68mph. We were 5min late arriving at and restarting from Thurles, but by Droichead Nua (the former Newbridge), 81.4 miles from Limerick Junction, we were 1min early. We left there exactly on time and without exceeding 71mph on the almost entirely downhill run into Dublin, pulled up at Heuston at 15.02, 3min ahead of time. In all we had gained 10min covering the 107 miles, with two stops, in 112min actual running time.

CHAPTER ELEVEN

The Great Northern 4-4-0s

ASKED TO NAME the typically British steam locomotive most people would probably plump for either the 4-4-0 or the 4-6-0. Ireland possessed few of the latter but the former were to be found all over the country, in great profusion and in all shapes and sizes. The GNR was the most devoted of all in its adherence to the 4-4-0, developing it in several different directions but always maintaining the family likeness, and if one wanted to find the type in its purest form one could hardly do better than visit Dundalk, despite the fact that those works were not in the United Kingdom at all.

The very first of the breed, the Js, came out in the mid-1880s. There were six of them, built by Beyer Peacock, and like so many of the 4–4–0s then going into service they were enlargements of a previous 2–4–0 design. Their driving wheels were only 5ft 7in in diameter and they were not intended to work the fastest trains, these being entrusted to two 6ft 7in 4–2–2s, built by Beyer Peacock at the same time as the Js and the only bogie singles ever to run in Ireland. The designer of both types was James Park, who had come to Dundalk from the English Great Northern and who produced engines so alike in some respects to those of Patrick Stirling that many people were convinced that the Irish GNR was a junior partner of the English one.

In fact the only link the two companies ever possessed was a visual one, Park bringing with him a Doncaster-type chimney, cab and other external features, as well as pretty exactly copying the English company's livery for his engines and coaches. Mechanically there was no close resemblance, for Park's bogie singles had inside cylinders and owed rather more of their inspiration to Beyer Peacock than to Stirling. The six J class engines were withdrawn between 1921 and 1924, but two saw further service with the Sligo, Leitrim & Northern Counties Railway, the last of these surviving almost until the outbreak of World War II, although I doubt if either ever did much work under their new owners.

The first express 4–4–0s on the GNR, the Ps, came out in 1892. There were two of them, with 17in by 24in cylinders and 6ft 7in driving wheels, and they were intended to replace the singles on the Dublin–Belfast Mails. But the singles were having none of it, and it was not until the introduction of dining cars in 1895 that they had to give way to something more powerful. This was the first design of Park's successor, Charles Clifford, but it was no break with tradition and the PP class was no more than an enlargement of the P. In all sixteen PPs were built, at intervals down to 1911, although the later ones were considered branch line rather than express engines. Immediately before these had come the P 5ft 6in class, a small-wheeled version of the P. All the varieties of Ps and PPs lasted into modern times, many rebuilt with larger boilers, and the last, PP No 74 of 1898, was withdrawn in 1963 as No 42x of the Ulster Transport Authority.

The next step was the Q class of 1899. There were 13 of these, with 4ft 6in diameter boilers pressed to 175lb, and 18in by 26in cylinders, but still retaining many characteristic Stirling features, including the Spartan cab, and the tender with springs inside the frames. Something bigger yet was needed, for with the continuing improvements in carriage design it was all the locomotive department could do to keep pace. The successors to the Qs, the QLs, were given larger boilers of 4ft 9in diameter and a 7in longer firebox. The increase in boiler size was particularly noticeable, for it required a considerably shorter chimney. The last two Qs, from Beyer Peacock, came out in 1904, the earlier ones being of either Neilson or North British manufacture.

The same year the QLs, with yet larger boilers and fireboxes, went into production. There were eight of them, and by 1910 when the last was put to work the Great Northern could consider itself very well off for express engines. The Qs and QLs were more or less confined to the Dublin–Belfast main line and one wonders if they were all able to find sufficient employment there. They would not be needed for anything save the faster through trains, as there were plenty of smaller 4–4–0s to work the main line stopping trains, while the Dublin and Belfast suburban services were largely in the hands of 4–4–0Ts and 2–4–2Ts. Goods services were the domain of an army of 0–6–0s of varying sizes and capabilities, each class corresponding to a 4–4–0 type; the newest were the LQGs with QL type boilers and cylinders.

Soon after the last QL came out the Q class were allowed to work over the Portadown–Derry line for the first time and most of them eventually migrated there. It was thought desirable to provide replacements and the result was the S class. Although there were only five of these, together with the three slightly modified S2s of 1915 they were considered by many to be the finest of all the GNR 4–4–0s. They had Schmidt superheaters and 8in piston valves, two innovations for the GNR, and whereas from the start they were good engines, like their contemporaries on the English Great Northern, the Ivatt Atlantics, they really blossomed late in their careers. Five small 5ft 9in U class 4–4–0s, tender engine versions of a 4–4–2 tank, also came out in 1915 but from then on there was then a long pause.

In the meantime a number of modifications were made to the earlier types. Clifford had retired in 1912 and been succeeded by G. T. Glover from the North Eastern. The first changes of the new *régime* were in the livery, the apple green gradually giving way to black for all classes. Cab roofs were extended backwards and lost something of their Stirling look, which probably did not greatly upset the enginemen, while nameplates were transferred from the boiler sides to the more usual position on the splashers. The cylinders of the PP, Q and QL classes were reduced in diameter, and all these, together with the Qs, were given superheated boilers. When the new boilers were fitted to the Qs they were pitched higher in order to clear the valves on top of the 8in piston-valve cylinders which were adopted at this time, and the cylinder diameters were opened out to 18½in, after having been reduced from this size some time earlier. The higher boilers improved the looks of an already handsome design, and these modified engines proved to be extremely speedy. They spent most of their time north of the Border working on the Belfast–Derry line where there was little scope for fast running, but on one occasion in 1932 No 135 came down to Dublin and during the return journey with a two-coach special covered the 31.7 miles from Dublin to Drogheda, start to stop, in 24min 4sec, at an avearge speed of 79.2mph and the fastest run ever recorded in Ireland up to that time.

The similar QLs were also given superheated boilers and piston-valves, but in order to keep the cost down and to disturb the motion and boiler as little as possible the valves were placed on top of each other in between the cylinders. The disadvantage of this arrangement was that the valves had to be restricted to 6½in diameter, and with the cylinder diameter restored to 18½in these valves proved rather small. The consequence was that the QLs were rather slower than the other modern 4–4–0s, although with their large boilers they were capable of plenty of hard uphill work.

The next stage in the development of the 4–4–0 was the raising of the boiler pressure, from 175 to 200lb. The S class were so altered in the late 1920s, as also were the S2s. Possibly this might have been the final development and the next step would have been a 4–6–0, but in 1932 the viaduct across the Boyne at Drogheda was renewed and the permissible axle-load on it was raised from 17 to 21 tons. It has been said that anything larger than a 4–4–0 would not have been able to get inside the erecting shop at Dundalk, and perhaps this was the reason the GNR remained faithful to the type; maybe the success of the Schools class on the Southern Railway also had something to do with it, but whatever the reason the raising of the axle-load restriction enabled the GNR to bring out a 4–4–0 which in size and power was a great advance on all previous types.

While at Gateshead on the North Eastern Railway Glover had worked with Smith and inevitably had become interested in compounding. At the same time a former General Manager of the GNR, John Bagwell, who had been employed on the Midland Railway earlier in his career, extolled the system, and so it was that the new 4–4–0, No 83 *Eagle*, emerged from Beyer Peacock as a three-cylinder compound. She was similar to the Deeley and Fowler engines of the Midland and the LMS, the change-over from simple to compound working being automatic, but she had a higher boiler pressure, 250lb, and high and low pressure cylinders 2in smaller in diameter than those of the Derby engines. The NCC also was considering building LMS compounds at this time, but rejected the idea in favour of a simple 2–6–0.

Eagle and her four sisters were handsome engines, not perhaps as elegant as the earlier inside-cylinder types but sturdy and powerful looking. They were built for a specific task, the new timetables introduced in the summer of 1932. The 112.5-mile run from Dublin to Belfast, with four stops, was allowed 125min running time, while the southbound run, which involved $16\frac{1}{2}$ miles of almost continuous climbing from the start at Great Victoria Street, and the steep $8\frac{1}{2}$ mile ascent to Adavoyle summit, took 26min longer. The load varied between 7 and 11 bogies, vehicles being detached at Dundalk and Goraghwood going north and at Portadown going south. These were tremendous tasks for a 4–4–0, even one boasting a tractive effort of 25,245lb, but the most spectacular piece of timetabling was reserved for the 3.15pm out of Amiens Street which had to reach Dundalk, 54.3 miles, in 54min, the first scheduled mile-a-minute run in the country. The Drogheda stop was omitted on this run, but passengers were still conveyed there by means of a slip coach, the last but one such working in the country. (The very last was on the GSR, the 9.30am Dublin–Cork continuing to slip a carriage at Kildare until 1940.) After the 1933 strike the fast timings were resumed but they were really rather more than the compounds could manage comfortably. At certain spots speeds were uncomfortably close to the limit compatible with safety, coal consumption rose to uneconomic proportions, and within two years it was found that the locomotive boilers needed retubing.

Reluctantly the Great Northern decided that the 1934 summer timetable would have to be eased out a little in places; also the boiler pressure of the compounds was brought down to 200lb, reducing maintenance costs, although it was later found possible to raise it again to 215lb. There was still plenty of high speed running on the main line, 80mph being common, while occasionally maxima up to 88mph were recorded. Perhaps to compensate for the loss of glamour with the disappearance of the mile-a-minute timing a new livery was introduced in 1936, No 87 *Kestrel* being the first to appear in it in January of that year. She was painted sky blue with black and white lining, red frames edged in gold, the initial GN in shaded gold letters on the tender sides, and the GNR emblem between them and on the leading splashers. *Kestrel's* four sisters were soon similarly adorned and were always kept in spotless condition.

In 1938–39 the S and S2 class 4-4-0s were almost completely rebuilt. There was now no need to keep axle-loads down to 17 tons so they were given heavier frames, new driving wheel centres and completely new or retubed boilers; the valve-travel was extended from $3\frac{3}{4}$in to 5in, and exhaust injectors were fitted. All but Nos 170 and 190 were equipped with new larger tenders, these two retaining theirs so that they might continue to use the turntable at Warrenpoint. The Ss, which had lost their names in World War I, had them restored and the S2s acquired the ones they had been allocated when new but up till then had never received. Both types were painted in the blue livery, hitherto exclusive to the compounds. Apart from this the renewed engines had changed very little in appearance, but they now had a tractive effort virtually equal to that of the compounds, as their boiler pressures also had been raised to 215lb, and there is evidence that they were preferred to the latter.

In late 1938 only two of the compounds remained in regular service on the Dublin–Belfast line, one being in the shops and the other two held at Adelaide shed, Belfast, as spares, while most of the still tightly timed express running was being carried out by the two-cylinder engines, these being reckoned to be easier on coal and oil. It was even proposed to take all the compounds out of service during the winter months, but although this did not happen the Ss and S2s handled the great proportion of the Dublin–Belfast traffic, the compounds being restricted in the winter of 1938 mostly to the 5s Sunday excursions. The war changed all that however, and with loads growing steadily heavier, the compounds came back into the picture. Sometimes trains would be made up to as many as 14 coaches, and the only engines with sufficient power to tackle them unaided were the compounds. So the latter proved of great value during these arduous times, and after the war they were given a new lease of life when they were fitted with Belpaire boilers carrying a slight increase in pressure from 215 to 220lb.

It is often claimed that the last new design of 4-4-0 in Britain was the Schools of the Southern Railway, but this is hardly so, for although the GNR compounds worked in Ireland, half of their time being spent outside the United Kingdom altogether, they were completely British in concept, were built in Britain, and worked upon a railway which deviated in no significant way, apart from its gauge, from typically British practice. And after the compounds, there was still to come the last of the long line of Great Northern 4-4-0s, the eleventh variation, or the seventeenth if one counts the variation in cylinder sizes of the various Ps, PPs and QLs as constituting separate classes. This was the VS of 1948. In the years immediately following the end of the war there was a very heavy traffic passing between the Northern and Southern Irish capitals, a train leaving Amiens Street for Great Victoria Street every hour from 2pm to 11pm and *vice versa*, and the Great Northern urgently needed more locomotives. So 15 were ordered from Beyer Peacock, five more UG goods engines, five more U class light 4–4–0s, and five of a new class of express engine, a simple version of the compounds. The first of the 15 arrived on board the British Railways steamer *Slieve Bloom* at North Wall on January 6, 1948, in partly assembled condition and was carefully towed up to Dundalk at a very low speed. The rest followed at weekly intervals, and by early February all the VSs had been completed and were at work. They were named after Irish rivers and numbered 206–210 inclusive, the highest in numbers that the GNR ever reached, apart from the MAK diesel of 1954, No 800. Other than reverting to simple expansion the VSs also differed from the compounds in their Walschaerts valve gear, self-cleaning smokeboxes, higher-sided tenders very similar to those of the LMS and NCC, and, later, smoke deflectors. They were painted blue, a livery which was at this time extended to all except the smallest GNR 4–4–0s, and were a splendid sight in those days of generally sombre and restrained colour schemes. They had little chance to show their paces, for schedules on the GNR never returned to their pre-war standards, but they had the reputation of possessing somewhat greater power than the compounds though not being quite such free-running machines. Their designer was H. R. McIntosh, the CME of the Great Northern from 1939 onwards.

All the Great Northern 4–4–0s were capable machines, their performance equalling their looks. The shortest lived were the later Us and the VSs, for dieselisation caused their premature deaths. The others averaged well over 30 years apiece, the oldest of all being PP No 74, which was withdrawn at the venerable age of 66. However, S No 171 *Slieve Gullion* may remain in steam the longest in the end, for she now belongs to the Railway Preservation Society of Ireland and makes a number of trips each year. The preservationists have done pretty well by the GNR 4–4–0s as there are two others still in existence, although neither is likely to be steamed again. Compound No 85 *Merlin* is scheduled to go to the Transport Museum at Belfast; and Q No 131 has been repainted in the old lined black livery by CIE and the last time I saw her she was at the back of Connolly shed, although she has since been moved up to Dundalk.

The performances of the compounds on the Dublin–Belfast line during 1932–3 have already been referred to. The Ss were also fully capable of maintaining time on these schedules, providing that loads did not exceed eight bogies. In 1938 Cecil J. Allen published six runs between Dublin and Dundalk, the 31.7 miles to Drogheda being allowed 35min start-to-stop and the 22.5 miles from there to Dundalk 25min. On the first four runs, with loads varying from 222 to 283 tons tare weight, three with compounds and one with an S, there was no trouble in keeping time, but on the last two the loads were much heavier, 338 and 345 tons tare. Compound No 86 *Peregrine* kept time on the first but on the second No 83 *Eagle*, with boiler pressure reduced

NCC railcar No 3 which was built in 1936 and destroyed by
fire in 1956, seen crossing the Greenisland Loop Viaduct.

CDJC Walker railcar at Barnesmore Gap in County
Donegal.   [P. B. Whitehouse

CIE Sulzer 960hp Bo-Bo No 1101 in charge of a Dublin and
Cork train.

CIE former GSWR D4 4-4-0 No 335 (1907–55) at
Woodenbridge with a Rosslare Harbour–Dublin train.

[Seaton Phillips

CIE former MGWR J18 0-6-0 No 589 (1892–1963) at the
Ballinrobe end of the branch line from Claremorris.
[Seaton Phillips

CIE 0-6-2T No 671 (1933–59) at Dun Laoghaire with a train
of new corridor coaches in March 1951.   *[Bestwick Williams*

Above Left: One of CIE's last remaining steam worked passenger services was the 10.40am Waterford–Macmine Junction seen leaving Waterford in August 1959. The locomotive is J15 No 157 (1872–1963) and the carriage is an ex-GSWR clerestory composite. *[Michael H. C. Baker*

Left: CIE former CBSR Beyer Peacock 4-6-OT No. 464 1920—65) at Glanmire Road shed, Cork in August 1961. *[Michael H. C. Baker*

Above: CIE 4-6-0 No 801 *Macha* (1939–62) leaving the tunnel north of Glanmire Road, Cork with a lightweight goods for Thurles a few months before her withdrawal in August 1961. *[Michael H. C. Baker*

Above: A BCDR six-wheeler at Queens Quay, Belfast in
May 1950.   [H. C. Casserley

Below: CIE former MGWR six-wheel second No 45mS still
in passenger service at Cork in August 1961.
                                            [Michael H. C. Baker

Foot: CIE ex-GSWR corridor second No 1124 at Inchicore.
This carriage was built in 1914 and withdrawn in the late
1960s.   [G. M. Kichenside

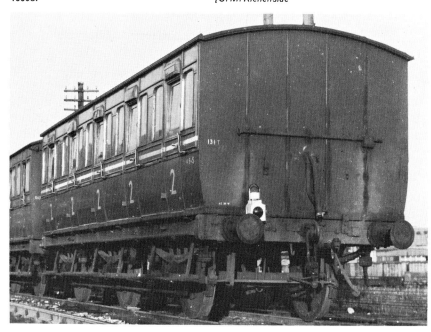

PLEASE DO NOT SPIT IN THE CARRIAGES
IT IS OFFENSIVE TO OTHER PASSENGERS
AND IS STATED BY THE MEDICAL PROFESSION
TO BE A SOURCE OF SERIOUS DISEASE

Notice from a GSWR carriage. *[Michael H. C. Baker*

A **TPO** being loaded at York Road on the **NCC**.
[General Post Office

A view of Heuston station from across the Liffey.

[Michael H. C. Baker

to 215lb, lost 35sec to Drogheda and a further 1½min between there and Dundalk.

In the opposite direction Cecil J. Allen recorded the performance of No 84 *Falcon* with a very heavy 12-coach train weighing 400 tons gross. The 24.9 miles from Belfast to Portadown took 32min 45sec, against a scheduled 32min, but time was kept from Portadown to Goraghwood and from there on to Dundalk, a tough section which includes 6½ miles at 1 in 100–113 to the summit at milepost 65½, just north of Adavoyle. Again the engine was working with reduced boiler pressure, and it would seem that while cutting it from the original 250lb reduced maintenance costs it meant that the compounds no longer had anything in reserve for loads much above the normal. Finally one must mention a run from Dundalk to Dublin with No 190, an S, in which she lost 35sec to Drogheda with a 305-ton train, but from there on to Dublin ran the 31.7 miles in 33min 45sec, despite a severe permanent way check, beating the schedule by 15sec, and covering the 28 miles to Raheny in less than even time. The highest speed was 79mph down the bank from milepost 16 past Rush & Lusk.

The majority of the engines led fairly uneventful lives, none of them attracting quite the attention lavished on the Great Southern's *Maeve* and her sisters, but one or two performed feats somewhat out of the ordinary and there was the occasional unfortunate accident. During the 1933 strike, when few trains continued to run, the driver of one which did, hearing what he thought were rifle shots just south of Dundalk (a not uncommon sound at the time) accelerated in order to get his train out of trouble, but ran straight into it, for the engine passed over a section of track from which one of the rails had been removed. Engine, tender and several carriages were derailed and rolled down an embankment, killing two passengers. It transpired that the supposed rifle shots were fog detonators which had been placed on the line in order to bring the train to a halt, for it was the intention of the supporters of the strike who had put them there to remove the passengers and crew from the train before derailing it.

The same engine, S2 No 190, was again involved in a fatal accident, in December 1945, while hauling the noon Belfast–Dublin express. Approaching Donabate at between 50 and 60mph a connecting-rod snapped and, flailing around, pierced the firebox. Despite the scalding steam which enveloped the footplate the driver managed to bring his train to a halt, without any injury to those in the train, although the leading coach was derailed. The passengers made an immediate collection in recognition of the great bravery exhibited by the crew in remaining on the footplate, but sadly the driver died almost at once from his injuries, and an inspector who was also on the footplate died the next day, the fireman alone recovering. A similar accident took place on one of the small 4-4-0s on the Clones line in November 1937; both enginemen suffered severe injuries, the fireman later dying.

Locomotives were sometimes lent by one company to another in order to help out for a limited period, but there are very few instances of engines being exchanged for the purposes of comparing one with another. The only one involving a GNR 4-4-0 took place in 1911, when GS&WR 4-4-0

No 322, a Coey 6ft 7in 4–4–0, worked for a week between Amiens Street and Belfast while a Great Northern 4–4–0, either a Q or a QL (the record is not clear) was tried out between Kingsbridge and Cork. Nothing of importance seems to have resulted from the encounter, and both Inchicore and Dundalk continued on their individual paths. An experiment carried out in the spring of 1936 saw the conversion of S No 172 to oil-burning. She apparently performed quite satisfactorily, but the trials were not extended, although a number of GNR engines were temporarily so fitted in 1946–7 during the coal shortage.

Although diesel railcars first appeared on main line services as early as 1951, steam did not disappear from the GNR with anything like the same rapidity as it did on CIE. In 1959 a variety of inside-cylinder 4–4–0s were still employed on stopping and semi-fast trains, although most of the compounds were at Dundalk awaiting breaking up, and express services by now were almost exclusively in the hands of the diesel multiple units. Nevertheless at the height of the summer steam had a few through workings and I particularly remember watching one of the three-cylinder simples, *Lagan*, pulling out of Amiens Street with a heavily-loaded express for Belfast. She had by then been renumbered 58 by the Ulster Transport Authority but retained her blue livery, as did all the 4–4–0s at this time, and in the bright September sunshine she made a magnificent spectacle as she accelerated her train of brown Great Northern carriages past the locomotive sheds and up the long elevated stretch of track across the Grand Canal and the River Tolka, and away through the North Dublin suburbs.

At the dissolution of the GNR in 1958 the surviving 4–4–0s were divided up between CIE and the UTA, a number of the Ps, PPs, Qs and QLs having already been withdrawn. CIE kept its allocation mostly on the GNR section, although these engines did venture elsewhere; some were stationed at Broadstone until its closure, but the UTA engines were seldom seen on the former NCC lines. When steam finished entirely on CIE in 1963 a few former GNR engines were sold to the UTA and these included three Ss and the VS *Boyne*. As late as 1964 *Boyne* still appeared on Dublin–Belfast through trains, but by the end of the following year she and her smaller sisters had been withdrawn, leaving the three preserved engines as the final representatives of the Great Northern 4–4–0s.

CHAPTER TWELVE

Railcar Development—
the Experimental Years

THE CLASSIC SOLUTION to unremunerative branch lines has for long been the self-propelled railcar, and Ireland, having a plethora of the former, was a pioneer of the latter. The story of its progress is one of ingenuity, persistence and, ultimately, of success, which was just as well for had it not been so it is doubtful if Ireland would today have a railway system.

Between 1900 and 1910, a period when the steam rail-motor enjoyed a considerable vogue in Britain, a number of Irish companies purchased examples, although hardly any survived in 1916 in their original form. Three Belfast & County Down rail-motors built by Kitson with Metropolitan RC&W bodies were put into service in 1902–3 and lasted until 1918, when the locomotive sections were detached and the bodies put to further use; There were two Manning Wardle rail-motors on the D&SER which lasted for no more than a year, chiefly on account of their extreme discomfort; while the G&SWR possessed the only rail-motor of the period actually built in Ireland. The power sections of the D&SER cars subsequently pursued varied careers as 0–4–0WTs. One, *Imp*, went to the Dublin & Blessington Tramway and then to the Great Southern, whilst the other, *Elf*, went direct from the D&ESR to the GSR; both were scrapped around 1930.

The G&SWR motor was designed at Inchicore by Coey and came out in 1904. The locomotive section was an 0–2–2T with outside cylinders, the first in Ireland, and a vertical boiler. The carriage part seated 40 third-class passengers and six first. It bore the standard GS&WR carriage livery of the period, which was rather splendid and is worth describing; it comprised lower panels painted in crimson lake, upper panels cream and white, and a lining of gold and vermilion. Coey's motor was tried out on various lines, from Kingsbridge via Glasnevin and Drumcondra to Amiens Street, and the Cashel and Killaloe branches, but it proved no better than the imported vehicles used on the other lines, frequently breaking down, gulping up coal at a fearful rate when it was working, and yet possessing insufficient power to haul a trailer. It lurked about Inchicore in disgrace for a number of years and was cut up there in 1915.

Inchicore tried again in the mid-1920s, buying ten Sentinel and Clayton steam railcars and putting them to work over a large part of the system at different times, Limerick being a favourite haunt. They were somewhat more successful than their Edwardian predecessors, one, No 356, still being at work on the Foynes branch in 1939, while there were four officially on the books in 1940, although they were probably in more or less permanent retirement. The other six had been withdrawn in 1931, when the carriage sections were still quite new. These were converted into two-car articulated sets and sent down to the Waterford & Tramore line, where they worked for a while behind the old 2–2–2WT No 483.

Nevertheless it cannot be said that the Great Southern got its money's worth from the cars, for it was clear by the end of World War I that if a really successful railcar was to be developed it would be powered by the internal combustion engine; indeed, one wonders why Kingsbridge bothered to persist with steam. Admittedly both the LNER and the Southern used similar vehicles in the 1920s, but it cannot be said that they obtained any better results than did the GSR, and anyhow they could far better afford to spend money on doubtful experiments.

A brave attempt in a different direction, also extensively tried out on the Great Southern, very nearly succeeded, but it failed in the end as much through the perennial bugbear of the Irish railways, lack of funds, as through inherent faults. Electrification had often been mooted, rather wistfully, for the Dublin and Belfast suburban lines, and no doubt if either of these cities had happened to be in England the money would have been found. As it is, third rail or overhead electrification is totally unknown on the main line railways of Ireland, although there have been a number of electric tramways, some of them railway-owned. Yet for nearly 20 years electric trains ran between Dublin and Bray along the former D&SER lines.

During the late 1920s a group of scientists at University College, Dublin, headed by Professor James Drumm, a Monaghan man, were working on a revolutionary type of battery, the basic characteristics of which were a high voltage and low internal resistance, enabling it to be charged and discharged many times each day at rates greatly in excess of what was then common. The Government, anxious to promote any scheme which might lead to the establishment of industry in the country, saw its possibilities, and in 1930 the Great Southern agreed to try out, with the backing of the Government, a former Drewry four-wheeled railcar, No 386, equipped with Drumm batteries. Working at 30hp the car was able to run at speeds up to 50mph, and after exhaustive trials with it the decision was taken to produce a full-sized two-coach train powered by Drumm batteries.

Numbered "A" it came out in February 1932, and was put to work on the Amiens Street–Bray run, covering 100 miles per day; its 15-ton battery powered two 200hp motors operating at 500V. The traction motors and all electrical equipment was supplied by Metropolitan–Vickers and were compact enough to be kept with the batteries below floor level.

Further progress was made in 1932, when a vacant shop and a small adjoining plot of land inside the works at Inchicore were leased to the Drumm Battery Company, which set up its headquarters there. A second train, "B", went into service in August 1933, and this could work for 80 miles before the batteries needed recharging. The horizon was not without clouds, however, for a report by a firm of consulting engineers, Merz and McLellan, on the Drumm trains proved rather disquieting. It discovered that the initial cost of the batteries was so great that it was likely to prove prohibitive unless substantial economies could be assured. One battery, of which the life was unknown, cost as much as an express locomotive assured of a life span of 40 years, capable of hauling ten bogie carriages carrying 700–800 passengers over any part of the system, whereas the Drumm train was confined to areas where re-charging plants had been set up.

The report could not agree with the Drumm Company's estimate of an annual saving of £9,130, but comparing like with like on suburban lines, this came out at the very much lower figure of £3,850, and then only if the battery was properly maintained. Of late there had been doubts about this, for although the company estimated that the batteries would last ten years there had been a definite loss in ampère-hour efficiency. The batteries also took too long to charge and the timetable was often upset, steam trains having to be substituted if the Drumm train was not ready to take up its scheduled working.

Nevertheless the Great Southern persisted with the Drumm trains and by 1935 had spent £27,147 on them, which was £7,000 more than the company spent in the following year on the five new D4 4–4–0s. In 1937 an agreement was drawn up between the Drumm Company and the Great Southern for the repayment of this money, and in April the Dail was asked to provide £30,000 for "electrical battery research". It was explained that the experimental work was almost over and that the future of the company now depended on sales of the battery. The money was granted and used for reconditioning the two existing batteries and providing two new ones. These were put into two further trains, "C" and "D", which began work in October 1939.

The electrical equipment of these was identical with that on the earlier sets, but improvements in manufacturing techniques ensured higher efficiency throughout the ten years guaranteed life of the batteries. A partial charge was received at the end of each 14½-mile run, a full charge giving the trains a range of 40 miles. They could accelerate at the rate of 0.8mph per second, and their maximum speed was 47mph. The coaches themselves were considerably more modern in appearance than the earlier sets, and were similar to the latest steam-hauled suburban stock. They remained the property of the Drumm Company, rental being paid to it by the GSR for the use of the trains. At this time charging facilities were withdrawn from Amiens Street but those at Harcourt Street and Bray were improved.

The arrival of the two 1939 sets meant that there were 13 weekday departures of Drumm trains from Harcourt Street, the number of steam engines required dropping to four. Usually the Drumms worked as two-car units, although it was possible to couple two units together and sometimes a trailer coach was added; this practice rather overloaded the motors, however, and was not resorted to in later years. The Drumms were worked hard and by 1935 the first two had covered over a million miles between them, a vastly greater total than two steam engines could have achieved in the same time.

In that year set "B" was involved in the most serious accident which befell the Drumms, and although it was fairly spectacular it fortunately resulted in no injuries. On the evening of June 26, during one of those severe thunderstorms which sometimes occur in midsummer and had already caused considerable damage at Westland Row, bringing down a section of the glass roof, the Drumm train had just left Dalkey when it ran into floods. These were 4 to 5ft deep and concealed a large fall of earth and rocks. A passer-by who had heard the landslide, which was caused by a burst sewer bringing down a 20ft high wall, had just time to run to a signal-post and wave at the driver of the train. The latter was able to slow the train down but not to stop it, and the obstruction was hit with considerable force, riding up over it. The train stayed upright and no-one was hurt, although a number of passengers were shaken, particularly by rapidly bailing out from the train and dropping into the deep, muddy water. Smoke began to pour from beneath the carriages and for a time a severe fire was feared. However, it chanced that Professor Drumm was at Dun Laoghaire at the time, and heard the crash; running to the scene he made a quick inspection and found that the smoke was coming from rubber cables attached to the batteries, rather than the precious batteries themselves, and was not serious. No vital damage was done to the equipment and after repair at Inchicore the train was put back into service.

Although the four Drumm units spent nearly all their days working between Amiens Street, Harcourt Street and Bray, one unit did work through to Donabate on the GNR main line, 10 miles north of Dublin, and Nos "C" and "D" were tried out on the Cork–Cobh and Mallow–Tralee lines, temporary charging points being set up to service them. No doubt the GSR would have liked to extend their use elsewhere but the World War II prevented this and in 1941 the Government announced that no more aid would be given to the Drumm Company. It was "no time for subsidising inventions" was the reason given. The company had little success in selling its batteries outside Ireland, and so a highly original and sophisticated attempt to provide a new form of railway traction progressed no further.

The Drumm trains were certainly popular with the general public and are remembered today with affection. While I was reading an article dealing with them in a 1935 newspaper in the National Library in Dublin an elderly man looked over my shoulder and said, "They could have been the saving of the railways, but it was all hushed up". This was not very well-informed comment, but of the kind that tends to be made when seemingly successful innovations don't quite make it.

The Drumms continued in service throughout the war, when they were invaluable during the coal shortage, and survived until 1949–50, by which time their batteries had reached the end of their useful life. They were removed, but, following the example of the old steam-powered Sentinels and Claytons, the coaches found further use as ordinary steam-hauled stock; they have all gone now. People are still experimenting with battery powered motor vehicles and London Transport, for one, uses battery locomotives. But the Drumm trains of the Great Southern were unique and it might have been that, but for the war and insufficient research funds, Ireland would by now be leading the world in this particularly clean and self-contained form of motive power.

The GSR showed little interest in the 1930s in other forms of self-propelled vehicles, preferring to concentrate on the Drumms, although it did own four Drewry four-wheeled petrol-engined cars, two broad gauge and two narrow. The narrow-gauge cars worked on the West Clare line, alongside a converted Model T; the 5ft 3in gauge ones, 30-seaters, went initially to the Goolds Cross–Cashel branch, but one was almost immediately converted into the pioneer Drumm car. This worked for some years between Inchicore and Kingsbridge, conveying staff, while the other car continued in its original form into the 1940s, when it was withdrawn.

The Great Northern and the NCC chose different paths from that of the Great Southern; theirs were the ideas which ultimately proved to be the way all Irish railways would have to go. Each began in the early 1930s with petrol-engined vehicles and then switched to diesels, carefully developing them to the point at which they became both economical and reliable. Ultimately they proved so attractive to management and public alike that the diesel railcar became the standard type of vehicle for all passenger traffic in the North.

The GNR and the NCC had both operated steam railcars in the 1900s and it hardly needs to be said that they were not of much use. The Great Northern tried out two varieties from British firms while Bowman Malcolm of the NCC designed his own and had them built at Derby. The locomotive sections of these latter were scrapped in 1913, but the two carriages were converted for ordinary use and as Nos 79 and 80 worked on the Larne line for many years.

The next NCC railcar was again steam-powered, unless one counts a converted bus which worked for a short while on the Coleraine–Portrush branch in 1924. The railcar was a Sentinel, similar to those on the Great Southern and the LNER, and no great shakes. It didn't care much for the many gradients it was expected to tackle and was scrapped after some seven years service. Then in 1933 the NCC, together with Leylands, came up with something altogether better, and to show their confidence in it gave it the number 1. This was a 54ft car with six first and 55 third-class seats, two Leyland 130bhp petrol engines, and capable of being driven from either end. It went to work in the Belfast area and performed all that was asked of it but Major Speir, the Manager, was not entirely satisfied and, in a typically high-handed manner passed over his own engineer, Malcolm Patrick, and got someone else to build him a lightweight car with diesel engines.

The result was No 2, which came out in June 1934, and although it incorporated several advanced features, such as the extensive use of aluminium and integral construction with the body and frames forming one unit, as sometimes happens when untried theories are put into practice with too little regard for the opinions of people who know what they are talking about, it did not turn out to be quite what the Major wanted. For one thing it sagged noticeably, despite some last-minute strengthening, and the weight reduction as compared with No 1 was nothing startling, actually rather less than four tons. The driving positions took the form of turrets, projecting upwards and outwards, one at either end, and were rather remarkable, if not very beautiful, appendages. They were so located to enable a number of railcars, together with trailers, to be worked in one train, the driver being able to see over the rooftops even if his car was marshalled in the middle of the train. As it happened traffic never warranted such a formation, and as the railcar proved incapable of keeping to the timetable with more than one trailer the rooftop view was never needed anyway. The revolutionary No 2 was hardly an unqualified success, but while it did not last as long as the other pre-war NCC cars it more than earned its keep, and Major Speir and its designer should at least be given credit for seeing the possibilities of the multiple-unit diesel train.

Two further cars followed, No 3 in 1936 and No 4 in 1938. Their engines were identical with those of No 2, two 125bhp Leyland diesels, and they also had turrets, although these blended in rather more happily with the overall design than did those of No 2. Two trailers were built in 1934, and these saw service with all the power cars. Certain workings called for the trailers to be pushed, a practice not popular with drivers, for, despite the turrets, visibility was not all that it might have been. It ceased when a cow caused the derailment of a trailer during the war, as the driver was unsighted until it was too late to avoid the animal.

During the 1930s the NCC had another go with road buses adapted to run on rails, this time using on one of them the Howden–Meredith patent wheels developed on the GNR. A couple of 1928 Leyland Lions were bought from the LMS and they worked up until the war; a regular duty of one of them was on the Coleraine–Derry section of the main line, where it ran close behind an express, stopping at all the small stations the express omitted so that the latter's schedule might be speeded up.

The railcars and buses provided the 'NCC's engineering and operating departments with valuable experience, which was used in developing the post-war diesel fleet. In actual terms of hard cash the effect they had on the Company's position up to 1939 was marginal, and the GNR was the one company to build up a substantial fleet of self-propelled railcars in the years before World War II.

The Great Northern was joint owner of the County Donegal Railways and the first internal combustion railcars built at Dundalk were two narrow gauge petrol-engined ones, in 1931. The following year the company began production of broad gauge railcars for its own use. AEC, of Southall, was early in the diesel railcar field and at the time was starting work with Park Royal and Swindon on the successful series of cars for the Great Western. An AEC engine of 130bhp powered the first GNR car, "A", which was a fairly small vehicle with 32 seats, intended for branch line duties and capable of hauling a loaded wagon or horsebox at 40mph, or two such vehicles at 35mph. A similar car, "B", but with a Gleniffer engine and electrical, instead of mechanical, transmission, came out in the same year. A contemporary account credits the Gleniffer car with "compressed paper" sides; whether these were disposable like handkerchiefs and underwear it did not say!

The next car, "C", was different again. It was driven by a Walker power bogie, a device particularly popular on the narrow-gauge, and had a separate driving compartment which was articulated to the rest of the car. The engine this time was a Gardner six-cylinder, 96hp, diesel. Car "C" could be driven from one end only, and was put to work on the Enniskillen to Bundoran line where it was a great success, covering 1,000 miles in a six-day week and 185,000 miles in a 3½-year period, before requiring overhaul. Although seating 12 more passengers than "A" or "B" ,"C" was considerably more economical; its fuel consumption averaged between 8 and 10mpg, while its operating costs worked out at less than 4d per mile. At this rate it could hardly fail to make a profit, and the GNR pressed on with further railcars, delighted with the results so far achieved.

Two similar cars appeared in 1935, "C2" and "C3" (the earlier one becoming "C1"), and these were the first to be used in the south, being put to work on the Dublin–Howth and Dublin–Balbriggan sections, each working over 250 miles per day. Walker power units were embodied in the next railcars, but Gardner engines of considerably more power were used, and the cars were quite different in a number of other respects. They were made up into four units, "D", "E", "F" and "G", two coming out in 1936 and two in 1938. Each unit consisted of three vehicles, the short power unit in the middle flanked by the trailer cars. These had timber bodies on steel frames and seated eight first-class passengers, 50 second-class and 101 third-class between them. Each unit was really a complete train, and "D" and "E" went into service on the suburban Dublin–Howth route, where they rapidly found favour with the the public. Dundalk was not too happy, however, about the transmission, which was by means of coupling rods, and it also felt that the 160bhp power output could be improved upon.

The two final pre-war units showed clear evidence of the great advances made since the emergence of the first car in 1932, each one being powered by two six-cylinder Gardner engines producing 204bhp transmitted to two pairs of non-coupled wheels. Each unit seated 164 passengers in three classes and was capable of a top speed of 48mgh. Cars "F" and "G" took over from the earlier articulated cars on the Howth line, which went to Dundalk for overhaul and then to the Belfast area.

In addition to the many railcars the GNR also owned some rail-buses which were used on lines where there was not sufficient traffic to justify a full-sized car. They were fitted with a unique type of rear wheel, the Howden–Meredith patent, in which a steel rim was fitted over a pneumatic tyre, giving a very smooth ride and at the same time keeping the cost of conversion down to £100. The buses retained their original interior fittings, headlamps and many other features from their road days, but their petrol engines were replaced by diesels, and with these they were able to return the excellent fuel consumption figure of 16mpg. They were far cheaper to run than a steam train, and, additionally, were more popular with passengers. Indeed, they actually succeeded in reversing the trend of branch line closures, and enabled the line from Scarva Junction, on the main line just south of Portadown, to Banbridge, in County Down, to reopen in 1934; on other branches the buses generated so much extra traffic that they eventually did themselves out of a job, being replaced by the larger capacity railcars.

The most casual observer would have been aware that the railcars combined the characteristics of both road and rail practice. The attractive blue-

and-cream livery was that used on the GNR's road fleet, and the large number of small windows, some with half droplights, and the bus type seats, also were inherited from road practice. Visually they were not at all unpleasant, the bowed fronts continuing the lines of the sides, and their uncluttered simplicity was considerably more effective than some of the blatantly over-designed examples produced in various parts of Europe in the post-war years.

The earlier GNR vehicles were usually to be found in the Portadown area, working on the Border lines, and neither they nor the Dublin and Belfast suburban units were ever called upon to perform express duties, although one of other of the first two cars was, for a time, attached to the rear of a morning stopping train from Belfast to Portadown, at which latter station it was detached and sent off independently to Armagh. The cars performed admirably on the services to which they were allocated, and there is little doubt that, but for the war, further vehicles would have been developed for main line use, leaving steam to concentrate on freight work.

A great deal of credit for the design of the whole series belongs to the GNR's Chief Mechanical Engineer, G. B. Howden, who took over from Glover in 1933. A Scotsman, Howden began his career on the North British, and he remained with its successor, the LNER, until 1929, when he came to Dundalk as Chief Civil Engineer. In this capacity he was responsible for rebuilding the Boyne Viaduct at Drogheda. On assuming the post of CME, he retained his former appointment, and delegated the locomotive side of the Mechanical Engineer's Department to H. R. McIntosh, while he and his Chief Locomotive Draughtsman, H. E. Wilson, concentrated on the railcars.

Howden was one of the outstanding figures in Irish railway history. In 1939 he became the General Manager of the GNR, and 11 years later he moved to a similar post with CIE. He went back north three years later, to head the Board of the UTA, at the same time taking over the joint Chairmanship of the Board that administered the GNR. For over 30 years he was at the centre of affairs, guiding the railways of Ireland through the most difficult period of their history, neglecting neither the interests of the railways nor of the men who worked on them. His death, in 1966, three years after his retirement, was widely regretted.

By 1939 the Great Northern was in severe financial straits, and excellent though its stud of passenger engines might be it was uncomfortably obvious that the continuation of steam haulage, with its limited availability and excessive use of manpower, was going to bring the company into the bankruptcy courts. The war put off the problem for six years, and by the time diesel railcars did take over the principal passenger services the fortunes of the GNR had sunk so low as to be irredeemable.

CHAPTER THIRTEEN

The World War II Years

FROM THE NARROW viewpoint of financial returns World War II was a godsend to the Irish railways. Passenger and goods receipts had been steadily declining on all of them, and on the big three were fast approaching the point where they would meet, and presumably thereafter exceed, expenditure. The NCC, largely through the efforts of Malcolm Speir, its Manager, had tried everything it knew to hang on to its passenger and goods traffic, despite which the number of passengers that it carried in 1939, 3,556,000, was noticeably less than the 1937 figure, 3,707,000, although both these were well in excess of the 1925 returns. Costs, however, had risen appreciably since then but fares had not.

The GNR was in a still shakier position. Passenger train miles in 1938 were greatly in excess of those in 1925, yet passengers carried dropped by 382,000. On the goods side loaded wagon miles in 1938 had dropped from 24,164,000 to 15,878,000 in 13 years, with the consequence that profits were down from £224,000 to a mere £40,000, a dismal slide which if continued would certainly result in a net loss within the next two or three years.

The Great Southern, never having reached the heights of the two Northern companies, could hardly fall so far, but like the GNR its passenger trains travelled further and carried fewer passengers in 1939 than they did in 1925, while loaded wagon miles had also declined, though not by very much, except for the head of livestock carried. This most important branch of the Great Southern's business had dropped heavily, partly on account of the economic war and the drastic reduction of cattle exports to Britain, from 2,169,000 head in 1925 to 1,394,000 in 1938. The excess of receipts over expenditure in 1925 was 9.11 per cent and in 1938 7.9 per cent; on the GNR, however, the decline was from 13.2 to 3.6 per cent—a dramatic indication of the company's fall from grace.

The war changed all this. The NCC, whose territory was entirely within Great Britain, was immediately affected, as was the northern section of the GNR; the GNR's southern section and all of the GSR's network for the time being carried on as before. Two reports had recently been published, one the McLintock, on the Six Counties' railways, the other the Transport Tribunal's, on those of the 26 Counties. The former had proposed, among many other things, that the NCC and the County Down should amalgamate and enter into a pooling arrangement with the GNR, while the Eire tribunal had made various recommendations concerning the structure of the Great Southern, its capital and restrictions on road competition. The war caused all these proposals to be shelved.

Eire determined to take no part in the war. DeValera was offered a deal
by the British Government in 1940, whereby all of Ireland would be united
as an independent country with the capital in Dublin, if he would bring the
26 Counties into the war and make Southern Irish ports and airfields available
to Allied forces, but he was not interested, which was hardly surprising as
one of the conditions of the deal was that Stormont had the power to veto
going in with the South if it so wished. Germany and Japan maintained
embassies in Dublin throughout the war, which sometimes proved useful to
Britain, and Ireland kept her neutrality. It might be argued that a victory
for Nazi Germany would hardly have been in the best interests of Eire, but
it was equally true that, historically, Ireland had no quarrel with Germany
and she certainly had no cause to feel under any obligation to come to the aid
of the British Empire. For all that it is probably true to say that, whatever
the actions of a minority, the population of Ireland as a whole wished the
average Britisher no harm and welcomed the entry of the USA into the war and
the eventual Allied victory. The minority, the IRA, chose to take advantage of
the situation and attempted to carry out, and in some instances succeeded in
perpetrating, bomb outrages on the civilian population in Britain. Brendan
Behan's book *Borstal Boy* gives an insight into the muddled, idealistic thinking
of some of the young IRA members, the same sort of people who to this day
plant bombs under the Belfast–Dublin railway line in what they believe to be
the furtherance of Irish unity and independence.

As in 1914 many Irishmen from both sides of the Border were already
members of, or hastened to join, the British armed forces. At the same time,
when it was clear that war was about to be declared, telephone calls from
London during the last week of August 1939, brought British soldiers on
holiday in Ireland back to their camps, while on the 26th of that month over
800 mothers and children, mostly Irish or of Irish descent, arrived from
England on their way to relations in the South and West. Throughout that
week refugees from England poured into Rosslare and Dun Laoghaire. The
harbour staff at Rosslare had to be doubled to cope with the rush, and Boy
Scouts volunteered to carry buckets of water up and down the platforms so
that the weary travellers could quench their thirst whilst they waited for their
trains. Numerous specials were put on to all parts of the 26 Counties, from
Cork in the South to Donegal in the North. In Waterford, through which the
trains from Rosslare passed, the ladies of the city formed a voluntary committee and offered tea, milk and biscuits to the women and children as their
trains paused at the station. By September 7 some 10,000 refugees had been
landed at Rosslare within ten days.

The traffic was not all one way. The liner *Athenia*, carrying evacuees from
Britain to America, was torpedoed almost within hours of the outbreak of
war and 237 of the survivors were landed from the rescue ships at Galway,
whence they were conveyed by train to Dublin. There they were given lunch
by the Great Northern at Amiens Street station and then taken on to Belfast,
a special compartment being provided in the train for two injured crew
members of the *Athenia*.

On September 11 a permit system was introduced which immediately cut down the number of travellers between Britain and Ireland, and sailings on most of the routes were reduced, releasing a number of ships for war service elsewhere. The Irish based B&I line cut its Dublin–Liverpool sailings to three a week in each direction, the LMS its Dun Laoghaire–Holyhead ones to one a day each way, and the GWR its Fishguard–Rosslare service to thrice weekly each way.

Eire was not unprepared for war and it was recognised that she might find herself drawn into it. James Larkin, still the most respected trade union leader even if no longer always the most powerful, had proposed a tunnel under the Liffey which would have provided employment and would have been less vulnerable to air attack than a bridge, and he also suggested covering the railway in between Westland Row and Dun Laoghaire and draining the Grand Canal as far as Mullingar to provide deep shelters. The Dublin City Engineer estimated that a 2,200yd long tunnel under the Liffey would cost around £1,800,000, and said this was only a rough estimate, as there was no exact data available on the underlying strata. The tunnel, of course, was never built, although there have been other similar proposals at various times since.

On September 3 and 4 blackout regulations were tried out. Buses in Cork started running with no interior lights and only side exterior ones. On NCC trains dull blue bulbs were fitted in the carriages, while on the mostly gas-lit County Down stock the globes were painted either blue or black with a small circle left clear at the bottom through which a minute yellow beam shone down. The GNR fitted blue bulbs similar to those on the NCC, and switched over to them when trains in Eire crossed the Border into the North. Various other blackout measures were tried at this time in the North, signal-box windows being covered in brown paper and station and yard lights tinted purple.

As people became used to the "Phoney War" and the expected air attacks failed to materialise blackout restrictions were relaxed and the drastically reduced timetables on the NCC were modified somewhat, a number of seasonal trains reappearing in the 1940 summer timetable. Major Speir had been appointed Railway Liaison Officer for Northern Ireland on September 1939, and the NCC bore the brunt of the vast amount of War Office traffic generated by the forces installations in the Six Counties, keeping in constant contact with the GNR and the B&CDR by means of a private and secret telephone link set up between the three Belfast termini.

On the Great Southern the peacetime timetables continued through the summer of 1940, both passenger and goods traffic increasing appreciably as the restrictions on petrol and oil supplies to road operators began to bite. The Anglo–Eire trade agreement signed by DeValera and Chamberlain in 1938 had also meant more business for the railways, as did the buying up of materials in Britain by Irish traders who feared that these would soon be unobtainable. On the passenger side restrictions on travel abroad kept holiday-makers at home, and the Great Southern and the NCC, also to a lesser extent the GNR and the minor lines, reaped the benefit.

Restaurant car services, including the four Pullmans, which the Great Southern had bought in 1936 from the Pullman Car Company, continued to run on the GSR during 1940, while the GNR and the NCC maintained dining and buffet cars on their principal routes throughout the war. A number of carriages and wagons were built for the Northern companies during this period, but by the end of 1940 Eire was feeling the effect of wartime shortages, for Britain had virtually nothing to spare for a neutral country, and there was really no other source to which she could turn. Construction of the third 800 class 4–6–0, *Tailte*, was held up and she did not go into service until June 1940, while the building of a new class of engine for the Dublin suburban lines, a three-cylinder 4–6–2 Tank, had to be shelved and eventually abandoned.

The year 1941 brought the war much closer. Not only was there an almost total halt in the flow of manufactured goods necessary to keep the Great Southern working at peacetime standards, but more seriously still coal supplies fell drastically and passenger and goods services were seriously curtailed. Britain saw to it that NCC, B&CDR and GNR trains in the North always had sufficient fuel, but the population of the Six Counties, and particularly the citizens of Belfast, had their lives disrupted in an equally effective and vastly more violent manner.

Belfast was one of the key ports in the Battle of the Atlantic, the nearest large harbour in Europe to the United States and the assembly point for convoys. As such it was an obvious target for enemy bombers, and in April and May 1941, they struck. Great damage was done, and although GNR and County Down property was relatively unscathed, the NCC at York Road took a fearful hammering. On the night of April 15–16 a number of NCC employees were killed, and the offices of the General Stores Department and the Parcel, Audit and Civil Engineering Drawing Offices were set on fire and completely gutted. The running lines opposite the engine shed also received two direct hits. Worse followed on the night of May 4–5. The remaining offices, together with many records, went, the station itself was bombed and set on fire, and the hotel was almost completely burned out. Twenty carriages standing in the station and on adjacent sidings were a total loss as were numerous wagons.

Outside the city high explosive bombs cut the line in two places, and for a time no trains ran closer to York Road than Whitehead, passengers having to transfer to buses for the final three miles. A railway company of the Royal Engineers, trained on the military railway at Longmoor, immediately got to work clearing up the wreckage and managed to effect temporary repairs which got passenger trains running into York Road again within 48 hours, and goods trains within four days. Temporary offices were set up at various places outside Belfast, and as far as was possible passenger trains from then on were stabled at night away from the city. The LMS made good the rolling stock losses, building 40 5ft 3in gauge bogies at Derby and fitting them to twenty non-corridor third class bodies dating from between 1925 and 1939, while goods wagons were obtained from various sources. Later another 24 coaches which had seen service on the other side of the Irish Sea were sent over to help deal with the great many extra troop specials the NCC was having to run.

For the rest of the war Ulster suffered little from enemy action, although there was still plenty of action at sea. One of the worst incidents involving a ship sailing from an Irish port occurred on June 13, 1940. The Great Western's 1,922-ton steamer *St Patrick* was nearing Fishguard, well within sight of land at the end of its 3½hr voyage from Rosslare, when it was spotted by a German aircraft. The planes repeatedly dive-bombed the ship and she was hit four times. There was no time to lower the boats, and the passengers and crew jumped overboard as the ship went down, clinging to rafts which some of the crew managed to launch or which floated free as the *St Patrick* slid under the waves. In all, 66 persons were saved but at least 23 died, most of them when the bombs struck the ship. All except one of the first-class passengers lost their lives, as did two stewardesses and the captain and mate.

Later in 1940 another railway-owned vessel sailing from an Eire port, the LMS *Cambria*, was bombed, this time with less tragic consequences. She was 40min out from Dun Laoghaire, bound for Holyhead, when she was attacked, but none of the bombs hit the ship; her decks, however, were sprayed with machine gun bullets, resulting in the death of the 3rd officer, slight injuries to one passenger, and numerous holes in the decks and upper works.

A more legitimate military target would have been one of the ships sailing between Northern Ireland and England or Scotland. The steamers from Belfast to Glasgow, Heysham and Liverpool, and the Larne to Stranraer services, were much used by troops coming or going off on leave, and in addition the Larne–Stranraer route, the shortest of the Irish cross-channel crossings, was the principal one for the movement of stores and personnel.

The section of line down to Larne Harbour found itself carrying vastly more traffic than ever before, the most spectacular working being that of a 17-coach train to Antrim which was broken up there and sent off to a variety of destinations on the NCC and the GNR. Throughout the war an average of seven extra trains was run each day on the NCC and in the space of two years the number of passenger bookings more than doubled; in 1939 the figure was just over 3½m, while by 1941 it was nearly 7¾m.

On the Great Southern the situation was totally different. Many of the factors which provided the NCC, and to a lesser extent the GNR, with so much extra business existed; nearly all the 50,000 private cars in Eire were off the roads, only 156 motor cycles were licensed, and commercial vehicle operators were restricted, yet the GSR carried one million less passengers in 1944 than in 1939 and not very much more freight. This apparent staring at a gift horse in the mouth came about through factors quite outside the Great Southern's control.

During 1941 coal supplies shrunk to little more than a trickle and most of that was hardly better than dust. It was quite impossible to run a normal service, and the disruption brought about was greater than anything previously experienced on the Irish railways, the 1916 and Civil War periods included. The lowest point was reached in April 1942, when eleven branch lines were temporarily closed and passenger trains on all other lines, main and branch, ran on two days per week only, while goods trains were confined to four. There was a distinct possibility that railway services would shut down altogether, and there were a number of occasions when this was averted only by the timely arrival of a collier at Dublin Docks. On one occasion in October, 1941, no more than a single day's supply was left, and the Government had to release its emergency stocks, some of which were kept in a dump in the Phoenix Park, trusting that it would be able to replenish them before the country was completely denuded of coal. If that had happened, power-stations and industry, as well as the railways, would have been brought to a complete standstill.

The trains which did run had to contend with coal of a quality hardly sufficient to provide enough steam to boil a kettle, and any semblance of a time-table disappeared. There were instances of goods trains taking 14 days to reach Dublin from Cork, and during the winter of 1942 a Killarney to Dublin passenger train took 23hr to complete its journey, whilst the Up Cork Mail bettered this by no more than 2hr. A typical run with the latter train was that of May 11, 1942. It left Glanmire Road station, Cork, at 11 in the morning, and apart from scheduled stops it came to a halt on a number of occasions to enable the engine to be detached and to run up and down the line to build up steam. A number of engines had charge of the train at various times, including *Maeve*, which in palmier days would have completed the journey in around $3\frac{1}{2}$hr unaided. On this occasion the Mail reached Kingsbridge at 6am on the 12th, 19hr after leaving Cork. Despite the length of the train many passengers were unable to find seats and spent the entire journey in the corridors. The dining car shut at 9pm after all the food had been used up, and when the tired and hungry passengers eventually arrived in Dublin most had to walk with their luggage to their destinations in the city, for the few taxis had been immediately snapped up, and the first trams and buses had not yet begun their day's work.

Bus and tram services in any case were also severely restricted in Dublin and the rest of the country. The first GNR double-deck buses, AECs, had gone into service towards the end of 1937, shortly followed by comparable Dublin United Tramways vehicles, Leyland Titans with bodies built at the company's works at Spa Road, Inchicore. Until then the DUT had relied mainly on trams, but between 1937 and 1940 a number of routes went over to buses. As in London and other British cities further conversion had then to be postponed, and it may be thought that trams, needing no imported fuel, had an advantage over the motor-bus during the war years. While this was true in Britain it was not so in Dublin, for the power-stations were not able to provide as much electricity as was required, and it was impossible to obtain spare parts for the trams.

The situation on the railways grew worse and a number of trains failed to reach their destinations at all, lorries with wood and coal having to be sent out to rescue them. The chief problem, once fuel had been obtained, was the clinker which formed on the firebars and fused with them, so preventing any draught getting to the fire and eventually putting it out. The engines then had to be abandoned by their crews and this became known as "bailing out". It was a term used so often that it began to appear in official documents, and one telegram from a depot foreman to his superintendent, informing

A CIE Walker Bo-Bo diesel No F502 (later with Bord na Mona) backing down on to its train at Kilrush, West Clare section.   [R. N. Joanes

The memorial set up in the forecourt of Ennis station to Percy French with the preserved West Clare 0-6-2T in the background.   [Michael H. C. Baker

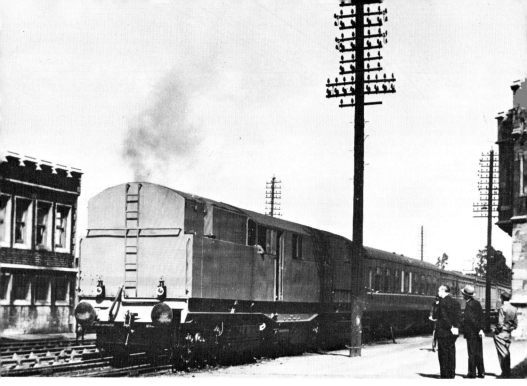

O.V. Bulleid (third figure on the right) watching the turf
burner undergoing trials at Inchicore. [CIE

CIE A class diesel No A21 at Youghal with the 7.45pm
train for Cork on June 19, 1956. [B. K. B. Green

Top : CIE–Park Royal railcar unit forming a Wexford–Rosslare train, seen running along the quay at Wexford. *[P. F. Winding*

Above : A six car CIE former GNR railcar set headed by a 1958 built BUT vehicle leaving Dublin Connolly for Drogheda.
[Michael H. C. Baker

Below : NIR five car MP railcar set with an additional parcels van at York Road. Note variety of types and ages of vehicles. *[Michael H. C. Baker*

Above: CIE rebuilt two-cylinder 4-6-0 No 405 (1923–55)
leaving Mallow with the Dublin–Killarney "Radio Train" in
1950.   *[Bestwick Williams*

Above right: CIE rebuilt Metro-Vickers Co-Co No A40r
passing Limerick Junction wih the Dublin–Killarney
"Radio Train" in 1970.   *[Michael H. C. Baker*

Right: CIE C class Bo-Bo on passenger train emitting usual
cloud of exhaust seen passing Grand Canal Street. The
leading coach is open suburban second built just before
World War II and the remainder are wide bodied Park
Royals.   *[Michael H. C. Baker*

NIR former SLNCR 0-6-4T *Lough Erne* shunting at York Road on May 13, 1967. *[M. Dunnett*

Preserved DSE 2-6-0 No 15 standing outside Inchicore
Works in August 1970. This locomotive was built in 1922
by Beyer Peacock.   [Michael H. C. Baker

NIR 2-6-4T No 51 passing Whitehead with a spoil train in
October 1969.   [J. D. Mills

The CIE Dublin–Cork Liner Train headed by single cab
GM Bo-Bo No B126 seen leaving North Wall.

[Michael H. C. Baker

A CIE Dublin–Greystones train approaching Bray with
GM Bo-Bo No B170 in charge.   *[Michael H. C. Baker*

him that he had bailed out another crew, fell into the hands of the detective department, causing great consternation until its meaning was explained.

Many attempts were made to obtain fuel from other than the usual sources, not all of them strictly legal. At Amiens Street GNR crews would sometimes take pity on their Great Southern comrades and move their engines alongside GSR ones, passing over some of the vastly superior coal with which they were supplied, while less obliging GNR men might still find themselves a few lumps short if a GSR locomotive was in the vicinity and they failed to keep a sharp eye on it. Anything burnable left close to a railway line was likely to be removed, and boxes, planks, wooden buckets, timber blocks and bags of turf all used to disappear into fireboxes if their owners failed to keep them well out of sight. Sometimes the population got its own back by removing the wooden keys placed between the rails and the chairs. Being soaked in oil these burned splendidly and were much sought after; but the practice was severely frowned upon by the authorities and some heavy fines put a damper upon this bit of private enterprise.

More official substitutes for coal were timber, turf, Irish coal from the Arigna mines and "duff". Of these timber was the most expensive, whilst turf and Arigna coal were little better for locomotive purposes than coal dust, which the Great Southern was reduced to buying at one point. Duff was produced in briquetting plants which the company obtained second hand in the spring of 1942, and was a mixture of dust and pitch; it was hardly ideal but it did save the railways from coming to a complete standstill, and by late 1942 some 1,500 tons of it were being produced each week. In August of that year there was a general reduction of 15 per cent in train loads, increased to 25 per cent on severely graded sections of line, and this, combined with the improved fuel situation, brought about a distinct improvement in timekeeping. Less than a quarter of the timber and turf consumed in 1942 was needed the next year, and a fairly regular, if much reduced, service was maintained for the duration of the war.

With train and road services so decimated people looked around for alternative means of getting about. An obvious one was the canal barge. The two principal canal systems in the country, the Grand and the Royal, had carried over 1m tons of merchandise between them as late as 1905, but by 1940 they were almost unused. On the GSR-owned Royal Canal, which was still having £10,000 spent on it each year, less than half-a-dozen boats shared what business there was, and although there was rather more activity on the Grand Canal it also made a sizeable loss. In 1942, however, its fortunes revived a little and orders were placed for 20 new wooden barges; the first of them completed its maiden voyage on October 28, arriving back in Dublin after a 5½-day round trip to the Midlands with 61 tons of turf briquettes.

The most colourful answer to the lack of public transport was a horsedrawn stage coach. This was a 25-seater *charabanc*, drawn by four horses, and ran between Adare and Limerick. The 11-mile route was normally served by Tralee to Limerick trains, but whilst these were suspended the coach proved a great success and was extended to Rathkeale, 19 miles from Limerick. The cost to each passenger was 2d a mile.

The one development in the transport field at this time which had any lasting effect on the railways took place in the air. In August 1942, Aer Lingus inaugurated a regular service, thrice weekly, between Collinstown and Rincanna (now Shannon). Although Collinstown, now simply called Dublin Airport, was a considerable distance from the city centre, as also was Shannon from Limerick, the overall time was still very much less than by rail, and in the first four weeks of its operation the Dragon Rapide biplanes were booked to capacity and carried a total of 250 passengers at £3 per head single, £5.10s return.

While the Great Southern struggled along as best it could, the Great Northern found itself raking in more money than its directors could have imagined possible three years earlier. Fuel was no problem, for the British Government kept the company well supplied in order to cope with the military traffic in the Six Counties, and could hardly stipulate that none of it was to be burned on the other side of the Border. There was no possibility of taking a holiday outside Ireland and yet, now that the war had wiped out unemployment, more people than ever in the North could afford to go away. So they went to the South and the West and so great was the demand for railway tickets at Great Victoria Street during the summer of 1942 that controls had to be introduced. People queued ten deep, and over a single weekend more than 5,000 passengers arrived at Amiens Street from the North. It was a similar story each summer while the war lasted and virtually every record relating to traffic density and receipts between Dublin and Belfast was broken over and over again.

Since the setting up of the Border there had always been a certain amount of smuggling across it, but the unnatural conditions obtaining while the state of war existed in the North meant that certain commodities were in short supply up there, whereas others were difficult to get hold of in the South. It was a smuggler's paradise and one gets the impression that almost the entire population at one time or another was involved in illicit trading, not the least backward being employees of the GNR. Within a few days of each other cases were brought before the courts in February 1942, in the first of which a restaurant car attendant was fined £250 and imprisoned for two years for offences under the Defence Regulations, which included bringing into Northern Ireland two letters from Eire, while in the second two men were fined £750 at Dundalk with the alternative of six months inside. An onion smuggler hardly sounds a very romantic figure, but no doubt there was money to be made out of the business; indeed, two Dundalk men attempted to infiltrate five tons of the vegetable into the North by removing the wagons containing them from the main part of the train in which they were marshalled whilst the customs officers were examining it, and then slipped them back in again.

A rather different case concerned an entire restaurant crew of five who had regularly been bringing two loaves of white bread from Belfast to Dublin each day. It was pleaded on their behalf that quite often the restaurant car stocks ran out and the men gave their own bread to the customers. Whether the magistrate's heart was softened by this or whether he did not regard the crime as a particularly heinous one in any case is not recorded but the men were let off with small fines.

There were numerous other instances of GNR men appearing before the law. A Dundalk driver was given 12 months for trying to bring in $3\frac{1}{2}$cwt of tea amongst the coal in his tender, while on other occasions bags of the precious beverage were found sewed into the upholstery of carriage seats or stuffed into fire extinguishers. But all these exploits were as nothing compared with the amount of contraband found about the persons of the GNR's passengers. For sheer scale and ingenuity their efforts made those of the railway's employees appear quite amateurish.

On one memorable day in July 1942, the 5pm train from Bundoran was so delayed while its occupants were searched that it was 4am before it pulled into Belfast. Around this time customs officials were particularly vigilant, and a search of a Dublin–Belfast express produced something from practically every occupant of the packed train, 800lb of butter, boxes of chocolates, saucepans, kettles, knives, forks, boots, shoes, vast quantities of every commodity scarce in the United Kingdom and plentiful in Eire. Goodness knows where some of the larger items were concealed; the usual places for small articles were in pouches and belts which the women hid beneath their skirts.

In the 1940s shiny red lipstick was all the rage, yet it was almost impossible to get hold of it in Northern Ireland. The build-up of troops in the Province provided unlimited possibilities of attachments to eligible young men, and the young women of the Six Counties were determined not to let the chance slip. Lipstick was easily obtainable in the South and rapidly became one of the most profitable items in the smuggler's repertoire. The dummy fire extinguisher in the Great Northern carriage which had been used to smuggle tea into Eire made its return journey packed with cosmetics, and one of the biggest hauls the customs men ever made was at Clones, when they discovered 430 packets of lipstick in a train bound for Belfast.

Various measures were applied in an effort to cut down smuggling. Wire netting was put across seat spaces and floors and ventilators, and at one point the GNR went to the extreme of borrowing some MGWR six-wheel carriages from the Great Southern equipped with wooden seats, which made it impossible to conceal anything in the upholstery. One of the most cunning dodges, the mark of a professional rather than one engaged in the business merely "for the duration", was practised by the jewellery smuggler. Rings were slipped into a glass of stout in the dining car and then removed once the Border was past. This particular trick was halted by closing all the catering cars while they were in the vicinity of the Border. A measure which went some way towards putting the less dedicated smuggler out of business was the debarring at Drogheda and Dundalk of all intending passengers for stations south of Goraghwood. The chief inconvenience to the Great Northern of all this, apart from the incarceration of its employees from time to time, was the delays to trains, and this was eventually overcome by putting customs officers on board the trains and letting them carry out their searches whilst the train was in motion. But smuggling was such a profitable business that nothing less than the end of the war could greatly reduce it, and a fair amount has continued right down to the present day.

There were other ways of making a profit out of wartime conditions, one of the more unlikely being the resale of railway tickets, in which quite a black market sprang up in the South at different times. One such occasion was a Leopardstown Race Day, when a gang acquired a great many of the limited supply of tickets and offered them outside Harcourt Street station at prices well above their face value, a 7d third-class fetching 1s. Even when the worst of the fuel crisis had been overcome the Great Southern was constantly turning passengers away for lack of trains to put them in. No extra trains could be run at holiday times, but the GSR did what it could by circularising Dublin schools and colleges and asking students and pupils to let them know if they required seats to be booked for them on trains to the country. There were very few holidaymakers from England and Wales, but many more than usual from Northern Ireland, and although the Great Northern was able to get them as far as Dublin without much trouble numbers who wished to go to the South and West were left behind at Kingsbridge or Westland Row. One's only hope was to book beforehand, when one was given a voucher for a particular compartment, and the vouchers were usually snapped up within a few hours of going on sale. Fewer trains filled to capacity meant far better returns, and between 1940 and 1945 operating profits increased significantly, the 1945 figure exceeding the 1938 one by 400 per cent. The final profit for 1945, after payments of interest and to the sinking and pension funds, was nearly £500,000. But by then the Great Southern had ceased to exist.

CHAPTER FOURTEEN

A General Election, and the End of the Great Southern

THERE CANNOT BE many cases in history of the fortunes of a railway company bringing about a general election, but such was the case in Eire in 1944. One of the solutions to the problem of declining profits put forward after World War I had been nationalisation, and although the Government had had chosen not to follow this up the idea had remained in people's minds. By 1939 it was generally accepted that if the Great Southern was to continue the Government would have to provide financial assistance and inevitably this would entail some degree of Governmental control. Although war conditions improved the company's position it was clearly seen that with the return of peace the decline which had gone on through the 1920s and 1930s would be resumed. During 1943 it was announced that the entire transport system in Eire was to be reconstructed, and immediately there was great activity on the Dublin Stock Exchange, the value of Great Southern shares shooting up by £2½m. Given the fact that the Great Southern was presently making a profit it nevertheless seemed to some people that this was an enormouse increase in the popularity of shares which had formerly been difficult to dispose of. The matter required explanation, and at the end of November 1943, a tribunal was set up to enquire into the possibility of a leak of confidential information.

The tribunal met early in 1944 and heard a great many statements. Before this meeting the Principal Officer of the Transport Branch of the Ministry of Industry and Commerce had resigned consequent upon the discovery of his name on a number of transfers of GSR stock. The President of the Stock Exchange set out the story as he saw it. The general opinion of the Exchange had been that the company would pay a year's dividend on the guaranteed stock, but after a disappointing annual report and an even more disappointing annual general meeting there had been considerable selling, which had continued following a statement by Mr Lemass, the Minister for Industry and Commerce. Then the downward trend in the share prices had been reversed and when the terms of the Great Southern's reconstruction were published in October there had been great surprise.

According to the President, the Stock Exchange Committee felt that the GSR directors ought to have put out a definite statement of their intentions earlier; the fact that there had suddenly been a spate of buying well before the terms of the reconstruction had been announced indicated that "there was something amounting to certain knowledge". The Secretary of the Stock Exchange agreed and said that "Dealings during the period had been extraordinary and abnormal", but on the other hand a member of the Exchange stated that it was common knowledge that trains were crowded and goods traffic had increased, and the only tip needed by speculators was the statement by the Chairman of the Great Southern that its capital was to be reorganised.

Meanwhile the Transport Bill providing for the replacement of the Great Southern and its amalgamation with the Dublin United Transport Company was introduced into the Dail. The first reading was passed at the end of March 1944, but on May 9 the second reading failed to get through by one vote; DeValera immediately resigned as Taoiseach and a General Election was called.

The opposition Fine Gael party made great play of the alleged leak on the Stock Exchange, accusing the Government of favouring speculators at the expense of the people and proclaimed "None are so fearful of the result of the election as those who have bought GSR shares and have not yet unloaded". Lemass denied that the reorganisation would cause redundancy, and said he was satisfied that it was a measure which would protect the transport system of Ireland. The electorate took Mr Lemass at his word and Fianna Fail was returned with an increased majority; DeValera continued in power, and GSR shares, which had fallen once more since the dissolution, now regained their former attraction.

The Transport Bill was re-introduced into the Dail and this time got through its second reading with a thumping majority of 69 to 38, a couple of days before the Tribunal finished taking evidence. A number of Opposition members who had made statements during the election campaign about the alleged leak withdrew them, admitting that they had nothing with which to back them up, and the report of the Tribunal which came out in September 1944, declared that there had in fact been no leak. Two people outside the GSR and the Government departments concerned had prior knowledge, but as these were the Archbishop of Dublin and the Governor of the Bank of Ireland it was not felt that any impropriety had resulted from these quarters. There had been improper use of the information by the official who had resigned, but no Stock Exchange deals had resulted, and apart from a purchase of stock worth £500 by a GSR director, suspicion of anything untoward was non-existent. On November 29, 1944, the Transport Bill (No 2) was received from the Senate by the Dail and passed, leaving the GSR with just one month of independence. During that month there occurred the most serious accident in its history.

Straboe is a place which consists of a level crossing some three miles east of Portlaoise (formerly Maryborough) on the Dublin–Cork main line and very little else. On the night of December 14, 1944, a goods train from Dublin, partly composed of loaded cattle wagons, was standing near the crossing when the Down Night Mail, headed by two-cylinder 4-6-0 No 406 ran into it at some speed, derailing 15 of the 25 wagons and pushing the engine, which was having its fire cleaned out, 20yd along the track. A number of cattle were killed, while others were injured and had to be put out of their misery; worse still, two Post Office sorters were trapped in one of the vans of the Mail train which was telescoped by the leading passenger carriage. This Mail van was an ancient, fragile thing, 67 years old, built entirely of wood, and it splintered into fragments, crushed, like the two similar Post Office vans immediately behind it, under the heavy steel underframe of the coach. One of the occupants of the latter, a soldier, Joseph Conroy of No 4 Army Band, crawled into the wreckage and reaching the two trapped Post Office men he wedged an iron bar into the debris and held it for $5\frac{1}{2}$hr, so preventing further injury to the men until breakdown gangs accomplished the delicate task of clearing a way into the remains of the van and removing its unfortunate occupants.

One of the postmen died from his injuries and subsequently charges of manslaughter were brought against the driver and fireman of No 406, and a charge of endangering the lives of passengers was brought against the guard of the goods train. At the men's trial it proved almost impossible to establish the true facts. Two witnesses claimed that the Mail train pulled out of Portarlington against the signals, while the record of the signalman there contained no entry mentioning the offering of the Mail train to Portlaoise box. Nor was there anything to indicate that the goods train had reached Portlaoise and that the section between Portarlington and Portlaoise was clear. On the other hand both enginemen on the footplate of the Mail train engine were adamant that they had received a green light on pulling out of Portarlington. Despite the fact that it was a common occurrence for a train to stop in the middle of a section owing to the poor quality of fuel the GSR was then having to contend with the fact that no regulations had been drawn up instructing guards to place detonators in the rear of their trains in the event of a breakdown. The outcome was that the locomotive crew were acquitted while the unfortunate guard was found guilty. The death toll of the Straboe accident would undoubtedly have run into double figures but for the fortunate chance of the largely unoccupied mail vans being marshalled at the front of the train. As it was the Great Southern was able to end its existence with its record intact of no fatalities to ordinary passengers.

The title of the new company was to be Coras Iompair Eireann. A Labour member of the Dail asked why the English translation, Irish Carrying (or Transport) Company could not be included in it, but the Minister, bearing in mind his party's declared policy of promoting the Irish language, said that it was a simple name and would no doubt soon become common usage, as indeed it has. CIE began life on January 1, 1945, with a paid-up capital of around £13½m and with power to borrow the balance to bring it up to £20m, in order to carry out extensive reorganisation. Holders of DUTC preference or ordinary shares received £145 of redeemable debenture CIE stock, whilst GSR 4 per cent debenture shareholders were given an equal number of CIE 3 per cent redeemable debenture stocks. For each £100 of GSR guaranteed shares their holders got £50 worth of 3 per cent debenture stock and £50 worth of common stock. Great Southern shareholders had certainly done much better of late than DUTC ones, as the value of GSR ordinary stock had gone up in a year from £29 to £70, while £1 DUTC shares had risen only from 24s 9d to 28s 3d. But in the long term the DUTC had been a much safer investment, the Company having made a steady profit for many years. Its head, A. P. Reynolds, who had actually been in charge of both the DUTC and the GSR since 1942, was appointed Chairman of CIE.

Although generally welcomed Reynold's appointment was not universally popular. All his previous transport experience had been with Dublin road undertakings, apart from a period with Aer Lingus, and it was felt by some that he might not be particularly sympathetic towards the claims of the railway side of the business, and these forebodings in the event proved to be not entirely without foundation. The seven founding members of the CIE Board of Directors were drawn in equal numbers from the GSR and the DUTC (one having been a member of both), while the General Manager was E. C. Bredin of the Great Southern. His chief assistant was Frank Lemass, formerly secretary and accountant of the DUTC. When one reflects that the area served by the latter concern was confined to one city and its environs, while the GSR covered virtually the whole country, yet these two amalgamating parties were considered to be of equal status, one gets some idea of just how important Dublin was in relation to the rest of the 26 Counties. One might compare the situation with the head of London Transport suddenly finding himself in charge of affairs at such far-flung places as Thurso, Penzance and Great Yarmouth while still keeping an eye on the No 11 buses going round Parliament Square.

During the company's 20 years existence the locomotives of the Great Southern had run 226m miles at the head of 172m trains conveying 166m passengers, 1000m tons of merchandise and 72m head of livestock. In its final year the GSR grossed receipts of £6,854,615, and out of its net profit of £753,103, £228,264 was available for dividends. The total fees paid to the CIE Directors were fixed at £9,500 per annum. A union leader claimed that Reynolds had received £5,000, but CIE strongly denied this; as head of the Great Southern he had been paid exactly half this, and presumably it was deduced that he had received a similar amount by the DUTC, so that now that the two jobs were combined he would get both salaries.

The emblem chosen by CIE was the wheel *motif* formerly used by the DUTC. For a time it was painted on carriage sides in place of the old Great Southern crest, which had embraced the coats-of-arms of the cities of Dublin, Cork, Limerick and Galway, but after a while carriages were left unadorned and painted green, although locomotive tank and tender sides and goods wagons continued to wear it. Although replaced some years ago it may still be seen on a few wagons.

The Great Northern remained unaffected by the creation of CIE, and its blue-liveried buses ran alongside CIE ones in the City of Dublin, connecting with the Howth trams at Sutton and Howth stations. On the other side of the Border plans were also afoot for amalgamations, although again the GNR, on account of its working within two countries, was not to be included. At the end of 1943 an Agricultural Inquiry Commission had recommended the take-over by the Government of the NCC, the B&CDR, and the NIRTB, and suggested that although the GNR would have to remain independent it might take part in a pooling or other working agreement. No immediate action was taken, but it was expected that amalgamation or nationalisation along these lines would be put into effect once the war was over.

Meanwhile the three Northern companies continued to carry unprecedented numbers of passengers, straining their resources to the limits. They were kept pretty well supplied with fuel, although they were urged to be as economical as possible, and at times of very heavy traffic restaurant cars were left off Dublin–Belfast expresses in order to accommodate more passengers. Incidentally the NCC and the GNR both served lunches at 4s a head throughout the war, a typical *menu* consisting of hot soup, cold salmon and lettuce, milk pudding and coffee, while GNR staff at Amiens Street could obtain a substantial lunch for 1s 4d, cooked by the Italian *chef* just promoted from Bundoran, where he had made a name for himself.

One unlikely cause of the decline of GNR coal stocks was the small boys of Dundalk. Whenever a train was held up at the signals outside the station they would swarm all over it, begging pennies if it was a passenger one, and pinching coal from the wagons if it was a goods. The railway authorities were chiefly worried by the safety aspect of these antics, worries which proved well founded when one unfortunate lad was knocked down and killed by a non-stop express. At one time Dublin suburban services were slightly reduced, and in the spring of 1945 an overall speed limit of 60mph had to be imposed on the GNR, resulting in the easing of a number of passenger train schedules on the main line. All these were mere pinpricks compared with what the Great Southern and CIE had to put up with, and the greatest problem faced by the Northern companies was a shortage of rolling stock.

The NCC continued to turn out 2–6–0s of Class W until 1942, and bought a number of second-hand coaches from the LMS in addition to those sent over to replace the ones lost in the Belfast air raids, while the GNR was able to build a number of coaches at Dundalk, including some high-capacity workmen's non-corridor thirds. No new engines came out in this period. Both companies continued to build goods wagons of various types. Much as the NCC and the GNR were loth to turn traffic away they had to keep one eye on the future and there was no point in putting great numbers of vehicles into service, even if materials for their construction had been available, only to find they were redundant once the war was over and normal conditions returned.

The Belfast & County Down benefited as much as any Irish line from the wartime increase in traffic, but it was in the nature of an Indian summer, and one that was marred by the worst accident on Irish railways in modern times. In 1942 the B&CDR carried 3½m more passengers than in the last full year of peace, receipts going up to 188 per cent, and season ticket holders by no less than 252 per cent. At the same time train miles went up by no more than 25 per cent and this figure gives a very clear indication of how under-utilised County Down trains had been before restrictions on road travel forced the office and factory workers of Belfast to take to them. Even goods tonnage went up by 137 per cent, goods train mileages rising by only 20 per cent; as a result of all this a 3 per cent dividend was paid on baronial shares, while two years of arrears, 1929–30, were paid to the 5 per cent preference holders.

For a little while those who owned County Down shares were regarded as rather sharp fellows instead of the public benefactors that they had previously been taken for. The directors then had a real rush of blood to the head and went and ordered a brand new engine. They had had a former D&SER 2–4–2T on loan from the Great Southern, but for some reason best known to the locomotive department it had done little work, and the decision was taken to spend some of the unexpected profits on a new one. Beyer Peacock's were approached, and agreed to squeeze one into their war programme with the proviso that it was of a design identical with the last County Down passenger engine that the firm had supplied. This was a 4–4–2T No 16, built in 1924, and so in 1944 the first 4–4–2T to go into service in the British Isles since the LMS Tilbury tanks of the 1920s, and the last in the long line of this once most popular type, was delivered. She was put to work on the Bangor line where her services were much appreciated, and she also worked down the main line to Newcastle on the heaviest trains from time to time.

Push-and-pull motor trains were never used as extensively in Ireland as in some parts of Britain but the County Down found them handy for short working on the Bangor line, and one of these trains caused the deaths of 22 County Down passengers in the second week of January 1945. The accident took place at Ballymacarrett Junction, where the Newcastle, Bangor and Belfast Central lines converged, ½-mile from Queens Quay. The morning of January 10 was foggy, and the 7.11am from Bangor, a train of 13 six-wheel carriages headed by Baltic tank No 25, pulled up some 40yd short of the red outer home signal there, the visibility at the time being 150yd. Some distance behind was the 7.40am auto-train from Holywood consisting of the auto-coach, a 27½-ton steel-framed bogie vehicle which had once been a steam rail-motor, two six-wheel carriages, and the engine, 2–4–2T No 5.

Now the County Down employed a very peculiar automatic signalling system on the Bangor line, the basic principles of which were that a driver, after standing at a stop signal at danger for 2min, might proceed with great care to the next stop signal, wait another 2min there if it was against him, and then proceed again, and so on. During fog or falling snow the waiting period was extended to 4min. The significant point was that the driver was not required to telephone to the signalman after the 2 or 4min was up before he restarted his train, and this must be regarded as a somewhat dangerous practice. It had come about chiefly owing to the County Down's straitened financial circumstances, one signalman having to do the work of a number, and as the sections of line equipped with these signals were track-circuited it was felt that the system was foolproof so long as the safeguards incorporated in it were observed. It had worked well enough for some 20 years, but those who considered that this had proved its effectiveness were thoroughly dis-illusioned on that January morning at Ballymacarrett, the collision actually occurring just outside the limits of the automatic section.

The last-but-one station before Ballymacarrett is Sydenham, and both the distant and stop automatic signals there were on for the auto-train, the auto-coach of which was leading. The driver waited for the specified 2min at the stop signal and then, as there was virtually no fog at this point, moved his train slowly off and came up to Victoria Park Halt, the last stop before Ballymacarrett, where some passengers alighted; the train was nevertheless still very full. The distant signal for Ballymacarrett Junction, now only half-a-mile away, was on, so the auto-train moved off cautiously, especially as the fog had now closed right down, forcing the driver to open the front window of the auto-coach in order to get a better view. Suddenly a red light appeared in the murk some 30yd ahead, and the driver had only just time to apply his brake before his train ploughed into the rear of the stationary Bangor one.

As in the Straboe accident the collision might have been far less serious had modern steel-framed rolling stock been exclusively involved. The auto-coach was certainly highly resilient, a feature it owed to its self-propelled origins, but this only made matters worse, for it swept through the 13-ton six-wheeler at the back of the Bangor train as though it hardly existed, coming to rest 10ft into the next carriage. The only damage to the 27½-ton auto-coach was some slight knocks around the front end and the loss of its leading bogie, which was torn away. The six-wheeler behind it was rather battered, but only two people in the auto-train sustained any kind of injury.

In the Bangor train it was a fearfully different story. Eighteen persons were killed outright and over 20 were injured, four later dying from their injuries. The Bangor train had been packed with workers going into the city, many of them to the Harland and Wolff shipyard, and survivors from these assisted their injured and dying workmates along with firemen, police, ambulancemen and others who were soon on the spot. The track was undamaged, and the two smashed-up coaches of the Bangor train still stood on the rails, so it was possible to get one line back into use within 3hr and the other in time for the evening rush-hour.

A disaster fund was started by the Mayor of Bangor, to which town most of the dead belonged, and on January 29 an inquiry into the collision opened in Belfast, conducted by the Chief Engineer to the Minister of Commerce, the latter being responsible during the war for railway operation in the Six Counties. The driver of the auto-train estimated his speed at the point of collision at not more than 10mph, but he and the fireman, who was on the footplate of the engine, disagreed over a number of points, including the intensity of the fog, and it was presumed that the train was travelling considerably faster, possibly at anything up to 27mph. Calculations and tests carried out by the Inspecting Officer showed that the auto-train could not possibly have caused the damage it did if its speed had been as low as the driver had claimed, and if the brakes had been applied 30yd back from the point of impact. It also appeared likely that a number of passengers had moved into the driver's cab in order to give themselves more room, and might well have distracted the driver's attention. All these, however, were factors which merely contributed to the severe results of the collision and their absence could hardly have prevented it.

The Inquiring Officer did not much care for the condition of the control equipment of the auto-train; he found the action of the regulator imprecise and that of the brakes tardy, while there was no reverser fitted in the coach. But the ultimate cause of the Ballymacarrett accident, as returned at the inquest on its victims, was "the failure of a faulty signal". Fog obscuring the driver's vision contributed to it as did the absence of fog-men and of an assistant in the Junction signal-box. The faulty signal was the up Bangor branch outer home, the one at which the Bangor train, headed by the 4–6–4T, was standing. The signalman had tried to clear this signal as the train approached it, but finding that it would not move (a common occurrence in certain weather conditions), he allowed an up main line train to proceed over the Junction and enter Queens Quay. He then left his box and walked down the line, intending to signal the Bangor train on with a hand lamp, but the crash took place almost immediately, the sound of it reaching the signalman some seconds before he was able to see the trains through the fog. The guard of the Bangor train had been about to leave his van to place detonators on the line to stop the auto-train, which he knew must be somewhere in the vicinity, when it loomed up at him out of the fog, and although he was injured he did manage to put some detonators down whilst the fireman of the auto-train ran back further and stopped the next train, which was on the point of passing an automatic stop signal and very well might have suffered the same fate as the auto-train.

Not surprisingly the B&CDR immediately abolished the 2min and 4min waiting periods at the automatic signals, and substituted a rule stating that no driver was to proceed past any stop signal until he had used the nearest station telephone to ensure that the line was clear; telephones at the signals had never been installed. In addition, each train was to carry an illuminated number-plate, the numbers being sent from station to station by telephone, and no train was to be allowed to proceed into a section until the next one was clear. From April of that year telephones were installed at each signal, and no more auto-trains were run, a diesel railcar set from the GNR taking their place. Links with the latter company became much closer, and eventually the B&CDR Directors passed the management of their line over to the GNR. It was, however, much too late to save the County Down, and the claims for compensation as a result of the Ballymacarrett accident only added further to the financial problems weighing down the company now that peacetime conditions were returning.

CHAPTER FIFTEEN

The Post-War Decline

THE END OF the war in Europe was greeted with almost as much relief in the 26 Counties as in the Six, although a demonstration by students of Trinity College, Dublin, when they climbed on to the roof of one of the University buildings and put up the Union Jack in place of Ireland's Tricolour, did not go down too well. One small, but welcome, easing of restrictions, particularly to railway enthusiasts, was the lifting of the Emergency Powers (Restriction of Photography) Order of 1939, which had made it pretty well impossible to photograph anything to do with the railways, even if one had been able to obtain film. A railway clerk who ignored the order and had been charged with taking pictures of ships at North Wall was fined £1 and warned that the penalty might have been £500 or six months inside.

In June 1945, some of the restrictions on travel between Ireland and England were lifted although passports, identity cards, and visas were still required. There was a daily service between Dun Laoghaire and Holyhead, a twice-weekly one between Belfast and Liverpool, and, by the middle of July, thrice-weekly ones between Fishguard and both Waterford and Cork. The Larne–Stranraer service was also being worked but was still monopolised by the military. Small boys were offered 10s to stand in queues in Belfast to obtain tickets for England, and the services from other ports were equally in demand; during one Bank Holiday intending passengers queued in Glasgow for three days for tickets to Ireland. Some visitors had rather less trouble. The King, Queen and Princess Elizabeth came to Londonderry on July 19, 1945, and a special train, headed by No 99 *King George VI*, was provided for them. In the event, however, the royal party flew from Londonderry to Belfast and the NCC had to be content with carrying the Northern Ireland Premier.

Over half the ships at work on the Irish Sea routes in 1939 had been lost during the war and many of those which survived were at this time still under Government control and far away. Few could be spared for their normal peacetime activities, and when one of those which was, the LMS *Hibernia*, was discovered to have sprung a leak whilst tied up at Dun Laoghaire and was taken out of service, would-be travellers at Euston nearly rioted on hearing the news. The *Hibernia* was taken to the Alexandria Basin, Dublin, one of the very few occasions when a cross-channel railway-owned steamer entered an Irish dry dock, and it was there found that the poor old lady had worn her plates thin through overwork and lack of attention. She was patched up and sent to England for more extensive repairs, her place on the Dun Laoghaire–Holyhead run being taken by her sister ship, the *Cambria*. Both were veterans of the route, having being introduced, along with two similar vessels, the *Scotia* and the *Anglia*, when the LNWR took it over from the City of Dublin Steam Packet Company, the owners of the ill-fated *Leinster*, at the end of World War I.

In some ways they were the finest ships ever employed on the Irish Sea routes, with a gross tonnage of 3,440 and a top speed of 25 knots, which enabled them to do the crossing in just under 3hr 30min less than is usual today. They worked a double daily service in the 1920s and 30s, and proved so reliable that the LMS was able to dispose of the *Anglia* and keep the service going with the other three. The *Scotia* was sunk at Dunkirk, but the two survivors remained with the LMS, the *Hibernia* latterly working between Dun Laoghaire and Holyhead, while the *Cambria* moved up the coast to Belfast and was used with the B&I SS *Louth* between there and Heysham. The British & Irish line is the only Irish-owned company working the cross-channel passenger routes, although there has been talk from time to time that Ireland might take a share in the Holyhead–Dun Laoghaire mail service. The three 1928-built Duke class vessels normally used on the Belfast–Heysham run all went to the war, as did the brand new *Princess Victoria*. She was sunk very early in the war and her loss was particularly unfortunate for she had been in existence for barely a year. She was one of the very first stern-loading car ferries, and in her few months of peacetime service she had worked between Larne and Stranraer.

Her place was taken by the *Princess Maud* while the MV *Royal Daffodil* far from her normal duties of taking day trippers down the Thames from Tower Pier to Southend and Margate was pressed into service mainly for troop movements. The LMS had two turbine steamers on order in 1939 to replace the *Hibernia* and the *Cambria*, but these had to be cancelled, and it was not until 1948 that a second order was placed, with Harland and Wolff. Before that a new *Princess Victoria*, virtually identical with her predecessor, had entered service; she too was destined for a short life and a tragic end.

The old *Hibernia* went back into service towards the end of September and provided much-needed relief. But a journey between London and Dublin in the days just after the war was liable to be a very wearisome business. The elaborate customs and immigration formalities made disembarkation a lengthy chore, although prolonged protests by the public did something to ease this by the end of 1945. One still had to allow up to a month in applying for a passport from the Government department concerned, and one also needed a sailing certificate from the shipping company. The "Irish Mail" was taking 7½hr between Holyhead and Euston, and more if it was late, which it often was; one day the engine actually ran out of coal some miles short of Euston. The sea crossing was extended to 4½hr in order to conserve fuel and shorten the passengers' tempers, and when one had finally struggled through all this one was likely to find the train for the South or West had given up waiting and had gone off, empty, on its merry way.

Bit by bit as ships returned from the war things got better. The B&I *Kerry* was resurrected from the bottom of the Mersey, where it had sat for a year after being in a collision, and new ships went into service, although it was not until the blossoming of the drive-on-drive-off car ferries of the 1960s that the scale of pre-war traffic was reached once again. In 1945 the steamers found themselves faced for the first time, with competition, for Aer Lingus resumed its service between Collinstown and the old London airport at Croydon using DC3s.

The GWR, with fewer boats than the LMS, suffered relatively heavier losses during the war, two of the three Saint class boats which worked the Fishguard–Rosslare route being sunk. The three were turbine steamers dating from the early 1930s; the survivor, *St Andrew*, reopened the service in 1946. Replacements for the *St Patrick* and the *St David* came out the following year, but the new *St Patrick* went off to Weymouth in the summer to assist on the Channel Isles run. A fourth GWR boat was the *Great Western*, a somewhat smaller vessel of 1,742 gross tons, built in 1934 for the mainly cargo Waterford–Fishguard route. She survived the War and continued the service thrice weekly in each direction.

In December 1945, it was announced that all the CIE branches which had been shut since the fuel crisis of 1942 would shortly reopen. As some of them had not seen a train for over three years a great deal of work needed to be done, but one by one they came back to life, even if in many cases their hold on it was precarious. On the main lines dining cars reappeared, providing a substantial dinner for 3s 6d, sixpence less than on the GNR and the NCC. Inevitably the cost of living had gone up to some extent and the unions were campaigning for higher wages. At the annual general meeting of the GSR in 1943 Reynolds had complained bitterly that despite a fall in revenue the unions had "decided to take all they can at the moment". Naturally the men did not see the situation that way and a leading member of the Labour party, M. P. Linehann, retorted that they were asking for no more than a bonus of 8 to 10 per cent to counteract a cost of living increase of 58 per cent. He added that the increase in the working expenditure of the Great Southern was almost entirely due to the fuel bill, which had gone up by £300,000. This latter statement was certainly true. In 1939 the GSR spent £388,691 on 227,068 tons of fuel, the cost per mile working out at 7.77d. In 1945 CIE bought 307,672 tons at a cost of £1,055,247, despite running fewer train miles, and the cost per mile now came to 2s 7.36d, a staggering increase of 304 per cent.

The GSR Chairman was rebuked from another and more unlikely direction.

Lord Glenavy, Chairman of the Great Northern, in a reference to wages said, "Greater increases have been applied to the GNR than the GSR; yet the amount received by workers out of each £1 of gross receipts in 1942 was 8s 6d on the GNR as compared with 11s 8d on the GSR". One should remember, however, that if the Great Southern could have obtained all the fuel it needed it could have carried considerably more traffic without any increase in staff, and might therefore have come up with figures comparable to those of the Great Northern. This was borne out the following year when fuel supplies although far from adequate, were a little better, and the amount paid out in wages for each £1 of revenue fell to 10s 3d.

Reynolds further complained that he had more staff than he needed, many stations dealing with only a handful of trains, and yet if any of these were running late the men had to be paid overtime in order to wait behind and attend them. The trade union attitude was that their first responsibility was to their members, and if traffic had fallen and trains were running late through no fault of the men why should they be penalised by either being forced to work longer hours for no extra money, or getting the sack? There was little chance of a job elsewhere if a railway man was put out of work, and there was much competition to obtain the steady employment that a career on the railways offered. In 1944 691 young men sat the examination for the 80 vacancies in the clerical grades, and apparently one stood a better chance of being selected if one was a fluent Irish speaker. The language, which had almost died out by 1916, had been taught to all children since the 1920s, which is not to say, however, that everyone mastered it. Nevertheless even at the present time some schools teach all subjects, including science, in the Irish language, and anyone applying for a Government department post, in the civil service, or in one of the professions, has to pass an oral examination in Irish. Of those who chose to answer the written paper for the 1944 GSR clerkship examination in Irish 16.86 per cent passed, compared with a 10.85 per cent rate for those who answered in English.

The confrontation between the management of the GSR/CIE and the unions during the war was the classic one, each side paying little heed to the other's legitimate grievances. One can sympathise with the frustration Reynolds must have felt as he watched a large proportion of his work force drawing wages for spending most of the day standing around kicking its heels, yet any trade union leader who agreed to any of his men being singled out for dismissal, knowing the hardships this would cause to the man and his family, would have been branded, perhaps justifiably, as a traitor. The management was paying the penalty for having cried "wolf" too often in the past whenever a wage claim had been put in. But a solution had to be found sooner or later, and with the resumption of private motoring at the end of 1945, although at first on a very limited scale, both men and management knew that the time left for them to come to terms was limited.

The first Annual General Meeting of CIE was held in March, 1946, and at it Reynolds made a number of proposals which heralded great changes, and apparently indicated a rosy future. Much the best received of these was one to reduce fares and rates and at the same time to make the railway side of the business more competitive; about the methods to be used to achieve these desirable ends Reynolds was more reticent.

One specific and highly revolutionary proposal concerned motive power. Passenger trains, all of which would be long-distance, would be diesel hauled, and to this end five diesel shunters had already been ordered, while two freight locomotives and a passenger one would follow from British firms, and two further freight diesels from Switzerland. Once any teething troubles with these had been sorted out wholesale dieselisation could take place. The end of the branch and main line passenger stopping train, and its replacement by the motorbus, was clearly heralded. Although this would mean the closing down of what once had been one of the most important sides of the railways business, it was a development which had often been predicted during the previous 20 years, and people were generally prepared for, although not necessarily happy, about it.

The only short-distance trains which were consistently well patronised were those on the Dublin and Cork suburban lines, the latter being a rather special case in that no buses competed with them. Yet even between Bray, Harcourt Street, Westland Row and Amiens Street the trains were not carrying the traffic they once had, more and more city workers preferring the double-deck buses which were replacing the last of the trams. The suggestion that the Harcourt Street line might actually close down was now being voiced, although one proposal that the tracks be ripped up and the track formation converted to a reserved road for buses was clearly impractical unless remarkably thin vehicles were employed.

In the last year before amalgamation the GSR and the Dublin United Tramways Company had made a combined profit of over £1m, but a year later this had fallen by £300,000, net rail receipts being £135,000 less. This was partly accounted for by there being more trains and thus less passengers for each one; unfortunately the more comfortable rail travel was the less economic it became. Although rail takings in 1945 came to twice those of the buses, bus services were four times as profitable, and one cannot deny that Reynolds, given that he was a bus rather than a railway man at heart, had every justification for expanding road services and contracting those of the railways, in the economic climate then prevalent. Lemass, the General Manager of CIE, estimated that £5 million was needed to modernise the railways, and it could certainly be argued that such a sum would produce greater returns if spent on the road services.

By the summer of 1946 the punctuality of CIE passenger trains had reached the point where a regular traveller on the main and branch lines was able to describe it as "remarkably good". The fuel situation was much better, and although schedules were not very demanding the fact that CIE could virtually guarantee an on time arrival for every train was an excellent selling point. Trains were generally well patronised, and on the August Bank Holiday No 800 *Maeve* demonstrated that the ravages of the war years had done her no permanent harm when she lifted the heavy second part of the 10am train to Cork, comprising 14 bogie carriages and a six-wheeler, out of Kingsbridge unaided, attaining 20mph by Islandbridge. CIE was again able to run specials for sporting events, for Gaelic Athletic Association meetings, and to the Curragh and other racecourses, while Sunday services also were resumed on a few lines.

Various administrative reorganisations were put into effect, the Traffic Manager becoming responsible for all operating and commercial rail activities, while the Running Superintendent was now answerable to him instead of the Chief Mechanical Engineer. This had the effect of ensuring that services would be geared to the requirements of the traffic, rather than to those of the motive power, and the CME's area of responsibility was further reduced by removing the Rolling Stock Engineer in charge of the Road Department from his authority. In actual fact there was no longer a CME, for the last one, Ginnetty, had retired in 1944. His predecessor, Bredin, had become General Manager in 1941, and on reaching retirement age in 1946 he was succeeded by Frank Lemass, the brother of the Minister for Industry and Commerce.

The task of the Chief Mechanical Engineer had not been an envious one of late, most of Ginnetty's activities being concentrated upon keeping some sort of service running in the face of the mounting fuel crisis. The only new design current during Ginnetty's tenure of the office had been the three-cylinder suburban 4–6–2T, which Bredin had originated, and although authorisation had been given for it to be built, lack of materials had caused its withdrawal, and there is no evidence that construction was actually started. The likelihood of dieselisation, and the contraction of suburban traffic, meant that there was now no chance of its being revived.

In an effort to attract passengers back to the suburban services fares were lowered; a third-class single from Bray to Tara Street, the station nearest the city centre, now cost 11d; in 1939 it had been 1s 2d. Then, just when it seemed that the railways were in sight of better times, that old bogey, shortage of fuel, dealt them a hefty wallop in the midriff. The winter of 1946–7 was severe in the extreme, the worst in living memory. Coal in Britain could not be moved from the pitheads, and export of stocks to any foreign country had to be banned, so that CIE trains once again came almost to a standstill.

In January 1947, passenger trains were reduced to one a day in each direction on the main lines, four days per week, while a number of branches closed altogether. Then in February, with the coal situation in Britain no better, further cuts had to be made. Passenger trains ran on only three days in each week, and all livestock specials were cancelled, causing a number of fairs to be postponed. Finally, on February 24, with one exception, all passenger services ceased. Goods trains still ran, but on three days a week only. The passenger exception was the Night Mails; four of these, the up and down Cork Mails, and the down Athlone and Wexford trains, each included one passenger coach which made connections for Limerick, Waterford, Tralee, Mallow, Bantry and Skibbereen. For all practical purposes, however, there was no way of travelling by train in Southern Ireland, other than on the Great Northern, a situation which had not been reached even in the worst days of 1942.

The heaviest of the snowfalls came at the beginning of March, and the West of the country was totally cut off. A County Donegal railcar left Killybegs around noon on the 12th, found that it could not proceed beyond Barnes-more, 25 miles distant, as snow had drifted across the line to roof height, and had to reverse to the previous station, Lough Eske. On another narrow-gauge line, the NCC's from Ballycastle to Ballymoney, a steam train with 14 passengers aboard stuck in a drift just after 7pm on the same day and stayed there, unable to communicate with the outside world until the following morning, when a rescue party managed to dig its way through. A light engine had twice failed in the attempt, finally imbedding itself in drifting snow. The passengers were got out but the train had to remain until the weather improved and a thaw set in.

Travelling by bus was still more hazardous. The experiences of one particular CIE crew and their passengers amounting to an epic worthy of a Holly-wood film script. The bus left Longford for Sligo, a 60-mile journey which normally took 6hr, although the trains, when running, did it in two. Within a short while a blizzard descended and the bus found itself surrounded by drifts 10 to 16ft high. As there was no chance of outside help the occupants set to work with shovels, an eventuality of this sort not having been entirely unfore-seen, and began to dig. At more than one location they took 8hr to progress one mile, but gradually they battled their way through. They stayed the night in a hotel and next morning recommenced digging. Bit by bit they moved on, stayed when they could in hotels, although these were rapidly running out of food. The telephone wires were all down, but news of their plight eventually reached Sligo, and three miles from their destination they were met by a party of 450 men, sent out by a councillor to clear the way. Six-and-a-half days after leaving Longford the bus entered Sligo in triumph, as the midday angelus was ringing, and at the head of a long convoy which had gathered behind.

Relief came to CIE on March 12, when 11,100 tons of coal arrived in Dublin from Baltimore, while more came to Cork, and about the same time a thaw set in. Even now the railways troubles were not over, for the lines which had previously been blocked by drifts were now inundated by floods and landslides brought down by the melting snows. The coast line between Grey-stones and Dublin was cut in several places, but was restored by March 18, when passenger trains began to run over it again. On April 21 it was announced that livestock trains would recommence to run, but it was another month before main line passenger trains came out of their 90-day hibernation, a four days per week restricted service beginning on May 25. It was then hoped that the arrival of more coal from America would mean a six-day service by the beginning of June.

CIE had taken various measures to counteract the fuel crisis, the most significant being the conversion of a number of engines to oil-burning, but notice of termination of employment were issued to some 10,000 railwaymen. The first move was a week's notice to 1,500 clerks and supervisors, followed by the suspension of most of the rest of the railway's employees. The white-collar workers in the Cork area refused to accept notice, claiming that as they were employed on a monthly basis they should have a month's notice. The manual workers were just as disturbed and equally loth to accept the notice, particularly as a dispute between CIE and the unions, over a wage claim by craftsmen at Inchicore, was already in progress. Then, in the middle of all this, James Larkin died.

For many years the pre-eminent position he had once enjoyed in trade union circles had been disputed, but he had remained a unique figure, a link with the great days of trade unionism and the struggle for a better lot for the working classes. Larkin continued at work almost until the day of his death, a familiar figure to Dubliners, travelling each morning on the bus to his office, or to the Dail, where he represented the Labour Party. He was a tall, handsome man, a pipe smoker, and by inclination easy-going and kindly, despite the abuse heaped upon him throughout his career by a varied selection of opponents representing factions of both management and the unions, men with lesser visions and for the most part with no great control over their emotions.

Larkin's funeral was a state occasion. All strike pickets were withdrawn so that they could attend, old differences were forgotten and thousands lined the route. Part of Larkin's appeal came from the breadth of his intellect. While he could totally immerse himself in trade union struggles when needs be, at other times he found the opportunity to pursue quite different interests, and numbered Sean O'Casey and Bernard Shaw among his friends. His proposal at a meeting of the Dublin City Council in 1946 that Shaw should be offered the honourary freedom of the city brought this reply from Shaw. "My Dear Jim, nothing could have pleased me more . . . than it's being initiated by you . . . you have been a leader and a martyr while I have never had a day's discomfort". O'Casey wrote a fine tribute on Larkin's death, declaring that his spirit would continue to lead the Irish workers, ending with the words "It is up to us to finish the work that Jim began so mightily and well".

In later years Larkin had been less directly concerned with the railways, following a bitter dispute with the other members of the executive of the Irish Transport and General Workers' Union which had resulted in a court case and his expulsion from the position of General Secretary. Both parties had some right on their side, although it is true to say that a number of Larkin's opponents were not unmindful of their chances of promotion within the union, whilst Larkin himself put the betterment of the rank and file before everything else. He set up another union, the Irish Workers' Union, but Larkin was really too much of an idealist and too careless of other people's reputations ever to be an effective member of a group, particularly at a time when most people had grown weary of continual fighting, and he was constantly frustrated by the readiness of the rank and file to accept less than he felt it was entitled to. For all that the great affection and respect felt for him by all sections of the community was amply demonstrated at his death, and it is primarily to Jim Larkin that the Irish transport worker owes his present relatively comfortable standard of living.

The strike at Inchicore ended after seven weeks with the men agreeing to accept an increase which would give them a basic rate of 3s per hour, 6d less than they had asked for. Meanwhile there had to be a number of demotions and dismissals; 81 craftsmen at Limerick Works were laid off, while 200 drivers were reduced to firemen, 200 firemen reduced to cleaners, and 200 cleaners sacked. On May 1 the Railway Wages Board was replaced by the Staff Tribunal which, with the agreement of the unions and CIE, was empowered to lay down wages and salaries for all grades, one of its first acts being the supervision of an agreement between the management and the Dublin clerks fixing a scale ranging from £350 to £500 per annum, a 65 per cent increase on the 1939 level. Women were to receive between £3 and £4.15s per week; equal pay with the men, one of the causes that Larkin had championed, had still be be achieved, as it still has in many Government and semi-Government departments. In Aer Lingus, for example, when a woman marries she is automatically demoted and may suffer a considerable drop in salary.

The coal from America had not come in time to save a number of the jobs of men threatened with suspension, although some had taken their annual holiday (holidays with pay had come in during the war) in order to postpone the evil day, and the unions felt that CIE was not restoring services as quickly as it might. A strike was threatened for June 16, if a guaranteed six-day, 48hr week was not in force by then, and although at first CIE could not promise more than five days, stocks of fuel built up so rapidly in the late spring that it proved possible to offer everyone a full working week before the deadline was reached. The United States guaranteed to send over 500,000 tons of coal within three months at a cost of £2m, and with the embargo on coal exports lifted by the British Government, fuel from that source was soon arriving at the rate of 11,000 tons per week.

One railwayman who could afford to remain aloof from all disputes over wages was Patrick O'Donovan, a ganger who lived at Skibbereen. He won £10,000 on the Grand National Sweepstake in April 1947, a windfall which seemingly had little effect on his way of life, for he declared that he had no wish either to leave Skibbereen or his employment by the railway.

The attractions of oil as a fuel to a country like Ireland, which had virtually no coal deposits, were glowing ever brighter, and towards the end of 1946 CIE set about converting a number of its steam engines to oil-burners. The first was No 264, a former GS&WR 0-6-0, by way of an experiment in 1945, and when this proved successful permission was given to convert another 89 locomotives. The expense, what with all the fuelling and ancillary equipment and the soaring maintenance costs consequent upon the excessive heat to which the boiler tubes and fireboxes were subjected, was considerable. However, CIE was able to guarantee that a train hauled by an oil-fired engine would arrive on time, and the smoke-box doors and tender sides of engines so equipped were painted with large white circles so that signalmen might know and give them precedence.

A great variety of engines worked on oil, including four 400 class and all three 500 class 4-6-0s; the 800s, however, continued to burn coal and remained in charge of the Mails, assisted when necessary by one of the oil-burners. Without oil-burning engines CIE trains would have ceased altogether during the crisis of 1947. But they were expensive, firstly on account of the excessive wear and tear they suffered, and secondly owing to the high price of fuel oil. On top of this supplies of oil were scarce, and nothing like sufficient for CIE's needs, so that by the middle of 1948 all the oil-burners had reverted to using coal; indeed, some of them lost their conversion equipment almost as soon as it was installed and before they had a chance to try it out on the road.

By then other oil-fueled engines, five 487hp diesel-electric shunters, the very first diesels to work in Southern Ireland, had gone into service, and six large diesel-electric passenger locomotives for the Dublin–Cork line, each powered by two 960hp Sulzer engines, were on order from Vickers Armstrongs. It seemed that the prophecies concerning the large-scale dieselisation of CIE, made in the 1946 Annual Report, were about to be fulfilled. But in the summer of 1948 an inquiry into internal transport in Southern Ireland was instituted by the Minister for Industry and Commerce, and its findings, published at the end of the year, were such as to suggest that the diesel locomotive after all was not the answer to CIE's problems.

CHAPTER SIXTEEN

The Milne Report of 1948

NOTWITHSTANDING THE fact that the South of Ireland had remained neutral throughout the war and that its railways had consequently suffered no damage as a result of direct military action, their plight was hardly less enviable than that of the four main line companies of Great Britain. In the latter case nationalisation was seen as the answer, and in Ireland no one was greatly surprised when the Inquiry of 1948 recommended a similar solution to the Republic's transport problems. We will go on to consider the effects of the 1950 Transport Act in a later chapter, but in this one we must look at the state of the railways as the 1948 Transport Inquiry, headed by Sir James Milne, the last General Manager of the Great Western Railway, found it.

The financial position had hardly been rosy in 1939, and by 1948 it was somewhat worse, although the point should be made that the deterioration was not as great as it had been in the period from 1914 to 1920. Passenger receipts in 1948 had actually increased quite significantly since 1939, but this improvement had to be set against a roughly equivalent decline in freight traffic, particularly in livestock, which for long had been one of the railway's principal sources of income. In 1945 the railways had made a small net profit, but by 1947 this had been turned into a deficit of over £1,000,000.

Services in 1948 were still severely restricted, due mainly to the continuing fuel shortage and to a lesser degree owing to the large numbers of locomotives,

carriages and wagons unfit for service; they were running at barely half the 1939 level. Despite this nearly as many people travelled by train in 1948 as they did in 1939, which would suggest that either trains before the war were very much under-patronised or that those afterwards were excessively so. If a full pre-war service had been restored by 1948 it is possible that CIE passenger train receipts would have been considerably higher than the actual total of some £2,000,000. People were rather better off and many more families were able to afford holidays; at the same time they were no as yet so affluent that many could afford a motorcar, and so they travelled by train. There had been a considerable drop in the number of season ticket holders, most of whom were commuters on the Cork and Dublin suburban services, and if we sub-tract these from the total of passenger journeys we find that there were more long-distance rail travellers in 1948 than in 1939. A curious aspect of these figures is the increase in the number of first-class tickets sold, both seasons and ordinary. There was a startling 300 per cent rise in the latter category, which strongly suggests that the third-class accommodation provided on some trains had got to be quite insufferable.

To demonstrate that this was indeed the case one can do no better than record the fact that the average age of a CIE carriage was 47 years, and that it was more likely to be a six-wheeler than a bogie vehicle. It might not have been overhauled since 1929, it was possible that it had no form of heating, and there were actually two splendid antiquities which had no light either. It is a wonder Sir James Milne, fresh from the splendours of the Great Western, did not faint clean away as he surveyed his task. The very newest carriages, four suburban brake seconds, were ten years old; there were thirty other relatively modern steel-sided vehicles, including the set built in the mid-1930s for the Cork Mails; and the rest, 1281 in all, were wooden-bodied types of obsolete, some of it very obsolete, design. At any given time over a quarter would be unfit for service, either awaiting or undergoing repair, or more likely, simply rotting away on some forgotten overgrown siding.

The wagon situation was not quite so bad. The average age of a wagon was 32 years, and only around 7 per cent of the total of 11,891 (broad and narrow gauge) was out of service. To this figure the members of the Inquiry felt able to add the rare comment "satisfactory".

A second fairly bright spot was the permanent way. It had not deteriorated to any marked degree, mainly because of the not very strenuous demands put upon it, and while speeds remained low it would serve well enough. How-ever, the rails on the Cork to Dublin main line were for the most part over 50 years old and would need renewing if continuous high speeds were to be introduced. That speeds would increase was certain if only because they could hardly go any further in the other direction. The fastest train between Dublin and Cork managed to attain the dizzy average of 37mph, while the Waterford trains ran the donkeys a close second in averaging 25mph.

The tone of the Milne report took on an extremely gloomy aspect when it summoned up sufficient courage to deal with the motive power position. The average age of CIE's 491 locomotives was 51 years. In other words, most of them went back to the days of Queen Victoria, and it would hardly have been surprising if they had found one or two which had made the acquaintance of King Billy. This was a situation which was delightfully refreshing if one was a railway enthusiast from the other side of the Irish Sea, bored with a surfeit of electric multiple-units, but it was not half so funny if you had to put up with it all the year round.

The cost of repairing the locomotives had doubled in the three years since 1945, and would obviously go on increasing as the years went by and more and more parts needed renewing. As with the coaching stock, over a quarter of the total number was always unusable. It took an average of 110 days to give an engine a general repair at Inchicore, a month longer than it had done in 1939, and heavy work in the outdated shops at Cork or Limerick was even more inefficient, in terms of expenditure.

One of the most unfortuaate aspects of the situation was the absence of a Chief Mechanical Engineer. M. J. Ginnetty, who had succeeded Bredin in 1942, had retired himself two years later, and since then the responsibility for construction and maintenance of engines, coaches and wagons had been divided between various people. With the best will in the world friction was bound to arise between departments and individuals where it was not clear who was responsible for what, delaying important decisions on renewals of equipment and reorganisation of the works. This situation was reflected in reverse at the very top of CIE. The six Directors were no more than advisers and almost the entire administration of CIE was carried out by the Chairman. However competent he was and considerate of the other directors' views, this was really much too much responsibility to put on the shoulders of one man.

Costs generally had risen since 1945, but perhaps the most startling increase was in wages and salaries. The total amount thus paid out by CIE in 1948 was £6,274,000, an increase of some 55 per cent in three years. While a proportion of this was brought about by higher salaries and wages, a great deal of it was the result of taking on more staff. The Inquiry commented that while on the road passenger side of the business this was reasonable enough, considering that there had been an increase of 22 per cent in the fleet, it was somewhat more difficult to account for in the railways, as neither traffic nor services had expanded.

The Inquiry found that there were more drivers, firemen and cleaners than were ever likely to be needed. A number of these were being kept on in the hope that services might eventually be restored to their pre-war level. Probably there was no one in CIE who thought they would be; even if broad-gauge services were maintained it was obvious that not much of the narrow-gauge network would survive, but the management can hardly be criticised for showing reluctance in dismissing men who had worked all their lives on the railway. A more practical immediate solution was to reduce the number of locomotives. Even on the busiest day in 1947 some 140 of CIE's 488 loco-motives (broad and narrow-gauge) were not required in traffic, and by careful selection it was found that withdrawal of some 100 engines would practically halve the number of classes in service. This, together with other economies in the locomotive department, would save some £250,000, and was considered to be much the largest sum that could be economised in any CIE department. The total loss made by CIE in 1947 was actually rather less than the loss made by the railways. Canals and docks were run at a loss, but the buses made a hefty profit, and the tramways, hotels and road freight were also in the black, helping to keep the total deficit down to £877,489.

To convert this into a profit and to pay the long-suffering Common Stock holders at least 4 per cent (something which had not happened since 1945), economies in maintenance and operating costs and fare increases would have to be made, amounting to around £1,650,000. It was felt that over a period of years this was possible, but that in the immediate future the Government could help by meeting the interest on capital works under construction on the grounds that they were in the national interest, and also by waiving the liability to repay sums advanced under the guarantee of debenture interest.

One of the more curious aspects of the report in the light of what transpired is that although it suggested a limited number of diesel railcars similar to those on order for the GNR should be purchased, it took scant notice of diesel locomotives. It did admit that having separate types of engines for passenger and freight traffic was uneconomical, and recommended that all future types should be capable of handling both, but it assumed that these would still be steam locomotives.

There were at the time five diesel shunters at work, the Mirlees engines, Inchicore-assembled, Nos 1000–1004 (now Nos D301–5); two main line 950hp locos, now Nos B113/4, on order; and six large 1,800hp machines contemplated, but the Report felt that, firstly, there were virtually no main line or shunting requirements in Ireland for a locomotive to work around the clock, which was one of the diesel's chief superiorities over a steam engine; secondly, that the steam engines in existence and contemplated would be quite powerful enough to cope with any demands likely to be made on them in the future; and, thirdly, that the enormous cost of diesel locomotives simply was not justified. It therefore recommended that the order for the six large diesels should be cancelled and that fifty steam engines should be built at Inchicore in the next five years. One paragraph noted that "a few engines with heavy axle-loads are confined to the Dublin to Cork route", and suggested that they should remain in service only for as long as this entailed no heavy renewal of the permanent way, thus heralding the end of the Queens and the other 4–6–0s.

The point should be made at this juncture that the Inquiry was undoubtedly biased in favour of railways. Of its seven members (three of them technical assessors) all but one, W. J. Elliott, the former General Manager of Hay's Wharf Cartage, were railwaymen from the four British main line companies. They hardly seemed to have considered the possibility of substantial closures; indeed, they were quite favourably disposed to the reopening of some lines already closed down. They do admit that stations and lines which were far from the centres of population, and could advantageously be replaced by road services, should not be retained, but even some of these they felt might be saved by that supposed panacea of all ailing railway services, the diesel railcar. They challenged the official figures put out for ten branches threatened with closure, and made the point, which has been repeated many times subsequently, that one cannot calculate a branch line's value as a feeder to the main line nor can one come up with a concrete figure for the actual amount of money saved by closing it. The crux of their argument was that a branch line should be retained if it was in the public interest to do so.

Just what "the public interest" is has occupied politicians, economists and the public itself for as long as people have paid rates and taxes, but the Inquiry pointed out that road transport had an unfair advantage in that it was partly subsidised by the rates, while the railways had to meet the entire cost of maintaining its track out of its receipts. To balance this situation it was suggested that a single authority responsible for roads, railways and canals should be set up, and that each form of transport should then make a fair contribution to the total cost. The income from road vehicles would be collected in the form of licence and fuel duties, and the railways and canals would pay a uniform charge per pound of gross receipts.

One of the final sections of the Report dealt with the GNR and the other four companies with lines crossing the Border. It found the GNR generally to be in a better state of health than CIE, but nevertheless likely to need Government aid if it was to balance its books. The company might well be left as it was, but both the Ulster Transport Authority and CIE were empowered to take it over if they cared to, and if this should happen the GNR's rail and road services should continue to be worked as one concern rather than divided at the Border.

Of the cross-Border lines all but the County Donegal were working at a loss. True to its traditions the Inquiry was in no hurry to close any of them, and suggested that their affairs be thoroughly gone into, and that if they were kept open they should be incorporated into the GNR.

CHAPTER SEVENTEEN

Nationalisation in the North

THE PLAN TO merge the principal rail and road undertakings in the Six Counties, put forward during the war, was published as a Bill in 1947 and passed by the Stormont Parliament in 1948. It authorised the new concern, the Ulster Transport Authority, to raise capital up to £10m, and granted it powers to take over the NCC, the B&CDR, and the Northern Ireland Road Transport Board. It was further given authority to "acquire or co-operate with" the GNR. The advantages of the former course were many, but for the time being the GNR was left, not altogether happily, to go its own way.

The price paid to the shareholders of the County Down for their railway,

£485,990, caused a great furore; indeed, a Stormont MP declared it to be "One of the greatest scandals ever perpetrated on the taxpayers", and that the County Down had no saleable value at all. Not surprisingly the shareholders were aghast at this piece of effrontery, and immediately countered with one of their own, proclaiming that the County Down's assets amounted to at least £1,175,000, "at pre-war prices". Indeed they actually had the nerve to broadcast to all and sundry, including, presumably, these citizens who still bounced their way to work in the company's ancient six-wheel carriages, that the "entire stock was in excellent condition". If this was not enough to bring a blush of shame to their cheeks their Protection Association went quite *berserk* and announced that the assets were really, in present-day terms worth £5m. This was, despite the Chairman's comment that "an angel could not make the railway pay", and a Directors' announcement in February of the previous year of their intention to close down all the company's lines, other than the Bangor branch. This they had been prevented from doing only by a timely word in their collective ear from the Minister of Commerce, who reminded them that they had certain statutory obligations to fulfil.

A Government official bravely went along to a meeting of the shareholders and rather took the wind out of their sails by stating that the company had no power to sell, nor the Northern Ireland Transport Board to buy. The 1947 Act laid down that the Government had sole authority in the matter, and as far as the purchase was concerned it was a fair one, fixed with due regard to current Stock Exchange prices and in relation to that paid to shareholders of the recently nationalised British Railways.

The County Down became part of the UTA on October 1, 1948, and some fifteen months later, on January 15, 1950, most of the former B&CDR's 80 miles of track, all except the Bangor branch, and for a little while longer a short section of the main line as far as Comber and the Donaghadee branch, closed down. Traffic had fallen right away again after the war, a typical complement of a train on one of the closed branches, that to Ardglass, consisting of one passenger. A bicycle rather than a bus would have been a more suitable replacement. A curious survival among the locomotive stock was a little 2-4-0, No 6. She had 6ft driving wheels, the largest on any County Down engine, and during the war, after lying out of use for some years, she was given a new boiler, and so enjoyed her unexpected lease of life that she was still at work on the last day, hauling the 10.45am express from Queens Quay to Newcastle, arriving back in Belfast at 3.04pm. Her train was not a very heavy one, five six-wheelers and a bogie coach, and the schedule was not too exacting, though a fairly stiff task for such a small engine, which did well to lose no more time than 2min, partly due to signal checks. Officially, No 6 lasted until 1956, as did most of the County Down engines taken over by the UTA, but it is doubtful if in fact she was ever in steam again after January 1950.

The very last County Down passenger engine to remain at work was one of the Standard 4-4-2Ts, No 17 of 1909; she finished in the summer of 1953. One of her sisters, No 30, dating from 1901, was later restored by the UTA at its York Road Works, and now resides in the Belfast Transport Museum.

Rather remarkably a number of the old six-wheel carriages survived the diesel-isation of the County Down section, and might be seen bouncing along behind NCC 2–6–4Ts and other unlikely motive power at times of heavy traffic until the late 1950s. One of the WT Class 2–6–4s, together with a rake of bogie carriages, worked for a short while on the Bangor line in 1949, and later others of the class put in some fairly lengthy stints, but all this was too late to save the larger part of the County Down system; the circuitous nature of its routes and the antiquity of its coaching stock had proved insuperable handicaps.

A tank engine version of the NCC's successful W Class Moguls had been on the cards for some while, and the end of the war made it possible for production to get under way. The first, No 5, arrived from Derby in the summer of 1946, and went into service on August 8. She was the most power-ful tank engine yet seen in Ireland, and a very much more successful machine than the previous holders of that title, the County Down Baltics. The last of the latter, NCC No 222, was given a heavy overhaul at York Road in 1951, and it was thus possible directly to compare the two classes, but this was like matching a bow-legged mule against *Arkle*. The Baltic was hardly able to exceed 60mph, although her acceleration was reasonable, and her front end arrangement was such that she could never hope to approach the free-running Derby-built 2–6–4Ts. Nevertheless No 222 was, by some margin, the last of her wheel arrangement to remain in service in the British Isles.

It might be thought that as the NCC Moguls were a tender engine version

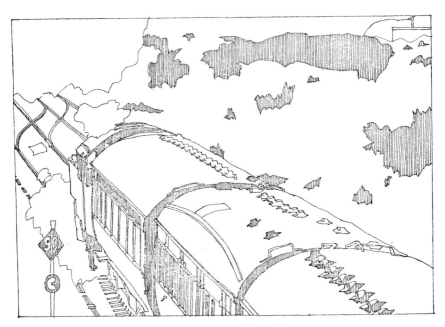

An NIR 2–6–4T pulling out of Larne with a Belfast train

of the original LMS Fowler 2–6–4Ts, and that the WTs would be virtually identical with these latter, but this was not so, and a number of dimensions, apart from those made necessary by the difference in gauge, were different. Cylinder sizes and boiler pressures were the same, but the driving wheels of the Irish engines were 3in larger, giving them a tractive effort of 22,160lb, compared with the slightly higher 23,125lb of the Fowler locomotives. With their cut-away front end framing and built-up bunkers the WTs looked more like the Fairburn versions of the type, with which they were contemporary, although they had parallel boilers and their circular smokebox handle was a typically NCC touch which was not to be found on any of the English varieties. Certainly a first glance at a WT revealed it to be a member of that closely-related family whose ramifications spread from the original Fowler engines to the BR standards, and it might be said, with no great stretch of the imagination, to extend even wider, starting with Churchward's first large 2–6–2T, and embracing Maunsell's Rivers and Ws, and the LNER L1 2–6–4s.

No 5 was put to work from Larne shed, where she was joined by three others, whilst the other six initial members of the class went to York Road. There were some steaming problems early on, but these were soon rectified, and the engines became very popular at both sheds. They were allocated to regular crews, some staying with them for years. At Larne they displaced all but two of the seven 4–4–0s previously resident there, and were a great improvement in that they could run around their trains and be ready to return to Belfast within ten minutes, as no visit to the turntable was needed, but at York Road the Moguls continued to predominate in the top link. Despite many similarities between the two classes there was a basic difference in the method of firing, the tanks preferring the "little and often" method, whilst the 2–6–0s steamed most successfully on a big fire well built up. They were designed for different tasks, so there is little point in comparing them, although it is true that WTs took over some of the duties of the Ws in later years as the latter class was withdrawn. By then, however, the principal passenger turns on the former NCC lines were all worked by dmus.

The greater coal and water capacity of the tender engines made them more suitable for the Belfast–Londonderry run, while the tanks were ideal for the shorter journeys, although when in the top-class condition in which they were maintained in their early days the latter were capable of covering the 95 miles between Belfast and Londonderry without taking water en route, and were well able to exceed 80mph. The livery of UTA locomotives, chosen after a number of experiments, was black, lined with gold and red, with the coat-of-arms of the Authority on the tender or tank sides; coaches were a darkish green, unlined.

One immediate advantage to the public of having rail and road services under the same management was the publication of them all in one timetable, which ran to 392 well-laid out pages, and was very good value for 4d. The UTA's first Chairman was Major F. A. Pope, who had previously been head of the NCC. Under his charge were 426 miles of railway, and a variety of passenger and goods road vehicles which covered 79,000 miles annually.

Very little of the narrow-gauge lasted long enough to become part of the UTA, the only sections still working in 1948 being the 10½ miles from Larne to the paper mills at Ballyclare, over which an occasional goods train ran, and the 16¼-mile Ballycastle Railway. Four engines were sufficient for all the traffic on these lines; these were Nos 41–3 and No 111, two-cylinder compound 2–4–2 tanks. They were the very last engines working on this system which was so peculiarly unique to the NCC, all the standard gauge engines of the type having been either withdrawn or converted to simples some time previously. With the backing of the LMS, the NCC had been able to go a long way towards standardising its locomotive fleet, and of the 28 classes extant in 1932 no fewer than 21 had disappeared by 1948. Nearly half of the NCC engines then in service had been acquired since 1933, all but six of them being either W class 2–6–0s or WT 2–6–4Ts. The remainder consisted of two standard LMS 0–6–0Ts, transferred to the NCC in 1944 and used for shunting in the York Roads yards, and four diesels, of various types, all built in Belfast by Harland & Wolff.

One tends to think of the latter firm as being solely concerned with ship-building, but from time to time, perhaps with one eye on the vagaries of the ship-building business, they tried their hand at diesel-powered railway engines. The first, in 1933, was a 270hp machine, officially a 2–4–0, which had a large steam locomotive type chimney and generally looked rather like a somewhat oversize toy tank engine. It went to the B&CDR, which used it to haul passenger trains on the Ardglass and Ballynahinch lines, apparently quite successfully, and it survived until these branches closed, following which it went back to Harland & Wolff. Their next passenger engine was a more conventional-looking 2–2–2–2, of 500hp and with electric transmission. It was rather underpowered for main line work, and not very fast, its top speed being 55mph, but the County Down persisted with it until 1944, when it was transferred to the NCC. Even then its career was far from over, indeed, hardly started, for it was put on to shunting duties and, still bearing its old County Down number, 28, lasted into NIR days, latterly on the GNR section at Adelaide shed and Great Victoria Street station. A 225hp 0–6–0 shunter, No 22, was built for the NCC in 1934, followed by No 20, an 0–4–0 of similar power, in 1945, and finally a very small 0–4–0, No 16, in 1951.

Apart from these Harland & Wolff built a few diesel engines, railcars, and sower units for export, some of them running trials on the NCC before sailing for foreign parts, but despite being one of the first British firms in the field, the company rather sadly seemed to lose interest at the beginning of the 1950s, a move that now in its present unhappy state it is perhaps regretting.

The experience gained with the pre-war NCC railcars and the Harland & Wolff diesel engines convinced the UTA that considerable economies could be effected, and a superior passenger service provided, if steam was abolished. This decision might seem rather curious in view of the highly efficient and almost new fleet of 18 2–6–4Ts, but it was the old story of rising costs and declining receipts, and now that there was no LMS to bolster the former NCC lines something had to be done immediately. Replacements had to be provided for the County Down rolling stock, and in August 1951, a three-car unit of former NCC coaches, powered by four AEC 125bhp diesel engines, went into service on the Bangor line. The unit was a direct development of the pre-war NCC railcars put together at York Road, the motor-coaches, Nos 6 and 7, being corridor brakes, one a composite the other a third, while the trailer, No 528, was a ten-compartment, non-corridor third. In all the unit provided seating accommodation for 272 passengers, a complement roughly equivalent to that of a train of six six-wheelers. The coaches used in this pioneer railcar unit were all originally steel-panelled vehicles, built in the 1930s, the compartment third coming from Wolverton, and the other two from York Road. In this respect they were unlike previous railcars in Ireland, all the earlier ones having been built as such. The UTA's move, however, was a reasonable one, in that it had inherited a considerable amount of up-to-date coaching stock from the NCC, and if it was going to dieselise on a large scale then it would be rather less costly to utilise existing equipment wherever possible, rather than to build everything new.

CHAPTER EIGHTEEN

The Aftermath of the Milne Report

THE PUBLICATION OF the Milne Report caused a considerable stir, and brought forth much comment from people and bodies that were involved, or concerned with public transport, as well it might, CIE being the largest single employer in the 26 Counties. Generally it was well received, although some were more than a little surprised that Milne had come down so heavily in favour of retaining the *status quo*. On the whole the unions were quite satisfield; indeed, Senator J. T. O'Farrell, a former Secretary of the Railway Clerk's Association and for long a prominent speaker on railway matters, congratulated the Report's compilers, while the President of the Irish Transport and General Workers' Union pronounced himself reasonably content, apart from a predictable reservation over the proposed 5 per cent cut in expenditure on wages and salaries. Another union man came to the somewhat sweeping conclusion that if branch lines were to be considered uneconomic, the fact that they mostly served agricultural areas must mean that the government should logically consider that agriculture also was uneconomic. What everyone wanted to know was whether the Government intended to accept the Report just as it stood, and if action would be taken upon it immediately.

Since the General Election of the previous year Fianna Fail had found itself in the unusual position of being out of office. It had, as ever, secured the largest number of seats, but not sufficient to give it an absolute majority, and a Government had been formed from an alignment of the right and left. John Costello, leader of Fine Gael, Ireland's second largest party, had taken over from DeValera as Taoiseach. It was felt that Costello would be rather less enthusiastic for state ownership than his predecessor had been, and consequently there was considerable surprise when the Government Information Bureau announced early in February 1949, that a Bill was to be presented to the Dail recommending that the Milne Report's suggestion that the status of CIE remain unchanged be ignored, and that the entire public transport system in the 26 Counties, excluding the GNR, should be nationalised. Dealings on the Dublin Stock Exchange in transport shares, including those of the GNR, were halted, pending the coming into force of the Bill. A Transport Board, retaining the title CIE, would be set up to run the new concern, and it would ensure that no employee would be dismissed on the ground of redundancy, normal wastage being allowed to take care of any reductions in staff found necessary.

The Honorary Secretary of the Irish Transport Stockholders' Union was not anywhere near as pleased at this piece of news as was the trade union side. While expressing his satisfaction that there was to be no free competition, which would have skimmed the cream off the traffic, leaving the dregs for CIE, he complained that the financial recommendations were grossly unfair to common stockholders, and claimed it to be a disgrace that Sir James Milne had not consulted any members of the Board of Directors before concluding his enquiries. One wonders if the latter statement was strictly accurate; in the introduction to the report Milne and the other compilers state, "In particular, the Chairman, General Manager and other Officers of CIE afforded us every assistance. . . .". So at least the Chairman of the Board knew what was going on, and it is also stated that the Stockholders' Association itself was consulted.

One dramatic effect of the publication of the Bill began to be rumoured early in February, and on 17th of that month it was announced that the Chairman of CIE, A. P. Reynolds, had resigned. In actual fact he had been asked to go, although it is doubtful if he would have wanted to stay on in the changed circumstances, as was made clear in a letter he wrote to the Minister for Industry and Commerce, published on February 19. Reynolds objected to the denigration of the diesel locomotive, and said that as it had been in use in America and on the Continent for 20 years it was not correct to say that it was untried and still in process of development. He could see no future for branch line rail traffic, and main line services could only be sustained if there was sufficient passenger density. As to short distance traffic, particularly in the Dublin area, the railways were indispensable to this only if it became considerably more intensive. Reynolds finished with the broadside that the public nowadays would "not travel by train if any other form of transport was available". This last statement sounded very much like an emphatic vote of no confidence in the system of which Reynolds had been in charge for seven years, and it was perhaps best for all concerned that he should relinquish his office.

His had been an unenviable task running a railway which was chronically short of fuel and modern equipment, and the men who produced the Milne Report were probably not the best qualified for the task, as their experience had been confined to the vastly different conditions obtaining in Britain. Nevertheless one cannot avoid the impression that Reynolds's early years in road transport had left him with a permanent bias in favour of the roads, and that he was prepared to see the railways virtually disappear from the 26 Counties.

Reynolds's career in public transport had begun with the ownership of one bus, and he had so progressed that when the Government decided that some order should be brought into the chaotic field of bus and tram operation in Dublin, his company, the General, was second only to the DUTC. He actually offered to take this over, and although that would have been rather like the Romney, Hythe & Dymchurch making a bid for British Rail, Reynolds eventually became Chairman of the DUTC. He initiated the tramway replacement programme, securing a very favourable contract with Leylands for the supply of bus engines and chassis, and it was on the strength of this, among other things, that he became head of the Great Southern. Unfortunately Reynolds was not very sympathetic towards the trade unions. He had a brush with Ernest Bevin, head of the Amalgamated General Workers' Union, in 1944, when Bevin refused to accede to certain demands made by Reynolds, and relations between the management and the workers of the GSR and the DUTC, and later CIE, were not always very happy.

Reynolds's comments on the diesel locomotive were correct in relation to the United States, but CIE found to its cost that Sir James Milne was equally accurate so far as Britain was concerned, for the early British diesels were giving a great deal of trouble. But there is little doubt that if Reynolds's line, rather than Sir James's, had been followed, CIE in the long run would have been spared considerable expense. The Mirrlees-engined shunters, originally Nos 1000–4, and the two main line Sulzer-engined goods engines, originally Nos 1101 and 1102, have given over 20 years trouble-free service, and the ten 950hp AIA-AIA diesels, powered by engines ordered by Reynolds, equally have remained clear of the problems which have beset the later standard A and C classes. The 950hp Sulzer engines had been intended for five main line, 1,900hp locomotives, two engines for each locomotive, and had actually been delivered to Dublin Docks when the decision came to reverse the dieselisation programme. They were left to languish in their packing cases for some years before finally going into service.

There was not really much of a case to be made for retaining many of the branch lines, and even Milne tacitly admitted this, but Reynolds's attitude towards main line and suburban services was, to say the least, arguable, while his summing up of the public's attitude was far too sweeping and defeatist. Obviously no one wanted to travel long distances in six-wheeled unheated non-corridor carriages which arrived at their destination hours late, but fast, comfortable, modern corridor trains with refreshment and buffet cars, such as the GNR and the UTA were still running, and the GSR had operated on the Cork line until 1941, were a completely different proposition. Moreover there was absolutely no reason why CIE could not soon have a number in service, either steam or diesel operated.

Reynolds's successor during the interim period before CIE was nationalised was T. C. Courtney, the Chief Engineering Adviser to the Department of Local Government, a one-time railwayman who had worked on the old Cork, Bandon & South Coast Railway. G. B. Howden of the GNR was appointed to act in an advisory capacity, and on September 30, 1949, the final senior appointment, following the Milne Report, was made. This was the appointment of Oliver Bulleid as Consulting Mechanical Engineer. Bulleid was, of course, the outstanding locomotive engineer of his time, and by a quirk of fate he took over the office his predecessor on the Southern Railway, R. E. L. Maunsell, had left to go to Ashford 36 years earlier. Bulleid, a devout Roman Catholic, found much which appealed to him in Ireland, and he stayed at Inchicore until his retirement. At the same time his position was a frustrating one, and his one new design, the turf-burning locomotive proved abortive. Bulleid had acted as technical assessor in the preparation of the Milne Report, and his hand could certainly be seen in the championing of the steam locomotive. Bulleid was not greatly opposed to diesels, but felt rather that the steam engine possessed a potential which had not yet been exploited. This attitude he had no doubt inherited from his former chief Sir Nigel Gresley, whose A4 Pacifics had proved capable of running at speeds equal to those of the contemporary German diesel railcars, and of hauling considerably greater loads. Bulleid's Leader tanks on the Southern, and the CIE turf-burner, were among the last completely new steam designs in the world, and certainly the most revolutionary, but they came out at a time when the facilities and money for the patient development necessary to achieve perfection were no longer available, and neither type went into regular service.

The new appointments meant that CIE had a team at the top entirely committed to improving the state of the railways, and the reasonable hope had been born that with nationalisation the modernisation programme, so long delayed, would be got under way. The Transport Act, 1950, setting up the new board, came into effect on June 1, 1950. The board was appointed by the Government and consisted of a full-time Chairman and six part-time Directors. It was empowered to fix its own rates, fares, and all other charges. The total amount of stock substituted for the securities of the previous CIE and Grand Canal Company was £16,400,000. A most important provision written into the Act, and one which caused some misgiving, was that the Board should make a profit, or at least should not make a loss. It had responsibility for all forms of public road, rail and water transport within the Republic (as Eire had become on Easter Monday, 1949), and was charged to see that they were worked in such a way as to provide an "efficient, economical, convenient and properly integrated system".

As yet the third of the principal railway systems of Ireland, the Great Northern, had continued on its independent way, untouched by the nationalisation schemes going on around it. During the war it had benefitted enormously from the restrictions on road transport, and from the increased mili-

tary activity in the Six Counties, turning a steadily declining financial position
into a highly prosperous one. Net receipts in 1938 amounted to £40,000,
whereas six years later they exceeded £625,000. Yet in a further six years the
picture changed once again, that splendid profit decaying into a deficit of
close on £250,000. It was often claimed that ever-increasing wages and salaries were bringing about the bankruptcy of the railways. This was never
really so, for other costs were rising just as rapidly, and wages just happened
to be the factor which attracted all the publicity. Certainly the GNR wage
bill had risen by 173 per cent between 1938 and 1950, but expenditure on
some other items had gone up by an even greater percentage. On others still
it was rather less, but the overall picture was that of wages and salaries
just about keeping level with the general increase in expenditure. In 1938
62 per cent of the company's outgoings was on these items, in 1944 it was
59 per cent, and in 1950, 60 per cent. Fuel costs were the second largest item in
the company's budget, 11 per cent in 1938, 17 per cent in 1944, and 16 per
cent in 1950; in this case there was a definite percentage increase.

As for revenue, 1938 freight train receipts, came to £486,000, while those
of 1944 and 1950 were roughly equal at around £1,300,000. The GNR had
done well in increasing its total tonnage from 779,000 in 1938 to 1,459,000
in 1950, livestock figures remaining more or less constant. However, rates
had gone up by no more than around 50 per cent, a figure much lower than
the general rise in prices in both the Six and the 26 Counties. The GNR would
dearly have loved to raise them very much higher, but dared not for fear of
driving traffic on to the roads. This partly explains why the company found
itself losing more and more money each year despite doing just as much
business. The other principal reason was the decline in passenger traffic.
While an improvement on those of 1938, the 1950 results were little better
than half those of 1944, and even though passenger fares had risen very
much more steeply than goods rates, this rise did little to close the gap between
expenditure and income.

In the setting up of the UTA powers had been written into the Act enabling
it to take over those sections of the GNR within the Six Counties, and similar
provisions concerning the southern part of the company's lines had existed
since 1945. Proposals for merging part or all of the GNR with various other
transport concerns in both the Six and the 26 Counties had been mooted off
and on since the 1920s, but the problem of the Border had always got in the
way, and there had never been sufficient incentive to overcome it. Now there
had to be, for the GNR was in dire financial straits and clearly could not
continue in business much longer. At the Annual General Meeting at Amiens
Street station on February 26, 1949, the Chairman, Lord Glenavy, announced
that "the curtain was about to be rung down on the GNR". But the Dublin
and Stormont Governments got together to see what could be done, and in
January 1951, it was announced that an agreement concerning the future of
the GNR had been reached.

A new joint board would be set up to take over the company, with effect
from September 1, 1953. It would consist of ten members, five appointed by
the Republic's Minister for Industry and Commerce and five by the Six

Counties' Minister of Commerce. The GNR stockholders agreed to be bought out for £4.5m, handing over for this sum a rail seating capacity of close on 22,500, a road seating capacity (all within the Republic) of almost 7,000, a road goods carrying capacity of some 1,000 tons, a rail one of over 53,000 tons, 543 miles of track (excluding sidings), a salary and wage bill of £2.9m, 6,490 employees, and receipts of £3½m. Not many years earlier either government would have been happy to have gained the possession of such a well-run enterprise as the GNR, but by 1953 it had fallen greatly from its once pre-eminent position. Yet even then it still managed, with its diesel railcars, comfortable steel-panelled carriages, well maintained locomotives and general air of stylish efficiency, to give the impression that any troubles it might have were merely temporary embarrassments which could have no permanent effect on the company's well-being.

CHAPTER NINETEEN

Line Closures

THE OBVIOUS solution to the financial problems besetting the railways, now growing ever more threatening as private motoring bit deeper into receipts, was to dispose of their most burdensome liabilities. These were the branch lines, and the 1950s saw the beginning of the fearful slaughter, so often predicted, finally wreaked upon them. A list of railway closures in Ireland will be found at the back of the book, but there is rather more to be said about this period of Irish railway history than a mere recital of dates and distances.

It might be well to deal first with a line which was an exception to the general closure pattern. Virtually all branch lines served rural areas, which was hardly remarkable, Ireland being very little else. Dublin was one of the only three centres of population large enough to warrant suburban rail services, and in 1958 the most vulnerable of these, that of the former D&SER from Shanganagh Junction, 1¾ miles north of Bray, to Harcourt Street, went out of business.

For many years the South Dublin suburban services had been losing passengers, mainly to public road transport. Electrification had come to the Dublin tramways in May 1896, earlier than to all but two other cities in the British Isles, Coventry and Bristol, and a highly efficient system, said by some to be unequalled by any others, was rapidly built up, making considerable inroads upon suburban railway services. Dublin trams were the first to have covered tops and drivers' screens, and the Dublin United Tramways Company developed a points apparatus which was copied by many other concerns. Trams seemed to add something to the character of Dublin and become an integral part of it, their principal terminus being in the heart of city at O'Connell Street. Two long lines of them flanked the Nelson Pillar, waiting to whisk Dubliners north or south along the shores of Dublin Bay or eastwards down the Quays to the Phoenix Park and the new suburbs which had sprung up round the railway works at Inchicore and their own near by ones at Spa Road.

Dublin trams played their part in Irish history; they were stoned and bombed and blown up during the troubles of the first three decades of the Century, and they fascinated writers, particularly James Joyce, descriptions and images conjured up by them recurring in *Dubliners* and *Ulysses*. They fought a fierce and largely successful battle with the railways, and when the time came for them to go and they were replaced by motor buses, the decline in rail passenger receipts steepened.

The last, those on the Dalkey route, went on July 3, 1949, a number being sold off as sheds and summer houses; some of these can still be seen in the gardens of houses in the Dun Laoghaire, Killiney and Bray areas, as well as further afield. An attempt was made to preserve two of them, but lack of suitable accommodation and shortage of funds frustrated the venture, and all that survives are the trucks. It is hoped, however, that these may one day be reunited with a body retrieved from someone's garden, and restored ready to go on show in the Dublin Transport Museum, now at last established after having been mooted for a great many years, but nothing much happened for a long time. The condition of the preserved pre-war DUTC double-deck Leyland Titan bus and the GNR AEC Regent standing out in all weathers in the yard at Broadstone growing steadily shabbier, had led one to feel dubious about their chances.

An indication of how uncomfortable rail travel on the suburban lines had become can be gained from riding in one of the buses which replaced the last of the trams. Some of these are still at work in Dublin, and although more than 20 years old, have been well looked after and are in virtually their original condition, apart from a change in livery. Their interiors are Spartan in the extreme, and the amount of leg room provided for each passenger might serve a leprechaun very well but could hardly be described as wildly extravagant for anyone else. Yet rail passengers, who flocked to try them out, apparently found them much superior to what they had been used to and deserted the railway for good.

In its latter days the Harcourt Street line was a purely suburban one, none of its trains going beyond Greystones. The Drumm battery trains, which had worked many of the services, were withdrawn around 1950, leaving the old 333 class 4-4-0s and the inevitable J15s, both former GS&WR types, to carry on, ex-D&SE locomotives having virtually disappeared in the 1920s. Diesel railcars took over in 1955-6, but even these modern and comfortable vehicles could do little to reverse the trend of falling receipts. If their introduction had resulted in a considerable speed-up of the timetable there might have been some hope, but CIE showed precious little enterprise in this direction. Trains which had previously been allowed 33min for the 12¼-mile run between Harcourt Street and Bray, including seven stops, behind a

60-year old J15, or one of the much later but no speedier J15Bs, could achieve nothing better than a 3min overall acceleration when worked by railcars, while the one fast up train, the 8.50am from Bray, stopping only at Ranelagh, the last station before Harcourt Street, could only cut its time by a similar amount.

At the end the line was carrying no more than 1,000 passengers per day. CIE reckoned that at this rate it was losing £50,000 each year, and said that it was not prepared to go on *ad infinitum*. The protests were many, numbers of them coming from people who travelled either by car or by bus but liked to feel that the railway was there should they ever need it, even though they were not prepared to pay anything towards its upkeep. Fond though CIE was of all its train services, it could hardly keep the Harcourt Street one running on that basis, and on the last day of 1958 the end came. The final regular passenger train to use the terminus was the 4.25pm to Bray, an eight-coach diesel, and most of the passengers who had come in that morning by train had to make their way home again by the replacement buses. Services on the coast line from Amiens Street were improved to cater for passengers between Dublin and Bray, but most switched to the buses, for those who lived in the area between Shankill and Ranelagh were too far away from the coastline for it to be of any use to them.

Part of the line was used in the subsequent summer by a film unit, but little time was lost in lifting most of it and dismantling the bridges. Some of the track saw further service, but not in Ireland; an enterprising Pakistani gentleman bought it up and shipped it back home. At about this time the boom in building in the Dublin suburbs was just getting under way, and there were those who predicted that road traffic might increase at a much greater rate than had been anticipated, making an alternate means of transport between the city centre and the south eastern suburbs essential. Such has proved to be the case and what CIE intends to do about it will be examined in a later chapter.

Cork, the second city of Southern Ireland, which was once served by a variety of lines, broad and narrow-gauge, has lost nearly all of them. This is partly due to the usual factors, road competition and increasing operating costs, but there is in addition one other. For a long period, between 1920 and the end of World War II, Cork as a business centre stagnated; it suffered badly from the effects of the depression and the economic war, and in such a situation railway business was hit even harder than it otherwise would have been. After 1945 Cork began to recover and has continued to do so, but while traffic between Cork and Dublin has increased, that between Cork City and the sparsely populated areas of West Cork has not.

The narrow-gauge lines serving the Cork area had gone before World War II, as had the passenger service on the broad-gauge Macroom line. A regular goods service continued on the latter until the coal shortage of 1947, after which the line's only use was to provide cattle specials for Macroom Fair. It closed entirely at the end of 1953, the last few miles of the line being submerged by the waters of a hydro-electrical scheme.

Although Albert Quay was used by the Macroom trains its principal services were those of the former Cork, Bandon & South Coast Railway, serving the far south-west. These continued to run until 1961, the passenger services latterly being worked by diesel railcars, although the distinctive Beyer Peacock 4–6–0Ts monopolised the goods trains right up to the end, and one or two survived at Glanmire Road shed for a short while after the closure. Freight trains still run through the streets of Cork between Glanmire Road and Albert Quay, and right up until the early 1960s six-wheel carriages might be seen trundling along this route in charge of diesel-electric locomotives.

The last of the Cork area closures was the Youghal passenger service. Youghal is an attractive seaside town, architecturally considerably better endowed than most Irish resorts, and popular with holidaymakers and day-trippers. It lies 26½ miles due east of Cork and is connected to it by a single line branching from the Cork–Cobh line at Cobh Junction. Regular passenger services ceased early in 1963, but the goods service remains, and at summer weekends and on Bank Holidays passenger trains are restored for the benefit of excursionists. These are well patronised, and one may hope that the future of the branch is reasonably secure.

Eastwards from Cork, beyond Youghal, Dungarvan and Tramore, one comes to the City of Waterford. Like Cork it lies some way back from the sea, on a wide river, and is a port of some importance. Although not so large, Waterford has done rather better than Cork of late so far as the railways are concerned, only one of the six lines which served it at the 1925 Amalgamation having gone completely. This is the Tramore line, which had its own station, Waterford Manor, on the opposite side of the River Suir, and was quite isolated from the rest of the railway system. All rolling stock movements to and from it had to be by road; the special railcars fitted out for it arrived that way and departed in a similar manner when the line closed down. Passenger and goods trains survived into the 1960s, the passenger ones doing a fair amount of business at peak periods right up to the end, which came on the last day of 1960.

Of the three routes which connected Dublin with Waterford only one is now totally intact. The shortest was that of the GS&WR through Kilkenny and Portlaoise and this closed in 1962, through trains from then on having to reverse at Kilkenny and go via Carlow and Athy, regaining the main line at Cherryville Junction. Actually they had been doing this for some while previously, and as there was more traffic on this route, no great hardship was caused. The old D&SER route to Dublin via New Ross, Palace East and Macmine Junction had never provided a serious alternative, and in later years was a purely local branch, with two passenger trains in each direction on weekdays only. These were among the last CIE steam-hauled services and each train consisted of one carriage, a four-wheel van and a J15 0–6–0. Until early 1961 the passenger vehicle was an ex-GS&WR clerestory bogie composite; it was replaced by a slightly less elderly elliptical-roofed carriage from the same company. Passenger services ended early in 1963, but the section between Waterford and New Ross is still open for goods traffic.

A less predictable closure was that of part of the former Fishguard &

Rosslare Harbour Company's line linking Rosslare with Cork. This was, perhaps, the most important of CIE's cross-country routes and had always been well patronised by travellers between England and the south-west of Ireland. Apparently it did not carry much other traffic, and as there was an alternative route between Waterford and Mallow, via Clonmel, Tipperary and Limerick Junction, it was decided that substantial economies could be effected by transferring the boat trains to the latter. This involved a greater mileage, but over an easier route, and there was consequently little alteration in overall timings, a 10min earlier departure from Cork being the only difference affecting passengers. This was just as well, for the journey from Cork to Paddington is a tedious one; no fast running is possible to any degree until the greater part of the journey is over and one is leaving Wales.

I once travelled in a boat train on the old route through Dungarvan on a summer Saturday, and although I had boarded it only at Waterford it seemed an eternity before we reached Cork. The carriages had mostly seen better days, creaking, wooden-bodied, sparsely-upholstered specimens, and our A Class diesel, despite being relatively new, hardly distinguished itself, surmounting the steeper inclines at little more than walking pace amid billowing clouds of acrid brown smoke and a continuous shattering roar. Many of the passengers were small children and mothers, most of whom would have spent the night sitting up on the ship with practically no sleep, and they must all have been quite exhausted by the time the hot, sticky journey dragged to its end.

The Mallow–Waterford closure was one of the last on CIE, taking place in March 1967. On the same day two other cross-country lines in that part of the world ceased working, the Patrickswell–Charleville line, which had provided the shortest route between Cork and Limerick, and that from Thurles to Clonmel.

A little over three years later there an event occurred which would have been thought highly unlikely not very much earlier; the reopening of a lengthy section of closed line. A large manganesite-producing plant had been established at Ballinacourty, near Dungarvan, one of the conditions being that CIE would guarantee to provide it with rail access and run a regular service of trains conveying the dolomite necessary for the manufacture of the manganese. This dolomite is quarried at Bennett's Bridge, 23 miles north of Waterford, on the Kilkenny line. So the line from Waterford to Ballinacourty went back into regular use, the first dolomite special travelling over it on April 3, 1970. There are two trains a day in each direction, and one a day to Cork with manganesite. No passenger trains have run over the line since its reopening; the rails from Ballinacourty to Mallow were lifted fairly soon after the original closure.

Belfast, like Dublin, was once possessor of a rather more extensive suburban rail service than is now the case. The first closures were the County Down lines to Newcastle, Donaghadee, Ardglass, Ballynahinch and Castlewellan at the beginning of 1950. These were the most extensive, and although there are now many towns and villages cut off by rail from Belfast which once had either a direct or connecting service, the only line actually within the city which has closed is the Belfast Central Railway. This went on July 1, 1965, and had the effect of cutting off what was left of the former County Down, the Bangor branch, from the rest of the railway network. No regular passenger services had worked over it, but it was a most useful link and the principal reason for its demise seems to have been that it was in the way of a proposed new road. Since then someone has been having second thoughts, and the 1970 NIR Annual Report referred to its possible reopening. Whether this comes about depends upon Government approval. Until very recently one could have been sure that this would never have been forthcoming, but there have been changes of late; talk of the oft-projected Central station is in the air again, and there is cause for a degree of guarded optimism. Nevertheless successive Unionist Governments have made no secret of their anti-railway attitude and one remains sceptical over the present one's professed change of heart.

Outside Belfast railway closures in the Six Counties have been savage, considerably more so than in the South, and carried out with rather less regard to the hardships caused to the community. Neither the Republic nor the Six Counties are wealthy by English standards, but their attitudes to their states of relative penury are rather different. The Republic in a sense may be said to have chosen its penury, having deliberately broken away from Britain. This is not to say that it was in any way prosperous under British rule; quite on the contrary, it was deliberately deprived of the means of improving its lot. But if it had remained as a part of the United Kingdom it could be argued that it would have been supported in later years in the way that the North has been. One is now stepping into that most dangerous of fields, Irish politics, but the topic must be broached, for it is one in which the railways, along with every other aspect of life in the Six Counties, have become embroiled.

The South, having gained its independence, has always seemed prepared to accept the sacrifices necessary to improve its standards, and this applies throughout the community, including the West Britons, the Anglo–Irish, who were the ruling class before 1916, and who chose to stay in Ireland after Independence rather than return to England. Until recently the government was carried on by people who had been at the forefront of the Independence movement, and although this generation has now largely gone, its successors in general sympathise with the old aims. Irishmen care no more for politicians' reputations than do the British, but there is a feeling throughout the country that the Government, generally speaking, is on the side of the people. When unpleasant decisions have to be taken care is taken to ensure that those affected are consulted, and when railway lines have been shut people have grumbled but have usually accepted the inevitability of the move, particularly as alternate road services have always been provided.

This is not to say there has been no opposition to DeValera's policies, but it has tended to be one of emphasis or degree rather than principle. DeValera retired as Taoiseach in 1959, being succeeded by Sean Lemass, the Minister for Industry and Commerce, who in turn gave way to Jack Lynch, but both these have continued to follow DeValera's policies. On his retirement DeValera became President, and in 1966 he was re-elected, at the age of 84, 50 years after the 1916 Uprising. From time to time he travels by train, in the splendid state coach, No 351, built in 1902, and refurbished at Inchicore and fitted with B4 bogies in 1966; one wonders if he ever reflects on the time he held up the train outside Westland Row at the start of the 1916 Uprising. People still disrupt rail services from time to time for political reasons, usually choosing to blow up the Dublin–Belfast main line; fortunately this has not resulted in anything more serious for passengers than inconvenience, and in the North railways have generally remained unscathed during the present troubles despite the proximity of York Road to much of them.

Since 1922 the North has been a divided nation, a large minority, a growing one, taking great exception to its Government. This minority is firmly convinced that it is discriminated against, and can quote the statistics to prove its claim. It has often gone about justifying its case with methods so lacking in subtlety that they have done more harm than good, and a general atmosphere of bloody-mindedness has resulted. The Government can hardly be accused of doing its utmost to soothe the situation, and its treatment of the railways has reflected its somewhat cavalier attitude to the community at large. One would not for an instant deny that motor transport was better suited to many of the tasks which the railways once performed, just as it was in the South, but there were occasions when an impartial observer must have found it difficult to rid himself of the impression that the Government was hell-bent to wipe the entire rail network from the face of Northern Ireland, regardless of the inconvenience and hardships this would cause, and of the economic consequences. Unlike the Dublin administrations, Stormont has always been able to lay its hands on considerable sums of money to build roads, and it is at present spending millions of pounds on a motorway system, which may look extremely progressive but is not so easy to justify from an economic point of view.

One of the clearest indications of the Northern Ireland Government's intentions was given in 1956 when it announced that much of the GNR system in the Six Counties would be abandoned. This provoked a mass of protest, not least from the Dublin Government, which was responsible for the rest of the GNR and would find itself with a number of branches ending in the middle of fields if the Stormont administration carried out its threat. The GNR itself wanted to continue to work the lines, but Stormont remained adamant. The Minister of Commerce said that £14,000 a year would be saved by the closures, a sum which certainly lent credibility to the feeling that the reasons for the closures were not economic, and he stated that the agreement with Dublin for the joint operation of the GNR would be ended unilaterally in October 1957. The last trains on the Clones–Omagh, Glaslough–Portadown, Bundoran Junction–Bundoran, and Fintona Junction–Fintona lines ran on September 30; the last-mentioned was the famous horse-worked tram. Dublin had no alternative but to close down the truncated remains within the Republic, and the poor old Sligo, Leitrim & Northern Counties Railway, which had been in desperate straits for years, and had only carried on with financial assistance from the Stormont and Dublin Governments, found itself with no outlet for most of its traffic and succumbed at once.

Those of its employees lucky enough to live in the Republic, all but 30 out of 137, received compensation. The SL&NCR's history in recent years had been a saga of total misery, remarkable even in Ireland. Although the largest part of its one line between Enniskillen and Collooney (it had running powers from there over CIE metals into Sligo) was in the 26 Counties, nearly all its traffic, principally livestock, passed on to the GNR at Enniskillen, and thence to the ports of Derry and Belfast. In recognition of the benefit thus derived by the Six Counties the Northern Ireland Government had granted the SL&NCR an annual subsidy since 1935, and the GNR had been giving it a rebate on charges since 1949. Even this, however, failed to prevent the SL&NCR from making a loss, so it turned to the Dublin Government in 1952 and the latter responded by granting it £3,500 each year, £500 more than Stormont gave, but £500 less than the GNR's rebate. Still the tale of woe continued, and losses grew; the company appealed again for help and Dublin promised to raise its subsidy to a sum not exceeding £5,000 per annum provided that Stormont followed suit. Not only did Stormont refuse to do this, but it said that it would cease to continue what it had been paying.

Consequently in September 1955, the Directors of the SL&NCR applied to both governments for permission to abandon the railway, and shortly afterwards came the announcement of the Northern Ireland's intention to close the GNR line through Enniskillen. A great many appeals were made by local people to save this and Dublin upped its offer of help to a maximum of £15,000. But the carrying out of the threat to close the GNR line killed the efforts of the Republic and the SL&NCR collapsed. Its assets were auctioned off, and its three most modern items of rolling stock, two Beyer Peacock 0–6–4Ts, delivered as late as 1951, and a Gardner–Walker diesel railcar dating from 1947, were purchased for further service in Ireland.

Two of these vehicles still exist. The 0–6–4T *Lough Erne*, having worked on the Belfast dock lines and around York Road for a number of years, along with her sister engine *Lough Melvin*, was retired by the NIR in 1969 and has been preserved, while CIE acquired the railcar, numbered it 2509, and has since used it on a variety of duties, including a long spell on the Limerick–Nenagh line. Actually the SL&NCR did not own either *Lough Erne* or *Lough Melvin*, as it was unable (not surprisingly) to raise the purchase price; until they were bought by the UTA they remained the property of Beyer Peacock, the SL&NCR merely hiring them.

The 1957 closures reduced the GNR mileage in the Six Counties to a considerable extent, but it had left its two main lines untouched. The Benson Report of 1963, an enquiry into all inland transport in the North, put the future of these in jeopardy, recommending that the entire rail network, other than the Belfast–Larne, Belfast–Bangor and Belfast–Dublin lines should be abolished; the latter was to be retained for "prestige reasons" only. As a corrective to this view a second Government-sponsored report, that of Sir Robert Matthew on trends of population in and around Belfast, published at the same time, said that Belfast was as big as it ought to be, and that other towns, particularly Londonderry, Newry, Dungannon, Omagh, Coleraine and Enniskillen, should be built up as centres of population and industry. Railways would be needed to transport workers and materials, and Sir Robert considered that the system was already reduced to its minimum size.

A month earlier the Minister for Home Affairs had announced a plan putting into effect the Benson Report recommendations, with the exception of the UTA's Londonderry–Belfast line, which would remain. Nothing daunted, he totally ignored the Matthew Report, with the consequence that by the end of 1965 of the six towns recommended for development two only, Coleraine and Derry, were left with rail connections, or three if one includes Newry, for the Warrenpoint branch closed on January 4, 1965.

Tyrone County Council complained bitterly about the closing of the former GNR Portadown–Derry line, but the Transport Tribunal decided against it and on February 15, 1965, the last train ran. With the severance of the Belfast Central line later that year all that remained of the old GNR lines in the Six Counties was the Belfast–Border section of the Dublin main line, and the line from Knockmore Junction, just south of Lisburn, to Antrim. This was no longer served by regular passenger trains, but was of considerable importance in that it was the sole connection between the former NCC tracks and the rest of the Irish railway system.

As during the previous spate of railway closures in 1957 the heart-rending cries of poverty filling the air did not quite ring true, for they were insufficient to drown the announcement that a cool £120m was going to be spent on building motorways. A thousand railwaymen lost their jobs as a result of the implementation of the Benson Report. They were offered compensation but the unions remained incensed and there was much sympathy in the country at large, few people outside Government circles caring for the radical changes in the transport scene going on around them. The UTA's statutory monopoly of public transport was abolished, and private hauliers were granted licences and allowed to compete with the Government-operated road freight services. Successive Transport Acts in 1966 and 1967 put these measures into effect, the road services of the UTA being taken over by the Northern Ireland Transport Holding Company. This supervised two subsidiary companies, one for freight and the other for passengers, Northern Ireland Carriers and Ulsterbus. By the end of 1967 380 road freight operators resident within the Six Counties had taken advantage of the Acts and obtained licences, in addition to 65 based in other parts of the United Kingdom, and a further 73 from the Republic.

The railways, such as remained of them, became Northern Ireland Railways, and were given money for approved capital expenditure and to cover any revenue deficits from Government funds as well as out of profits made by other public transport concerns. All the former railway-owned hotels were sold, and so anxious was the Government to remove all forms of catering from the railways' control, that it went to the length of contracting out the staffing of restaurant cars.

One further timid step backwards proposed at this time was the singling of

24 miles of the main Belfast–Dublin main line, no less, south of Portadown. This notion left CIE aghast, as it did many other people, but not for long. It tactfully suggested that perhaps the UTA hadn't quite got its costings right, and then not so tactfully offered to make up any alleged deficit that the retention of double track might incur. This proposal was so loaded with political overtones that the Government could hardly ignore it, and rather than let it be said that the transport company of the Republic was ensuring that Irishmen within the Six Counties were getting an adequate rail service, it rapidly let the whole matter drop.

The morale of railwaymen in Northern Ireland was now, as may be imagined, at a very low ebb, many of them looking for jobs elsewhere before their present ones disappeared. Their principal hope of a continuing future for the railways and employment for themselves lay in John Coulthard, Managing Director of the UTA since January 1966. He had long served the railways, beginning his career with the LMS, and on taking over as head of the UTA he had very quickly made his presence felt. It would seem that in appointing Coulthard the Northern Irish Government had made something of a miscalculation, for he made it quite clear that it was not his intention to preside over the last rites of the railways in the Six Counties.

Relations between the Managing Director and the Government steadily deteriorated, threatening a complete rift, which came about in May 1967, after Coulthard had agreed to grant the conciliation grades a five-day week. Members of the Railway Board claimed that he was not authorised to take such action, and a meeting of the full Board of the UTA was called for the 8th. After six hours the decision was reached that Coulthard should be dismissed, and when this became known four days later, on the 12th, there was a tremendous outcry. The men staged a two-hour strike in protest, disrupting the evening rush-hour traffic and causing considerable chaos in Belfast. Their spokesman described his former chief as a "perfect gentleman", and a number of Stormont MPs supported him in Parliament.

Coulthard's own feelings are best described by himself in a letter I received from him in September 1970. "The story would make a book in itself. . . . It was clear to me during 1966 that the Northern Ireland Government, which had already savagely hacked away most of its railway system, had decided to run the railways down and abandon them. There is nothing which they would have liked better than a recommendation from me to limit the life of the railways to ten years. After my dismissal they gave me an undertaking to keep the railways going, and I believe that their change of heart was fairly genuine."

Coulthard's dismissal stood, but the Minister for Development was forced to concede that the Government did not intend to abandon the railways, but to "maintain and increase their efficiency". Coulthard is now the head of a ferry firm working out of Warrenpoint, and the railway's loss was a double one, for not only were they deprived of the services of a very able Managing Director, but they also suffered financially as a two year legal battle resulted in Coulthard receiving substantial damages for wrongful dismissal and libel. His successor was another railwayman, Hugh Waring, who started out at the age of 14 as a porter on the County Down, and for a long time was an official of the National Association of Transport Employees.

The present and future prospects of the Northern Ireland Railways are dealt with in another chapter; we may best end this one by reiterating John Coulthard's hope that the Government's change of heart towards them has been "genuine".

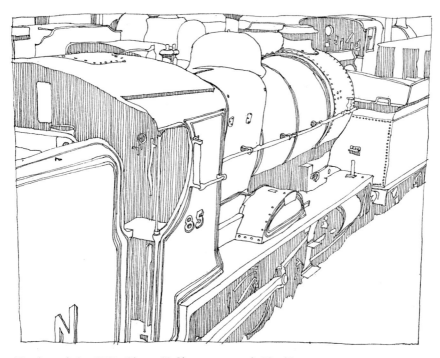

The last of the GNR Glover V Class compounds No 85
Merlin at Dundalk Works in September 1961

CHAPTER TWENTY

Dieselisation, the First Stage

WE HAVE SEEN that during the 1930s the three principal Irish companies as well as some of the smaller narrow-gauge ones had made determined efforts to perfect the self-propelled railcar, and that three of them, the GNR, the NCC, and the County Donegal, by 1939 had done so. Such a vehicle, doing away with the need for a separate locomotive, ready for action at the push of a button, economical, clean and modern, suited the lightly-trafficked Irish branch lines to perfection. Its principal disadvantage in the early days was its unreliability and rather short working life. As its design became more sophisticated and railwaymen became more familiar with its operation the first problem ceased to exist, and although railcars still tended to wear out rather faster than either locomotives or locomotive-hauled passenger stock the difference was not now very great, and in some ways was rather a boon, ensuring that out-of-date vehicles were not still trundling around when they had become obsolete.

The NCC, and in particular the GNR railcars, had answered the fervent prayers of their respective Boards of Directors by not only working far more economically than steam-hauled passenger trains but also by attracting passengers back from the roads to the railways. Their usefulness was somewhat reduced during the war years when loads increased out of all expectations, greatly exceeding the capacities of the railcars, but with a return to peacetime conditions and the mass migration of passengers back to the roads the railcar was seen as virtually the only card the railways had left to play.

Appropriately the GNR, which had made the greatest use of this type of vehicle during the 1930s, was the first of the big three to bring out a railcar after the war. Numbered 600, it was followed by 19 identical vehicles. They were based partly on the earlier GNR ones and partly on the pioneer cars of the English GWR type. Although their bodywork, like some of the latter, was of Park Royal design, it was rather less streamlined, and more a tidied-up version of the later GNR pre-war types. The cars were assembled at Dundalk, and each was powered by two 125hp AEC engines. All the working parts were kept below floor level, allowing the inclusion of 12 first-class and 32 second-class seats, a guard's and luggage compartment, and a steam generator heating unit. Nowadays rail travellers take the panoramic view through the front windows of a diesel unit for granted, unless they are unfortunate enough to live on the Southern Region of British Rail, but in 1950 it was quite a novelty, especially on a main line service, and the GNR cars excited a great deal of favourable comment. The only snag was that one needed a first-class ticket to obtain the full benefit of the view, these privileged travellers occupying the seats nearest the front. The top speed of 70mph produced by the two engines, placed symmetrically on either side of the main frames, was not particularly high, but the acceleration compared with that of a steam engine was meteoric, and was adequate compensation. The inaugural run by a train of railcars was made on June 1 to an admiring press and public and four days later it went into service between Dublin and Belfast.

Painted in blue and cream, the cars were used on every type of duty, taking over some of the principal "Enterprise" workings from the 4–4–0 steam locomotives as well as appearing on a variety of lesser main line and branch turns. A number of modern locomotive-hauled coaches were repainted in railcar livery to work with them, as each railcar was capable of hauling a trailer. The cars were all single-ended and fitted for multiple-unit operation; a train of them varied in length from two to eight vehicles, including trailers.

By 1950 the Great Southern's pre-war steam and Drumm electric railcars were all withdrawn and passenger services on CIE became 100 per cent steam-operated. The Milne Report had recommended the use of diesel railcars for branch line use, assuming that the branch lines were going to be kept open, and in September 1950, the CIE Management, noting the success of the GNR cars and the lack of it on the part of its own tired old steam engines and slowly disintegrating carriages, put in an order for 20 vehicles almost identical with those of the GNR. Before they arrived the order was extended to 60 cars, each costing some £18,500. They began to come over from England late in 1951 and the first four, Nos 2600–3, went into service on the Kingsbridge–Waterford line, enabling accelerations of between 15 and 25min to be made in the overall running time.

The section between Portarlington and Kingsbridge was covered in 47min at an average speed of 53.3mph, which at the time was the fastest in Ireland. They worked with a pair of new buffet cars, Nos 2405 and 2406, and thus the fortunate citizens of Waterford suddenly found themselves not only travelling faster than anyone else in Ireland, but doing it while wining and dining in the very latest rolling stock. When working with the railcars the buffet cars served as ordinary vehicles, meals and drinks being available throughout the train, served at tables between each pair of seats in all the coaches.

Delivery of the railcars continued until 1954, the first 48 being for main line use and identical in layout to the GNR cars. The subsequent ten, Nos 2648–57, were intended for the Dublin and Cork suburban lines, and although they differed little externally from their fellows their interior arrangements were modified; there were no toilets or tables, and the third-class capacity was increased by four. Both types were heated by oil-fired boilers in the guard's compartment, a rather old-fashioned arrangement and one which sometimes resulted in the odd sight of a diesel railcar wreathed in steam. The first boilers proved rather inadequate for main line use and were replaced by a more satisfactory design, which was capable of heating a four-coach train. It should be added that only half the cars (those with even numbers) were fitted with heating plants, so care had to be taken always to marshal an equal number of odd and even-numbered cars together; otherwise the passengers were likely to be either roasted or frozen.

Like their GNR relations the CIE cars in their early years were usually to be found on the principal main line services, as well as on the branches. Two however, Nos 2658 and 2659, were kept exclusively for a short-distance route, the Waterford and Tramore section. They were quite different internally, having no toilet facilities and no first-class accommodation, while the third-class seating capacity was increased to close on 100. As there was no rail connection between this line and the rest of the system the cars had to be taken by road across Waterford, and brought back the same way when the line closed down in 1960.

In August 1954, six more diesel transmissions and engines were ordered, the latter officially of BUT manufacture. BUT was the name of a selling organisation set up jointly by AEC and Leyland and the engines were actually AECs identical with the earlier ones. They were put into six new cars, designed by Bulleid, Nos 2660–5, and built at Inchicore. They were curious and rather ugly vehicles, with flat wedge-shaped fronts, and stood 4in higher than the earlier cars. This increase in height, although quite small, was very noticeable when the cars were marshalled into a train of normal-sized carriages, and caused the Bulleid vehicles to look quite out of proportion and rather top-heavy; certainly it in no way increased their elegance.

They came out in 1956, but did not last long in their original form, being converted in early 1961 to non-driving power cars. They lost their ugly cabs, the driving controls were removed, the windows panelled over, and corridor connections cut into the ends. Despite their considerably improved appearance, they retained the gawky look that those extra 4in had given them. These were the last railcars built by CIE and it seems doubtful if there will be any more, the emphasis of late having shifted back towards independent power units. They were not entirely suitable for main line work, from which they were gradually withdrawn; nevertheless they were an almost priceless asset to CIE in the 1950s, vastly more comfortable than most of the locomotive-hauled stock then in service, and if they were unable to prevent the closure of much of the branch line network they at least gave it a temporary reprieve.

The most ardent diesel railcar enthusiast of all the Irish companies was the UTA. Following the success of the pioneer three-car unit of 1951 it was decided completely to dieselise the surviving section of the County Down system, the Bangor line, and also to work much of the suburban traffic out of York Road with railcars. Two basic types were used, converted former steam-hauled ex-NCC vehicles and completely new cars. There were 15 new power cars and 14 trailers of a rather ugly design with recessed, sliding doors, but ideal for the Bangor line and a very great improvement on the worn-out stock the customers previously had to make do with.

The new cars were normally kept together, but might sometimes be seen working with the converted vehicles. There were 23 of the latter, all power cars, and of varying types, some compartment coaches, and others with centre corridors, or part-side-part-centre corridors. They mostly originated from the 1930s, but a few, including some compartment coaches sent over by the LMS, were rather older, going back to 1925. These were elaborately panelled, wooden-bodied, and very handsome vehicles of a type familiar all over the former LMS system in Britain until the early 1960s; nevertheless they were rather old-fashioned, and perhaps were a surprising choice for conversion, and therefore presumably many more years' service. Some were repanelled in steel but others retained their original wooden sides. The cars worked as either three-car or six-car units, each car being powered by two 125hp Leyland engines with the drive transmitted by means of a torque-converter. In 1956 it was decided that better use could be gained from the cars if they were run as four-car units, and to achieve this 14 more carriages were converted to work as trailers, while the engines were uprated to 165hp to cope with the additional weight.

This widespread adoption of diesel railcars meant that a number of elderly steam engines and carriages belonging to the three principal railways of Ireland could at last be retired. In 1951 CIE built the first new carriages to go into service on former GSR lines since 1938, and these and the railcars enabled Inchicore to start making serious inroads into the still numerous ranks of the six-wheelers. Although the Dublin commuter had been honoured with a few new bogie carriages in the 1920s and 1930s, and there had been the Drumms, he was as likely as not in 1950 to find himself bouncing to and from work around the southern shores of Dublin Bay in a six-wheeler, and was therefore particularly happy about the new carriages. The North Dublin commuter was not half so impressed, for he had grown used to such refinements long pressed upon him by the GNR, while the Belfast suburbanite living on the former NCC line was equally *blasé*, for he might still be going to work in the carriages to which he had grown used, the only difference being that they were now self-propelled railcars. The Bangor line commuters were probably the most delighted of all with the changeover from steam haulage, even though the old County Down six-wheelers did not disappear immediately. The few bogie carriages the B&CDR had possessed were transferred to the NCC section where the last of them may still be seen at work.

Despite the recommendations of the Milne Report, CIE continued the Great Southern's practice of scrapping one or two engines from a variety of classes rather than disposing of entire types, while there were not really enough railcars at work on the GNR or the NCC section of the UTA to enable any significant reductions to be made in steam power on those lines. The change-over to railcars meant that neither the UTA nor the GNR need build any more locomotive-hauled coaches. Both companies had done so until 1950 and 51, the last GNR carriages being catering vehicles, restaurant car No 403 and buffet car No 268. They were handsome and well-proportioned coaches, as was practically every carriage that the GNR had ever built, although a lot of the later ones had to be rather skimped in certain directions. Steel panelling was costly and a number of wartime and post-war coaches had sides of a composite construction, which was virtually indistinguishable from metal when new and painted in the GNR mahogany livery, but, not surprisingly, has not lasted particularly well; indeed, by the late 1960s this was causing some rather alarming looking warping and bulging.

The last coach built new for the NCC was an interesting vehicle, a saloon with all-welded sides, constructed by the LMS for its District Engineer's use. It was sent over to Ireland before being actually put into service, however, and maintained for the NCC Chairman to live in, in case air raid damage at any time should necessitate this. Further ex-LMS carriages went into service in Ireland around the time of the UTA's formation, but these were all second-hand, and the next new coach, a dining car, came out in 1950. Although of UTA design, it retained a typically LMS appearance, as did the 18 coaches of various types which were built by the UTA in 1951. Following these all new construction was confined to railcars, and it was nearly 20 years before the next locomotive-hauled coaches entered service in the North.

CHAPTER TWENTY-ONE

The End of the Narrow-Gauge

FEW IMAGINED IN 1945 that the remaining narrow-gauge lines in Ireland would last very long once restrictions on road transport were lifted. Had it not been for the war they might have disappeared already, for the 1930s saw the demise of a fair number of them, and in the event it was somewhat surprising that one or two hung on until the beginning of the 1960s. Some were shut down for most of the war through lack of fuel, but they resumed operation afterwards, only to close again in the severe winter of 1946–7. Even then all but one refused to lie down and struggled on for a few more years.

The once extensive network of lines belonging to the NCC in the north-east corner of Ireland had all but vanished by the time the UTA came into existence, and what remained went in July 1950. They comprised the attenuated remnants of the Ballymena and Larne (some seven miles from Ballyboley to Larne) and the 16¼-mile Ballycastle branch. The four compound 2–4–2Ts active at the end lingered on in a state of inaction for some time afterwards but were eventually broken up in 1954.

One line which kept going for the first year or so of the war and then closed down and stayed closed was the Clogher Valley. It had been under sentence of death for some time, the first step towards its condemnation having come in 1928. In that year the County Councils of Fermanagh and Tyrone had taken it over in response from an appeal from the company which owned it and was no longer able to pay its way, and had appointed a managing committee. This fared no better, and by 1937 decided that the line was altogether too great a drain on the ratepayers and called on the Minister of Home Affairs to step in. He, recognising the futility of continuing the farce, agreed that the Government should take over the railway and close it down, paying off the shareholders and improving the roads in the area so that they could cope with the large fleet of double-deck buses and articulated lorries which might (or just possibly might not) be needed to cope with the traffic until then handled by the railway. There seems to have been no great urgency to carry out these laudable intentions, and it was not until the end of 1941 that the Clogher Valley Railway finally went out of business. A momento of the line survives in the shape of a small four-wheel diesel (originally steam) tractor, sold to the County Donegal in 1932, but more of this anon.

Bits of the Londonderry & Lough Swilly Railway had been dropping off since 1935. As each one went it was replaced by the company's own bus and lorry services, and as these showed much better returns it was quite clear that the days of the trains were numbered. For this reason there was never any attempt to modernise rail facilities and the L&LSR remained a totally steam-operated line until the end. By 1950 some 31 miles out of an original length of 99 miles were still being worked. These were the lines from Derry to Buncrana and Letterkenny, and at the end officially carried freight only. By this time, however, the Lough Swilly apparently possessed no goods brake-vans, so passenger brakes were used instead, and if asked the company would issue one with a ticket to travel in them. Needless to say practically the only people who did so were railway enthusiasts, the locals preferring to take the much quicker and more convenient bus service. The seats in these carriages were made of wood, and as one had to be prepared to be shunted up and down goods yards every so often along the way one had to be particularly dedicated to take much delight in this form of travel.

Nevertheless the people of Donegal were not at all happy to see the Lough Swilly slowly fall apart, and at one point were roused to such a pitch that 200 of them descended on the gang sent out to lift the abandoned Letterkenny-Burtonport extension. They gained it a short temporary reprieve, which probably did something to salve their injured pride, for no one likes to think his part of the world is so unimportant that it can do without its train service. This section was of no practical use, however, and very shortly the demolition work was resumed.

Weekend excursion trains were run to Buncrana for Derry citizens wishing to spend a day beside Lough Swilly (the "Sea-Breeze Specials"), but even this traffic was capable of being handled by bus, and the end came for the Lough Swilly trains in August 1953. The last of the two unique 4-8-0s, No 12, had been repaired quite recently and was in steam on the final day, and for some time afterwards working demolition trains, and the two 4-8-4Ts also survived, though not in steam. Along with all the 4-6-0Ts and 4-6-2Ts still in the land of the living in 1953, they were all broken up within a few months. The name "Lough Swilly" still survives, for the company's bus and lorry services continue to operate and, rather curiously, "Railway" is still incorporated in the title.

One of the Lough Swilly 4-6-0Ts, No 14, withdrawn in 1943, had a particular claim to fame, or rather notoriety, for it was involved in the worst railway disaster to have occurred in Southern Ireland since Independence. One of the principal features of the Burtonport Extension was the 360yd long Owencarrow Viaduct, an impressive piece of architecture for a narrow-gauge railway. Like the West Clare, the L&LSR possessed sections of track which were exposed to the full force of Atlantic gales, and the stretch across Owencarrow Viaduct was one such. On the night of January 30, 1925, No 14 was crossing the viaduct with a train of one goods van and three carriages during a typically ferocious storm. She took it at the prescribed 10mph and was all but over when an exceptional gust of wind, later estimated at over 100mph, lifted two of the coaches from the track, one of them going right over the edge and hanging 40ft above ground level, miraculously supported by nothing but its couplings. Not so miraculous was the fate of its passengers, however. The carriage roof was torn off and they were tipped out; and to make matters worse some rocks from the embankment adjoining the viaduct rolled down on top of them. Of the 14 passengers in the train four were killed and five seriously injured.

The heavy engine stayed on the rails, and its crew, together with the guard, who was unhurt, did what they could for the passengers. The fireman, John Hannigan, struggled three miles through the storm to summon help. At the subsequent inquiry it was recommended that the guard rail, which extended part of the length of the viaduct, should be continuous, and more important, that a wind gauge should be installed and trains halted whenever the force of the wind became excessive. One wonders why such a gauge had not been used before; the West Clare, hardly the most progressive of railways, possessed one, and the Lough Swilly had been dropped a strong hint by Providence 17 years earlier when a similar accident had occurred at the same spot, though in this case without any loss of life or injury. It was regrettable that the lives of four of its passengers had to be forfeited before the lesson got home.

The far more vigorous County Donegal put up a fierce fight for survival, a fight conceived and pursued by the Company's Secretary and General Manager, Henry Forbes. Appointed in 1910, Forbes was a pioneer in the use of the internal combustion engine on the railways. His first venture was way back in 1920 with an inspection car. This was rebuilt with a 26hp Ford petrol engine, and although not really intended for public service it was used to keep the Glenties branch going during the 1926 coal strike. It was numbered 1, and originally seated six passengers. Later it was given a 27-seat trailer to tow around, which quite transformed its usefulness and Forbes, appreciating that he had got a vehicle which was cheaper to operate than a steam train, could stop between stations, and was able to provide a more frequent service, pressed ahead with more of the same sort. In 1926 he bought two further second-hand Ford-engined four-wheelers from the defunct Derwent Valley Railway, and then in 1928 came a much larger 36hp 22-seater with a body built by a local coachbuilder, Doherty of Strabane.

Further variations on the theme materialised, including the first diesel railcar, No 7, in 1931. In 1934 there appeared No 12, the prototype of what was to become the County Donegal's standard railcar. It was a bogie vehicle, built by Walkers of Wigan; it weighed 12 tons, seated 41 passengers, and had a four-speed gearbox and coupled driving wheels. Despite its projecting bonnet it was a neat-looking machine and further examples soon followed.

The final variation was a compact full-fronted car of 102hp, the last of these coming out in 1951.

During this period Forbes continued to buy up second-hand vehicles which caught his eye, and which he felt he could make use of. These included *Phoenix*, a four-wheel steam tractor from the Clogher Valley Railway which he converted to a diesel, two railcars from the Dublin and Blessington tramway, and a chassis from the Castlederg & Victoria Bridge line. Not content with *Phoenix* being the first diesel locomotive in the British Isles Forbes added further to its distinction by combining its locomotive duties with that of weed-killer by the simple expedient of turning its sooty exhaust on to the track.

The result of all this enterprise was that while the face of every other railway manager grew longer and longer, Forbes's countenance spread happiness and light wherever he took it. A great deal of equipment was obtained at very little expense from the parent company, the GNR, and with two-thirds of the mileage in the hands of diesel and petrol traction running costs were brought down until they were no greater than those of a road transport company. The lowest adult fare was twopence, visitors were encouraged and made to feel welcome, and net receipts rose to £16,000, 25 per cent of the gross receipts, a quite remarkable achievement in the stagnant days of the 1930s.

Henry Forbes was not merely a supremely successful manager of a railway; he also possessed a fund of knowledge concerning Celtic mythology and Irish history, and knew a vast amount about the flora and fauna of Donegal. He died in November 1943, and the County Donegal was never quite the same afterwards. Whether even Forbes could have ensured its survival after the war is arguable, but ultimately the railway found road competition too much, and the last section closed down on December 31, 1959. Quite a bit of it survives, however. The original railcar, No 1, and *Phoenix* are in the Belfast Transport Museum, along with steam engine No 2, while the two most modern Walker railcars are still at work, in the Isle of Man. An American bought engines Nos 4, 5, 6 and 11, together with some carriages, and was supposed to be taking them home with him, but for ten years now they have remained at Strabane, gathering rust and decay; their future is problematical.

The one narrow-gauge line which did not get up again after being hit by the 1947 fuel crisis was the Schull and Skibbereen section of CIE. If ever a railway faded away it was this one. The fuel situation first caused it to close down in April 1944. When it came to life again the Great Southern had passed away and it found itself a part of CIE. By then the bus service from Cork to Skibbereen and Schull had taken away much of its passenger traffic, and when the 1947 fuel crisis brought operations to a halt again, officially on February 1, but in fact a few days earlier, a good many people had the feeling that this time it was for good. So it proved. Although coal supplies were back to normal by the summer no attempt was made to revive the Schull and Skibbereen, although at the same time no one actually declared the line to be closed.

The engines, carriages and wagons dumped at Skibbereen grew rustier and mouldier as the years of neglect ate through, and soon grass covered the tracks on which they stood. At last, in September 1952, CIE applied for an abandonment order, and as there were no objections the granting of it was a mere formality. Demolition began in the autumn and the three engines, 4–4–0Ts Nos 3 and 4 and 0–4–4T No 6, which originally had belonged to the Cork & Muskerry Light Railway, were loaded on to standard gauge wagons and taken to Inchicore, where they were broken up in April 1954.

A line which lost its passenger service some time before the Schull and Skibbereen but kept going as a goods only concern for a while longer was the Tralee & Dingle. In the end its sole function was to serve the cattle trade, and every month on the last Friday one and sometimes two trains would set out from Tralee through the wild hills of the peninsula to Dingle. Next day they would load up with cattle and make their way back to Tralee, where the cattle would be sold at the Fair or transferred to the broad gauge and taken further afield. The line lasted just long enough to become something of a tourist attraction, but not quite long enough for anyone to do anything about preserving it as such, and it closed on June 27, 1953. Four engines were in use at the end, and of these two were broken up in 1954 while the other two were transferred to the Cavan & Leitrim Section. There they joined a further two former T&D locomotives which had been transferred earlier, including No 5T. This engine, the line's only 2–6–2T, still exists, as it was shipped for preservation, along with T&D coach No 21, to Wakefield, Massachusetts, in June 1959. Plenty of evidence that a railway once ran through the Dingle Peninsula survives, including gates where the track used to cross the main road, bridge foundations, and the terminus at Dingle, which is now a small factory.

The last steam-worked narrow-gauge trains in the Republic were to be found on the Cavan & Leitrim section. So long as coal from the Arigna mines continued to be sent beyond the immediate locality the railway was assured of a fair amount of traffic, much of it being to Belturbet where the coal was laboriously transferred by hand to broad gauge GNR wagons. What finished it off was the building of a power station near Arigna. This took virtually all the coal mined there, and in reducing transport costs to almost nothing was an undeniably sound economic proposition. Unfortunately without the coal traffic the railway had no reason for staying in existence, the passenger traffic never having amounted to anything very significant, and it closed down in April 1959. Two of its distinctive 4–4–0Ts were preserved, No 3 *Lady Edith* going with the Tralee & Dingle 2–6–2T to the USA, while No 2 *Kathleen* stayed in Ireland at the Belfast Transport Museum.

That CIE had no doctrinaire wish to kill off the narrow gauge merely because it wan't making money is clearly shown by its treatment of the West Clare. In 1952 it was decided to give the line a new lease of life and four diesel railcars were ordered from Walkers. They were almost identical with the latest County Donegal cars, and to work with them some bogie coaches were rebuilt with bodies very like those fitted to contemporary CIE single-deck buses. Three years later the West Clare was completely dieselised, when three 230hp B-B locomotives arrived, also built by Walkers, and fitted with

power bogies similar to those used on the railcars. It was a good try, but the 3ft gauge was inherently slow, and in the end CIE had to accept the inevitable; so the West Clare shut down on January 31, 1961.

At the end it was losing £23,000 each year; it was estimated that a replacing bus service would lose no more than £4,000, and CIE, much though it might love the last surviving narrow-gauge public line in Ireland, could hardly afford to whistle away a cool £19,000 annually. Many people regretted the West Clare's going, and there was an argument for its retention as a tourist attraction, particularly if one or two of the steam engines, which were still in existence, could be put back into service. If the railway could have been kept going on the same basis as the Welsh narrow gauge lines its future would have been assured, but one should remember that in 1961 few could have foreseen just how popular these would prove and in any case no one actually came up with a viable scheme for working the West Clare with volunteer labour.

One man who was not at all sorry to see the last of the West Clare was the CIE Chairman, Dr C. S. Andrews. Previously head of Bord na Mona, Andrews succeeded T. C. Courtney, who continued as a part-time member of the CIE Board, in September 1958. He was something of a Doctor Beeching and cared little for the railways as such. In his own words "It appears to me immaterial whether a required service is provided by truck, horse and cart, aeroplane, helicopter or hovercraft. In fact we find in many cases the horse and cart are still the cheapest way to carry goods and we use many horse-drawn vehicles for city deliveries. If stage coaches or cabs met the situation better, we would use them". Like Doctor Beeching, Andrews felt that if the railway system was to survive the unremunerative branches would have to go as quickly as possible, and on one occasion he got rid of a section of line with such rapidity (the West Cork routes) that he by-passed some of the due processes of the law and rather burnt his fingers. One should note that Andrews stressed that some form of public transport should always be provided when a railway line closed, and although he met with a fair amount of opposition both within and without CIE, given that he was expected to make it pay sooner or later the economic principles implicit in substituting road for rail services in the remoter rural areas were unimpeachable. At that time CIE was getting a grant of £1,175,000 from the government, which would go on until 1962, by which time it was hoped that CIE would be able to break even. The £19,000 saved by the closing of the West Clare was a step in this direction.

Andrews said that the railway was "probably the most expensive monument ever erected to a poet", but Percy French had the last laugh, for a permanent reminder of the gentle fun he poked at the West Clare now stands in the yard of Ennis station in the form of a statue of him, a few yards in front of one of the unpredictable engines which "Michael" used to drive. This is an 0–6–2T No 5 *Slieve Callan*, one of the locomotives with trailing wheels as large as the coupled ones, mounted on a plinth and protected from the weather by an awning. She is more cosseted now than she ever was in the days when she was active, receiving fresh coats of red, white and green paint whenever her gloss begins to fade, and probably also earning more money from the tourists

who come to Ennis to have a look at her and the Percy French memorial.

The assumption is usually made that with the end of the West Clare the 3ft gauge ceased to exist in Ireland. As far as public railways go this is true, but an extensive system of industrial lines continued and is still very active. Bord na Mona (Irish Peat Board) moves over 4m tons of peat each year, and to do this it relies to a large extent on light railways which can be laid over the soft boggy land, and taken up again and put down somewhere else when a particular bog is exhausted. The West Clare railcars and the diesel engines were taken over by Bord na Mona and were added to its fleet of 250 locomotives and 2,000 wagons.

It is surprising that so little interest seems to be taken by enthusiasts in the Bord na Mona railways, for they form a remarkably large and complex system in a country the size of Ireland; indeed, their 500 miles equal something like a quarter of the total 5ft 3in gauge mileage in the 32 Counties. While some of the Bord na Mona track is of a temporary nature, a great deal of it is permanent and includes some impressive engineering features. The latest of these is the recently completed 500ft long Garryduff bridge over the Shannon in County Offaly, an elegant reinforced concrete structure of seven spans. The Turf Development Board was formed in 1934, under Dr Andrews, and became Bord na Mona in 1946. While it is a state concern, it is expected to make a profit and does so, and the railways, in which some £4½m are invested, are a vital part of its operations.

In the years immediately after 1946 a large number of Deutz and Ruston four-wheel diesel engines of up to 48hp were put into service, but something more powerful was needed, and as there was nothing suitable on the market the Board's Chief Mechanical Engineer, W. A. R. Green, designed and built his own. This weighed 9.4 tons in working order, including two tons of ballast; its 80hp engine gave it a top speed of 20mph and enabled it to pull up to 100 tons of loaded bogie wagons. Tenders were put out and Hunslet was awarded the contract to build 53 of them, known as "Wagon-Masters". A fascinating little vehicle used by senior staff for getting about the bogs, and for moving maintenance men quickly to breakdowns, is a four-wheel railcar, designed and built by the board. There are ten of these, powered by Ford Prefect car engines, and they go buzzing about the workings like rail-borne jeeps. Turf-burning Barclay steam well tank engines were tried out in 1949 but they proved uneconomical, and all three were withdrawn. One is preserved at Stradbally and may be seen in steam at the annual Steam Fair there, and the other two are also still in existence despite their very short working life with Bord na Mona.

Track is constantly being lifted and relaid and repaired by three-man teams, who have the use of 12 electric rail-mounted track-layers, based on a Russian design, and various other pieces of equipment, including crawler tractors. The latter, however, can cause damage to the bog surface and are not employed if rail-borne equipment can do the job. The bogs are mostly in the Midlands, rather off the beaten track and not in the areas favoured by tourists, which probably accounts for much of the lack of interest in the railways. The Clonsast Group in County Offaly is perhaps the most accessible, and passengers on the CIE line from Portarlington to Athlone may well catch sight of one of the Bord na Mona trains at work as their train passes over the 3ft gauge line four miles west of Portarlington station. No road vehicle could move over the bogs nor pull the considerable loads with which the railway engines are required to cope, and as long as turf continues to be dug in Ireland Bord na Mona will need its railways.

The two narrow-gauge tram lines which survived World War II both succumbed in the late 1940s, the Bassbrook & Newry going in January 1948, the Giant's Causeway a year later. The last tram-line of all in Ireland was the broad gauge Hill of Howth route, belonging to the GNR, which lasted until 1961. There was certainly a case to be made out for retaining this as a tourist attraction, rather like the Blackpool trams but on a much smaller scale, for the open-top cars were popular on fine days right until the end. It was a very pleasant ride from either Howth or Sutton stations up the wooded slopes of the Hill to the summit, with its magnificent views across Dublin Bay and the open sea. The 5½-mile run from Howth up the Hill and back down the opposite side to Sutton took 30min, the track being single with passing loops. There were ten double-deck cars, eight painted blue-and-white and two with the teak finish once used on Great Northern railway carriages. Two survive, one in the Belfast Transport Museum and one at the Tram Museum at Crich in Derbyshire.

The last Irish railway to remain in the ownership of a British concern based in London was the Dundalk, Newry & Greenore. This, on January 1, 1948, became the property of the British Transport Commission, although it continued to be worked by the GNR as it had been in LMS days. It had been losing money for many years, despite the popularity of Greenore as a holiday resort during World War II, which had given the railway a temporary boost. By the end of 1945 much of this traffic was beginning to fall a way and with the cattle trade drastically declining from 114,000 head in 1938 to a mere 6,800 in 1949 and 1950 the BTC decided that the time had come to call a halt. It suggested to the Republic and to Northern Ireland that as they were discussing the take-over of the Great Northern they might like to include the Dundalk, Newry & Greenore in the deal. The BTC can hardly have been surprised when the offer was politely declined. There was nothing left but to come to terms over compensation and announce a closing date. This was December 31, 1951, and the last British Railways ship, the *Slieve League*, sailed from Greenore to Holyhead two days earlier.

Only one of the Ramsbottom 0–6–0STs, *Greenore*, was still in steam at the end, most workings being in the hands of GNR AL class 0–6–0s and JT 2–4–2Ts. Remarkably, the mid-Victorian six-wheeled carriages, also of pure LNWR design and still, in 1951, wearing that long-defunct company's purple-brown and spilt milk livery, lined out in yellow, predominated on the passenger trains. It was confidently stated at the time that one of the 0–6–0STs was to be preserved, but although the five lingered on for some while after the closure they were all broken up by the end of 1952. Happily a carriage was rescued, and is now safely ensconced in the Belfast Museum, where visitors may seat themselves on its studded cushions and marvel that such a vehicle was still in regular service with the British Transport Commission in 1951.

A total of £126,000 was realised by the sale of DN&GR property after the closure, but this was hardly sufficient to cover the arrears of interest which by then amounted to getting on for £500,000. The annual loss was £50,000, and one can hardly blame the BTC for getting shot of it as quickly as decency allowed.

CHAPTER TWENTY-TWO

Dieselisation, the Second Stage

IT HAD NEVER been the intention of CIE to make widespread use of diesel railcars on long-distance services, but they were employed on such duties in their early years and proved very popular with the travelling public. The heaviest passenger trains and virtually all goods trains continued to be steam-worked, hauled by locomotives of obsolete design, while the motive power situation was further handicapped by poor fuel and shortage of replacement parts. Despite the recommendations of the Milne Report and the CME's predilection for the steam engine, it was becoming increasingly clear that any new engines purchased by CIE would be diesel-powered. It was estimated that the annual economy in fuel costs alone would amount to almost £1m if the switch was made from coal to oil; also far fewer power units would be needed to do the same amount of work and, as the situation was critical and a great deal of money would have to be spent immediately on new locomotives, whether steam or diesel, the greater initial cost of the latter would be more than compensated for by the economies effected once the engines were in service.

A scheme was therefore drawn up for the entire dieselisation of CIE; this was passed by the Government and the capital expenditure necessary for the changeover was approved by the board. Three power groups of locomotives would be required to cover all duties, the first of between 1,100 and 1,400hp for main line passenger and goods services, the latter to run at night so that a locomotive could work one of the principal passenger expresses during the day and then take over a heavy night goods; the second a smaller 550–700hp type diesel for secondary mixed traffic duties; and the third a 350hp shunting and light goods design. It will be noted that even by the standards of the early 1950s the most powerful group of engines was not to be anything particularly impressive, considerably less powerful than the original LMS or Southern main line diesels, and well below the maximum capabilities of the 800 class Great Southern steam engines. Six or seven bogie vehicles were about the maximum for most main line passenger trains, the Cork Mails being very much an exception, and any unusually onerous tasks could be catered for by double-heading.

Tenders were invited in 1953 for the supply of diesel locomotives and 31 were received from many different countries. Some consideration was given to purchasing locomotives with hydraulic, rather than electric, transmissions, but this was found to have no economic advantage, and as its use was not very widespread it was decided to standardise on diesel-electrics. One rather gets the impression that the Chief Mechanical Engineer's Department would have liked the order to go to America, and the subsequent history of the diesel-electric in Ireland shows quite clearly why, but political and economic considerations determined otherwise. This, it must be remembered, was at a time when dollars were in short supply on this side of the Atlantic, and the contract therefore was awarded to Metropolitan–Vickers for 60 1,200hp Co-Cos and 34 550hp Bo-Bos, all with Crossley engines, at a total cost of £4,750,000. Subsequently CIE decided to go in for some small diesel-hydraulics and ordered 19 400hp Maybach engines and Mekydro transmissions from Germany for assembly at Inchicore.

The A class, as the 1,200hp diesels were to be known, were erected in the former LNER carriage and wagon shops at Dukinfield, Manchester, the mechanical parts having been built by Metro-Cammell in Birmingham, while the engines came from the Crossley Works in another part of Manchester. Early in July 1955, they began to arrive in Dublin, and after the final touches had been carried out at Inchicore trials began on the Dublin–Cork main line. The As were neat, if unexciting-looking machines, painted in a metallic silver-grey livery, unadorned save for the CIE emblem on either side and the number on the sides and ends, carried on two six-wheel bogies and with a body length much shorter than that of contemporary English main line diesels.

With the trials completed the "As" began to go into service in the late autumn; by February 20, 1956, the first stage of the dieselisation of the Southern Section of CIE was complete. There were 14 locomotives operating 4,600 train miles daily between Kingsbridge, Cork, Youghal, Limerick and Waterford, each locomotive averaging 328 miles per day. This latter figure was much in excess of anything achieved by steam, and bore out the contention that the change-over would result in a reduction in the numbers of locomotives needed. The highest rostered daily average involved two As working three return trips between them on the main line, one going down from Kingsbridge on the 6.30am, returning from Cork at 11.55am and going back again on the 8.00pm, while its fellow came up from Cork on the 7.45am, went back on the 2.25pm and completed its day on the 8.30pm back from Cork. In all each locomotive covered 496 miles daily. By the end of February 66 per cent of the Dublin–Cork mileage, passenger and goods, was worked by A Class engines, 21 per cent by diesel railcars and a mere 13 per cent by steam.

February 1956 saw two more notable stages in the spread of diesel power. A class engines began to work over the Midland section, and the 950hp

Sulzer diesel engines, ordered before the Milne Report, at last went into action. Instead of working in tandem, as had been the original intention, they were used to power 12 A1A-A1A locomotives, with body-work by the Birmingham Railway Carriage & Wagon Company and Metrovick transmissions. Like the A class they had clean, but not very inspiring lines; it is difficult to detect any family likeness between them and the British Rail Birmingham-Sulzer Type 2s and 3s, although the front end is reminiscent of the Metrovick gas turbine. The CIE Birmingham-Sulzers, numbered B101-112, have always worked on the Southern Section, originally on the Dublin–Waterford line on goods and passenger trains, but latterly they have mostly been confined to goods workings on the Dublin–Cork main line. Like the first two main line diesels, also engined by Sulzers, they have given very little trouble and have proved to be an excellent investment.

By January 1957, the last A had been delivered and Metropolitan–Vickers switched to production of her smaller sister, the C class Bo-Bo. The types closely resemble each other in appearance, particularly from the front; from the side the 550hp type diesel is noticeably shorter. There were 34 Cs and they were put to work on a variety of secondary duties, including branch lines such as that to Valentia, the most westerly railway line in Europe after the closure of the Tralee and Dingle. By the middle of 1958 CIE had 138 diesel locomotives at work, including the three narrow-gauge ones built in 1955 for the West Clare. The broad-gauge fleet consisted of the 60 A class, the 12 Bs, the 34 Cs, the 19 Maybach-engined, Inchicore-built shunters, Nos E401–419, the five original shunters, the original main line Bo-Bos, and three tiny four-wheel 130hp Deutz diesel-hydraulics, Nos G101–3, which performed such lightweight duties as hauling the single-coach Loughrea branch train.

To cope with this rapid change-over from steam CIE had done some hard thinking and had carefully prepared the ground. A driver did not exactly step off the footplate of a steam engine one evening and into the cab of a diesel the next morning and drive it away; indeed, a great deal of patient training had to be gone through before that could happen. First of all the engineering staff—the men who were going to have to maintain the new diesels—were sent off on six-month courses to the various works where the engines were being manufactured; this was part of the contract, written in by CIE and accepted by each firm that supplied it with engines. Fitters and electricians visited factories in England and Germany between November 1954, and March 1956, and while all this was going on preparations were being made to get drivers ready for the change-over. A few had already gained diesel experience on the early main line locomotives and shunters, and many more were familiar with the railcars, but now Inchicore had to look towards the time when every driver would be qualified to handle diesels. Four technical assistants and four locomotive inspectors went on a course of training at Metropolitan–Vickers works, and on their return a simulator—a replica of a diesel cab—was set up and the training programme for drivers went into action.

It was divided into three parts. First the drivers were shown the principal features of a diesel locomotive, and exactly what made it tick; then they were tried out on the simulator; and finally they were taken out on the road and under strict supervision allowed to get the feel of a diesel in operation. A driver was examined at the end of each stage and not allowed to pass on to the next until it was clear that he was competent to do so. In fact most drivers took very happily to the new form of motive power, for the change offered prospects of far less physical exertion and much cleaner and more comfortable working conditions.

A serious problem, inevitably, was the fate of the fireman, the second man. Tied up with this was the question of redundancy, for not only was a fireman not needed, but with the greater availability of the diesels fewer drivers were required, and the contraction of the CIE network, which by the late 1950s was becoming considerable, aggravated the problem. With the introduction of diesel shunters and railcars agreements had been reached with the unions over single manning, but one-man operation of main line locomotives was another matter, involving loss of employment on a much larger scale. Eventually CIE pushed ahead, presenting the unions with a *fait accompli*, but at the same time providing that all drivers should retain their grades and all firemen no longer needed for footplate duties would be transferred to other departments with no loss of pay. Drivers between the ages of 60 and 65, a considerable proportion of the top-link men, were persuaded to retire early on full pension, which many of them did, and in this way, together with natural wastage, many of the redundancies were absorbed without too much hardship or ill-feeling.

A number of major alterations were carried out at Inchicore at this time. The boiler and tender shops, which were totally unsiitable for handling diesel traction, received particular attention. A total of £64,000 was spent on converting the boiler shop into the Diesel No 2 Shop, where railcar engines and transmission parts from locomotives could be dealt with, and on one side of it were erected four bays, with ramps where servicing on diesel locomotives could be carried out without removing the engines. The erecting shops, put up in 1935 and used for the building of the 800s and for heavy repairs on all types of steam engines, were also adapted for dealing with diesels, although here the reconstruction had no need to be so extensive, such equipment as the overhead cranes and traverser serving steam and diesel locomotives equally well.

Despite all this steam had not yet vanished from Southern Ireland. In mid-1958, on completion of the initial dieselisation programme, CIE still possessed 242 steam engines, and the small boys of Ireland still had something for which to go train-spotting. As a matter of fact, train spotters did not form a particularly large section of the juvenile male population, and the hobby, even in steam days, never caught on as it did in Britain. Whether the absence of a model railway manufacturer who based his products on Irish prototypes had something to do with it is a moot point; it may be that the converse applies. There have been many scratch-built Irish models, the most celebrated collection being C. L. Fry's Dublin layout, and recently a model railway shop has opened in Grafton Street, Dublin's most exclusive shopping thoroughfare. Among the usual British and European products here has been some splendid GNR ones, so it may be that an attempt is being made by the trade to open up the Irish market; one wonders if it is ever likely to prove large enough to be lucrative.

In anticipation of the arrival of the diesels, and because CIE had always had far more steam engines than it was ever likely to need, the withdrawal programme was put into effect in late 1954. Amongst the first victims were four of the older 4-6-0s and two Woolwich Moguls. All were extremely run-down and would have needed extensive renewals to keep them in the land of the living much longer. On the other hand seven Maunsell Moguls were given overhauls in the winter of 1954-5, to enable them to continue to work the principal Midland goods and passenger services, and certain Southern Section duties. It had been recommended in a report drawn up by the CME's office in 1954 that 20 of the class be kept in good condition for a while longer, and that one 4-6-0, No 500, which shared heavy freight duties with the 2-6-0s on the Dublin-Cork line, should be similarly treated. In the event the Traffic Department concluded it could get by without going to such expense, and with the withdrawal of No 502 in 1957 the class became extinct. Two of the Queens, Nos 801 and 802, were relegated to goods trains on the arrival of the first As, and after a boiler inspection early in 1956 No 802 *Tailte* was not steamed again. A year later she was cut up at Inchicore, one or two parts being used to keep her sister, No 801, on the road for a little longer. No 800 *Maeve*, probably because, even in her twilight days, she was regarded as something special, was seldom reduced to the indignities of her sisters. She was repainted in GSR livery for an exhibition at Inchicore in 1956, and she was also on show there two years later; in between she worked a few seasonal extra passenger trains on the main line.

Although there were officially 35 4-4-0s on CIE's books in 1958 very few were capable of earning their living; most of them were dumped at Waterford, Limerick and elsewhere awaiting the cutter's torch, and by 1960 the only one remaining at work was a Coey D11, No 301. She had been distinguished in her early days by bearing the name *Victoria*, a rare distinction for a GS&WR engine. One of her three sisters, No 304, had an even greater honour bestowed upon her, for she had been named *Princess Ena* by a grand-daughter of Queen Victoria, Princess Victoria Eugenie, who had accompanied the old Queen on her tour of Ireland in 1900. The Princess, who was in her late teens and a popular figure with the general public, was prevailed upon to visit Inchicore and name the then brand new No 304 after herself, Princess Ena being the name by which she was affectionately known. The Princess later became Queen of Spain and as such was rather a tragic figure. On her wedding day an attempt was made on the life of her husband, and although the Royal couple escaped Princess Ena's white dress was spattered with the blood of a less fortunate bystander; later she was forced to flee Spain before the Civil War in 1936. She lived to be a very old lady, dying in 1969, ten years after the engine she had named in 1900 had passed to the scrapheap.

A great onslaught was made about this time on CIE tank engines. Old and not so old, they disappeared almost while their driver's backs were turned, and only 28 were still intact in 1958. Of these ten might be said to have been relatively up-to-date, six Bandon tanks, the Bandon goods still being steam-operated, and the four GSR 0–6–2Ts, which found employment on the few remaining steam-worked Bray suburban trains. The big Inchicore 2–6–2T, No 850, went in 1955.

By far the commonest type was the 0–6–0, which still found plenty to do in the way of branch line and secondary goods work and a few passenger turns. Not surprisingly, most of these 0–6–0s were J15s, the oldest of them by now having got within ten years of its centenary. Throughout their Great Southern and CIE careers they had borne the same livery, unlined grey, although this soon came to resemble a faded shade of black. From about the end of World War II the numberplates on the cab sides were removed and replaced by large painted numerals, and in the mid-1950s any engine it was considered worth repainting had the grey livery replaced by black. Athough not often repainted, and in most cases rather run down, Southern Irish steam locomotives in their last years did their best to put a good face on their decline, and were noticeably cleaner than most of their counterparts on British Railways.

Before dieselisation had been decided upon certain of the larger engines were considerably brightened by the acquisition of a coat of green paint, rather similar to that of the Queens. All the 400 and 500 class 4–6–0s and the Woolwich Moguls were so adorned, as was a motley collection of passenger tank engines working the former D&SER suburban services. In the latter case such an engine might be the only one of its class so treated; Bandon tank No 467 was one. There were also three ex-GS&WR 4–4–0s painted green. Not all these engines retained their green livery until their demise and some reverted to black before withdrawal.

Bulleid had little to do with the design of the main line diesels, these chiefly being the responsibility of Metropolitan-Vickers and Crossleys. He had kept a close eye on their progress, however, as they neared completion, and at one point had refused to accept delivery of the 'As' unless a particular modification was carried out. With coaches and wagons Bulleid's hand was more clearly seen although in broad outline Inchicore practice was continued.

The first post-war CIE carriages came out in 1951, three years before Bulleid's reign at Inchicore began, and were conventional vehicles, side-corridor, wooden-framed, steel-panelled, 60ft long composites. They looked very like the last pre-war GSR coaches, and were pleasant enough both to look upon and to travel in, although they were not quite as well proportioned as contemporary GNR corridor stock. Many more similar carriages followed, some of them open seconds, and there were also 14 buffet cars, built at Inchicore in 1953 and 1954. Nothing like so many catering vehicles had ever before been built in Ireland in so short a time, and their advent meant that many older ones from the pre-amalgamation companies could be withdrawn. Amongst these was No 343, one of the four original, clerestory-roofed, GS&WR dining cars which had worked the first services, between Kingstown, Kingsbridge and Cork in 1898.

When Bulleid arrived a number of composites and seconds were in process of construction, and he immediately put his own stamp upon them by introducing triangulated underframes and Commonwealth bogies. The latter are familiar enough to English readers but the former may need some explanation. The ends of each all-welded frame were arranged, as the name suggests, in the shape of a triangle, the purpose being to increase the longitudinal strength of the frame. A quick glance at the framing above the bogie of any modern CIE carriage will give one a good idea of the principle employed.

With these interim vehicles out of the way Bulleid got down to producing an entirely new carriage, 40 coming out in the summer of 1955. In their own way they were as ugly as the suburban multiple unit electrics that Bulleid built for the Southern, but at the same time they were ideally suited for high capacity, short-distance work. It is curious how Bulleid seemed almost to go out of his way to produce locomotives and carriages of rather repulsive aspect, and one can hardly claim that this widely held opinion is the automatic reaction to something new, for many innovations on the British and Irish railways subsequent to Bulleid have been much more happily accepted.

The 1955 carriages were of integral construction, very light in weight (26 tons) while being unusually wide. The two features which chiefly made such a mess of any aesthetic pretentions they might have had were the variation in width between the outer vestibules, which were 9ft 6in, and the main centre section, which was 10ft 2in, and a bulge protruding over the length of the latter. This was a strengthening waist rail, put on the outside to allow the maximum space inside. These coaches had corridor connections but no lavatories. Whilst not looked upon with favour by the enthusiast, who regretted the demise of the older wooden-bodied stock which they replaced, they were greatly appreciated by the general public. Later on another ten were built for main line service and these had lavatories. The entire batch was assembled at Inchicore from prefabricated parts supplied by Park Royal, by which name the carriages are generally known.

Some similar but much less peculiar-looking coaches came out in 1956. The exteriors were tidied up, the sides being flush and the 10ft 2in width extending over their whole length; internally they were little different from the Park Royals. In appearance they set a standard for the next few years, although their unpainted aluminium livery was not perpetuated. At this time all third class vehicles became seconds, and for a time carried a large "2" on their doors.

Although the non-bogie passenger-carrying vehicle was at last disappearing from the Irish scene new four-wheel vehicles designed to run in passenger trains were coming out of Inchicore in considerable numbers. These were the steam-heating vans introduced in 1955 to work with the diesel locomotives. The problem of heating carriages in winter was one which gave rise to considerable rumination when the decision was taken to replace the steam engine with the diesel, and CIE, unlike British Railways, came to the conclusion that the most satisfactory answer was to provide separate units. This had the advantage of flexibility, doing away with the need for the locomotive to be encumbered in the summer months with a lot of unnecessary equipment, but it did mean that in winter it had an extra vehicle to haul. This was partly offset by incorporating a guard's van and luggage section in each heating van. When work on them was completed Inchicore went on to produce 66 similar luggage-vans without heating apparatus. Both types initially were unpainted and cannot be said to have looked any the better for it.

The celebrated triangulated underframe was applied to goods, as well as passenger stock, and has been used extensively since 1953. The standard postwar open and covered wagons were of all-metal construction, and generally without vacuum brakes; as in Britain at that time most goods trains were loose-coupled and proceeded at a funeral pace. The advent of diesels made it possible for them to be generally speeded up, although there was still little danger of one overtaking the average cyclist, providing he had the wind behind him. An example of the dangers of working unbraked goods trains at any pace occurred at Cahir on the Waterford to Limerick Junction line on December 21, 1955, when a beet special made up of 32 laden wagons got out of control coming down the bank above the station. The engine, Woolwich Mogul No 375, was apparently unable to hold it, and as there was a mail train standing in the station the signalman, seeing No 375's predicament, diverted her into a siding. Her pace, however, hardly slackened and she burst through the buffer stops at the end at a speed estimated to be between 30 and 35mph, plunged on to the viaduct across the River Suir beyond the station and through the floor of the first span and into the water below, taking with her 22 wagons and her driver and fireman, both of whom were drowned. With them went any satisfactory explanation of the accident beyond the obvious one that the train had got out of control. The viaduct was out of use for some three weeks, and although No 375 was recovered from the river it was not considered worth while to repair her and she was cut up.

By a curious coincidence a somewhat similar accident occurred half-an-hour later on the same night, at Mallow, not so very far away. This time the engine involved was a diesel, No A14. She was at the head of the night goods from Kingsbridge to Cork and ran into the back of a mail train. Although the rear four vehicles of this were destroyed they were fortunately empty, and as the mail train had just begun to move the impact on the rest of the train was not as severe as it might have been and no one was hurt. A somewhat remarkable epilogue to this accident was the fate of A14, for she was out of service for four-and-a-half years. Considering that she was only a few weeks old in December 1955, and that the class was still in production, one is at a loss to account for this prolonged licking of her wounds.

CHAPTER TWENTY-THREE

The Beddy Report

DESPITE THE dieselisation programme it was clear that CIE was still not making the hoped-for progress towards solvency, and in the summer of 1956 the Government decided to call for another report into the state of public transport in Southern Ireland. This time the members of the Inquiry were drawn from a wider field than those who served on the 1948 one, and were principally businessmen with a great deal of experience in commerce in Ireland; the Chairman was Dr James Beddy, a Dublin educated economist. They were asked to report back to the Minister for Industry and Commerce by November 1, 1956. This proved to be a highly optimistic date, however, for despite holding 37 full day meetings the Inquiry was not completed until May 4, 1957.

Its first concern was to examine the balance sheet of CIE. For the year ending March 31, 1956, the undertaking could show receipts totalling £14,615,389, an all-time high. Unfortunately an even greater effort had been put into spending the money and £15,130,995 had been paid out, another record. The saddest aspect of the balance sheet was the deficit recorded by the railways, £1,223,222, without which CIE as a whole would have come close to making a profit. It was not quite such a big deficit as had been recorded in the two worst years, 1952–53, but it was bad enough and almost twice the 1955 figure. The road passenger side of the business, on the other hand, as ever showed a handsome profit, of over £680,000; road freight netted £82,000, and hotels, refreshment rooms and restaurant cars made £29,000. But it seemed that CIE was not cut out for adventure on the high seas, for it lost money on its boats (on the canals, the Shannon cruises, and the Aran Isles service), and on its docks, harbours and wharves. The obvious conclusion was that if it wanted to make a profit CIE should give up any ambitions towards the railways, forsake its hankerings for the seafaring life, and stick to the more mundane business of providing the public with bed, breakfast, buses and road freight services.

But of course it was not as simple as that. Before we take a look at what the Inquiry suggested might be done to remove CIE from the red, we had first better see how it got there, or rather how it failed to get out, since the 1948 Report had also suggested various courses which ought to have achieved this end. Theory is one thing, practice another and the Milne Report's pious hopes for a "progressive increase in traffic and reduction in expenditure" had not materialised. The 1948 Report had seen little necessity for any significant reduction in the railway network of Ireland, and yet here was another report less than ten years later seriously considering the total abandonment of the railway system, for this was one of the solutions at which Beddy and his colleagues looked. How had circumstances altered so drastically?

Statistics will not give us the complete answer. If anything CIE's position had improved, for the excess of railway expenditure over receipts was less in percentage terms in 1956 than in 1947. What had changed was the attitude of the people. The railway was no longer the Nation's lifeline. The number of private cars in the Republic had risen from under 52,000 in 1947 to over 136,000 in 1956. In the same period the size of the population had hardly altered, remaining at around 2½m. Relatively, Ireland is a sparsely populated country, at least by Western European standards, and it has a greater mileage of roads per head of the population than any other. Consequently the likelihood of its roads becoming so choked with traffic that it would be necessary to keep the railways open as an alternate means of transport, whatever the cost, was extremely remote. Only Spain had less cars per mile of road than Ireland and there was no Western European country which even approached Ireland's extremely low figure of 0.75 commercial vehicles per mile of road. The men who compiled the Milne Report had had a lifetime's experience working the densely trafficked routes of England where without the railways commerce could hardly have continued. They did not see clearly enough that Ireland was a very different case. By the mid-1950s it was beginning to be realised that the modern motor vehicle operating on an extensive system of well surfaced roads might easily put the railways completely out of business.

With CIE as the operator of 88 per cent of the road freight mileage and 38 per cent of the road passenger mileage, as well as 84 per cent of the rail mileage, it might not have been thought unreasonable for the Republic to opt for the abandonment of its uneconomic railways, and to transfer their traffic to its profit-making road services. It could follow, if it chose, the example of the Londonderry & Lough Swilly Railway, which had done just that and had turned an overall loss into a profit. But CIE tried a different tack and asked, not for the first time, for a restriction on private road freight transport. One gets the clear impression that whatever the economic facts CIE was not really interested in road transport, either its own or anyone elses, and felt that the only civilised way for the population and its merchandise to move around the country was in a railway train. It was gracious enough to admit that if people chose to buy nasty little tin boxes for their own amusement, and drove these into the first traffic jam they could find, it was their own affair and there was no point in the Government trying to pass laws about it, but it objected strongly to competition from road hauliers on the long-distance routes between the principal towns.

In 1925 there had been 4,950 commercial goods vehicles, in 1947 18,736, and in 1956 41,597. From virtually nothing in 1925 the amount of merchandise carried on the roads had risen by 1956 to over 2,586,000 tons, *plus* 521,000 head of livestock. On the railways the merchandise position had remained almost static, 2,317,000 tons being carried in 1955 against 2,298,000 tons in 1925, but there had been a steady fall in livestock, for the 1956 figure was less than a third of that in 1925.

CIE suggested that if road haulage was restricted so that all long-distance traffic (initially 50 miles and over) was compelled to go by rail the trailway network could be more efficiently utilised and costs brought down. This sort of proposition has been put forward many times in many countries, and there is a good deal to be said for it. A continual procession of heavy lorries trundling through towns and villages and along narrow winding country roads never intended to carry such traffic is a hazard to children and old people, frustrates the private motorist caught up in it, and is an annoyance to practically everyone else. Unfortunately for CIE, however, such conditions do not apply in Ireland.

The Rev A. W. V. Mace relates the story of how one day in 1954 he met a policeman taking a short cut along a railway line because "These days the roads are so choked with traffic" as the constable put it. In the subsequent three-quarters of an hour Mr Mace counted on the road three cars, two bicycles and a woman with a pram. Possibly this was two cars and a bicycle more than he might have met 20 years earlier, but it still fell rather short of autobahn standards. This is not to say that there were not some Irish roads that did on occasion become congested, but these were all in the few large towns and cities and particularly in Dublin. The railways had lost a lot of short-haul traffic, but equally they had acquired a considerable share of the increasing long-distance business as the figures for the average lengths of haul bear out. In 1925 it was 59 miles, whereas in the year ending March 31, 1956, it was 85 miles.

Therefore the main effect of forcing traffic conveyed by road on to the railways would have resulted in increased handling costs, owing to the short distance that much of it would be travelling. Far from enabling the railways to reduce their rates they might well have had to raise them, and everyone would have been the loser. By increasing its long-distance goods traffic CIE had shown that there was a definite need for a rail network, but the catch was that it only kept this traffic by holding its charges at an artificially low level. If it increased them the traffic would go on to the roads, even if they were less suited to the conveyance of some classes of goods, and CIE's dilemma was thus not so much how to increase its traffic, but rather how to handle the traffic it already had more efficiently.

Passenger traffic was in a very similar position to freight, the figures for 1956 not being so very different to those of 1938. The latter was somewhat higher, 11,587,000 journeys against 8,920,000, but if the Dublin commuters will forgive my drawing a parallel between them and livestock, it was a similar decline in their numbers which was largely responsible for the difference. Suburban journeys had decreased by 2,829,000 per year, leaving a mere 253,000 passengers lost throughout the rest of the system. As this was 258 miles smaller it meant that there were actually a number of services doing more business in 1955 than in 1938. This had been particularly noticeable in the two years prior to 1956, passenger journeys increasing from 8,104,000 in 1953–4 to 8,188,000 in 1954–5 and 8,920,000 in 1955–6. This was an encouraging trend and was attributed to two principal factors, the introduction of the diesel rail-cars and the development of excursion traffic. Under the latter heading came the Radio Trains, the Knock Shrine pilgrimages and

Gaelic Athletic Association specials. Ireland's rail network being small in comparison to Britain's, really heavy excursion traffic can make a considerable difference to traffic returns and the Knock pilgrimage traffic is an annual source of very welcome revenue to CIE. It is an event which has no parallel on the English side of the Irish Sea; the Durham Miners' Gala might once have had something in common with it, and the annual excursion of the Orangemen from Liverpool to Southport might be thought something of the same order, but it really bears little resemblance to what happens at Knock.

Knock is a village in County Mayo, the nearest railway station being Claremorris, the junction for the Ballina, Westport, Athenry and Athlone lines. In the early 1930s the Knock Shrine Society was founded, and the annual pilgrimage which had begun in the 1880s, after a number of devout people had experienced a series of well-authenticated supernatural visions in the vicinity, began to assume a national rather than a merely local character. The numbers had increased to such an extent that by 1954 CIE was operating 232 special trains between April and October and conveying 102,899 passengers in them. The specials came from all over Ireland, from such centres in the Six Counties as Belfast, Newry and Lurgan, and from within the Republic along a number of branches not normally worked by passenger trains, as well as over the more usual routes. The longest distance covered by any of the specials was the 248½ miles from Great Victoria Street station, Belfast, via Amiens Street, Glasnevin Junction and Mullingar, followed by the 231¼ miles of the Wexford trains, which reached Claremorris by way of Dublin and Athlone.

As can be imagined a great deal of organisation was needed to cope with the specials at Claremorris. On the busiest day of all there were 22 trains, although the advent of the diesel railcar had reduced the number of engine movements and eased matters somewhat. Buses were laid on to carry the pilgrims the seven miles from Claremorris to Knock, and then to bring them back again, and a number of ambulances, some of them converted buses, were needed for the stretcher cases. Ambulance coaches, a feature of CIE passenger stock, were included in some of the trains and almost all of them were equipped with restaurant cars. These were an absolute necessity, for some of the pilgrims might have had to leave before midnight on the Saturday and would not arrive back home until the early hours of Monday morning.

The greatest number of passengers carried on the Knock specials in any pre-war year had been 15,508, so it will be seen that the 102,899 of 1954 was an enormous advance. Perhaps the busiest day the Irish railways ever experienced in peacetime was Saturday, June 26, 1949. On that date the Pioneer Total Abstinence Association, to which most young Catholics belong and almost as many subsequently leave, celebrated its Jubilee in Dublin, while there were two important Gaelic Athletic Association matches elsewhere. In all 45 specials were run, three to Kilkenny, 11 to Limerick and 31 to Dublin, and at Amiens Street no fewer than 27 trains (20 of them specials) arrived within 4½hr. The operational problems must have been colossal, but it all seems to have gone off smoothly.

Nevertheless whatever CIE did in an effort to increase its receipts was bedevilled by soaring fuel and labour costs. In a wider sphere the last-mentioned increase was to be applauded, for it meant that the lower-paid workers at last were beginning to achieve a reasonable standard of living. This of course applied throughout industry in Ireland, but whereas the bus services, ports, and so on were able to absorb rising costs by increasing their business and efficiency, the railways were unable to do the same. There were still many stations which saw no more than half-a-dozen trains daily, goods and passenger, and often fewer, and where the staff thus were considerably under-employed. In this respect Ireland compared badly with other countries, for whereas the number of employees in relation to the route mileage of line and the volume of traffic was 57, the average for Western Europe as a whole was 19. CIE wagons and carriages spent most of their time standing around on sidings, depreciating all the while and doing nothing to earn their keep. In fact in terms of passenger-miles per carriage per annum and ton-miles per wagon per annum CIE's rolling stock was the least-used of all Western European countries.

These figures lead one to the inescapable conclusion that the railways of the Republic were being run most inefficiently. This was not particularly the fault of the people then in charge of CIE, but was more the result of circumstances which had been building up over many years. In the first place Ireland had far more railway lines than she could possibly support. The population was thinly spread over the country; there were only two cities with more than 100,000 inhabitants; and nearly six out of ten people lived either in small towns of less than 1,500 inhabitants or out in the country. As things were when the railways were built in the 19th century there was not enough traffic to go round, and by 1956 they were faced with two additional burdens, competition from the motor and a rural population which had halved. If one excludes suburban traffic one finds that on average every man, woman and child in the Republic made slightly fewer than two train journeys each year.

One of the prime necessities of any railway system which hopes to make a profit is the possession of areas of heavy industry; CIE had none. Belfast was the only city in Ireland which came within that category and it was outside the Republic. Dublin had plenty of industry but little of it of a heavy nature; CIE's own Inchicore Works the principal exception, and what other industrial activity there was within the Republic was situated near the sea and therefore not likely to provide the railway with as much long-distance traffic as it might otherwise have done.

Large cities usually mean large suburban areas around them and therefore a great deal of coming and going to and from the centre, more often than not by underground trains. Few serious proposals had ever been made about a Dublin underground, for apart from the possible unsuitability of the soil for tunnelling the money required quite ruled out any such idea. CIE's share of the Dublin suburban services was confined to the two former D&SER lines from Greystones and Bray to Harcourt Street and Westland Row, and while in its heyday in the 1920s a 15min service throughout the day had been necessary to cope with the traffic—a very satisfactory situation from the operating point of view for it meant that most of the rolling stock was fully utilised—by 1956 it had greatly fallen away. The decline had really started in the 1930s. In 1938 the total number of passenger journeys made on the two lines stood at 7,350,000, and by 1947 this had actually increased to almost 8m, but by 1951–2 the figure had dropped to 4,825,000. Since then it has remained fairly constant.

The number of people living along the lines, particularly in the Dun Laoghaire area, had increased during the period, so what had gone wrong? The villain was not the motor car this time but the bus. In 1947 the trams serving the south side of Dublin had been replaced by faster and more comfortable buses and had lured passengers away from the trains in their thousands. Since 1938 the volume of traffic worked by CIE road services in Dublin had gone up by 60 per cent, so that the loss sustained by the railways was up to a point compensated for by the increased profits made by the buses. One's immediate reaction might well be to suggest that if all the rail traffic was transferred to the roads CIE would be in a very happy financial position. Putting aside CIE's traditional attachment to its trains there was another reason why the problem was not a straightforward one. Dublin was the one really big centre of population in the Republic, and already by 1956 serious traffic congestion was occurring in its streets at certain hours of the day. To suddenly let loose a great many more double-deck buses was hardly likely to prove a popular move in the long term.

There were two further suburban railway lines in Dublin, the GNR's Drogheda and Howth services. There were no separate figures published for these, but it was clear from the overall passenger receipts of the GNR that there was nothing like the loss on its suburban services to equal that suffered by CIE. It is difficult to pinpoint the reason for this difference, but no doubt the superior condition of the GNR rolling stock and the less extensive bus services north of the city had something to do with it.

So it can be seen that despite showing a fairly large deficit the railways within the Republic were managing to hold on to much of their traffic, losing some here, gaining some there, and what the Beddy Inquiry had to do was to find ways of cutting operating costs to the point where they were exceeded by receipts.

It came up with many proposals, some far-reaching and some detailed, but the principal ones, largely put into practice in the years subsequent to the Report, totalled five. The first, and most drastic, although long anticipated, was once again a reduction in the size of the railway system. The existing route mileage of line was 1,918, and the Report recommended that this should be halved; at the same time all but 56 of the total of 373 stations and halts would disappear. This would be a fearful slaughter, but was based on the principle that stations in general should be about 25 miles apart, leaving all but a few areas of the country no more than 20 miles from a station.

The second recommendation, relating to the first, was that there should be a much closer integration of the rail and road services, buses connecting with trains and serving the areas in between the stations. Tied up with this was a suggestion that more use could be made of buses and motorcoaches for peak summer travel; this would enable CIE to cut down on the number of railway coaches in its stock which earned their keep on a few weekends only in each year and for the remainder lived the life of Reilly. The Report did not much like the fact that there was only one full-time member (the Chairman) of a Board responsible for a labour force of 20,000, and dealing with receipts amounting to £15,000,000 annually, and suggested that two others, experienced in various aspects of public transport, should join him.

Fourthly, it pointed out that rather than the Government commissioning a detailed study of public transport every so often when things got particularly sticky, it would be better if a permanent consultative body should be set up as a branch of the Civil Service which would keep a permanent eye on what was going on, and supply ministers and anyone else interested with all the relevant facts and figures straightaway. The last important recommendation was that CIE's capital should be adjusted in various ways, the net result being that some £11½m should be written off.

The tone of the Report was not particularly optimistic, and one is left with the impression that at least some members of the Inquiry believed that sooner or later the entire rail system in the Republic would have to be abandoned. What it all boiled down to was whether the motor vehicle would one day prove itself capable of dealing with all types of traffic in all conditions, or whether there was a point at which the motor became less efficient than the railway train. Only a sentimentalist would insist that railways be retained if the former supposition proved correct; whether it would be or not was likely to be determined within a very few years.

CHAPTER TWENTY-FOUR

Dieselisation, the Third Stage

BY 1957 IT HAD become obvious that the Northern Ireland Government was intent on closing the larger part of the GNR system within its control, regardless of the effect this would have on the sections in the Republic, and it was therefore decided that the GNR Board should be dissolved. Legislation was introduced into the Dail and Stormont to effect this, and at midnight, September 30, 1958, the Northern half was absorbed into the UTA while the rest was taken over by CIE. The rolling stock was more or less evenly divided, including a series of railcars then currently in production, the final two of which were completed after the GNR went out of existence.

These were based on the earlier series but differed in a number of important respects. Of BUT manufacture, they had an uprated version of the AEC engine, with the capacity increased from 9.6 to 11.3 *litres,* and a four-speed non-preselective gearbox, air-operated; this gave a maximum speed of 80mph, a 10mph improvement over the earlier cars. Eight cars, Nos 901–908, were composites, identical in layout and appearance to the 1950 Park Royal vehicles, although built at Dundalk. The remaining 16, Nos 701–16, were quite different, in that they had a driving cab at each end; as with the Southern Railway Portsmouth electrics this could be divided off in order to allow passengers to pass through it and, by way of a corridor connection, into the next coach. The intention was that these cars should be either worked singly or, in such trains as the "Enterprise", in the centre of much lengthier rakes with a single-ended car at each end, which thereby presented a neater appearance—a concern for the look of things that was typical of the Great Northern. The company hardly had the chance to operate its new train before the dissolution came, and since then the CIE and UTA have seldom bothered to run the cars in the order prescribed, the 700 series cars as often as not taking the lead.

In all 20 of the post-war railcars went to CIE and 24 to the UTA, and the pre-war cars similarly were more or less equally divided up. The solitary GNR diesel locomotive, the MAK 0–8–0, went to CIE and eventually took up residence in Cork; as to the 166 steam engines, exactly half went to CIE and half to the UTA. Generally the classes were split up, so that CIE got two of the Glover compounds and three post-war VS 4–4–0s, and the UTA three compounds and two VS 4–4–0s, but in some cases all of a class remained under one owner. Such was the RT 0–6–4 tank class, four shunting tanks, all of which were employed in the Belfast area and stayed there under UTA ownership. They were deceptive engines, for despite their impressive wheel arrangement they were really quite small, with AL class cylinders and boilers, the latter of either 165 or 175lb pressure, which produced a tractive effort of from 18,074 to 20,230lb. Almost immediately after being taken over one RT, No 22, was condemned, as were 13 other former GNR locomotives, while the UTA put a further 35 on the duplicate list with an X after their numbers (a revival of a once common practice) and renumbered the rest, which were to be kept in service until dieselisation was complete.

At first the only visible sign of a change of ownership was a stencilled CIE or UTA on the buffer beams of locomotives and tenders, but coaches soon began to acquire the livery of their new owners. Those belonging to CIE had a C placed in front of their numbers, but the UTA took the opportunity of totally reorganising its system and both former GNR and UTA carriages were renumbered. Eventually a few UTA and CIE-owned Great Northern locomotives were given overhauls and repainted in black livery, but most worked out their days in GNR colours, the GNR initials and coat of arms persisting, particularly on CIE, for some time after 1958. Indeed, as I write a number of former GNR tenders are still at Inchicore painted in their original blue livery.

Some former GNR locomotives and carriages took advantage of their increased spheres of operation to visit parts of Ireland where they had never been before, but generally speaking they kept to their home territory. The UTA drafted a number of WT 2–6–4Ts to the GNR section, where they took over stopping and main line services from GNR 4–4–0s, and were generally liked by the GNR men once initial difficulties had been overcome. That some should have been less enthusiastic was only to be expected, for even in their final days the various types of GNR 4–4–0s were capable of excellent running and their drivers were loth to part with them. Normally the 2–6–4Ts worked the through Belfast–Dublin trains as far as Dundalk, and there handed over to CIE diesels; in GNR days, of course, one engine worked right through.

There were still one or two UTA-owned ex-GNR 4–4–0s at work on the main line, and these could be seen in Dublin from time to time, but the tank engines had not the coal capacity to haul a heavy train over the 112½ miles.

In an attempt to rectify this lack, one, No 55, was fitted in 1965 with a tender and made one or two trial trips over the full distance. The experiment was not persisted in, however, probably because by then there was little call for steam working on the main line; it came to an end in November 1966, and a special was run on October 29 to commemorate the fact. The eight-coach train was made up of GNR-built stock, but as there were by then no former GNR 4–4–0s available to haul it 2–6–4T No 54 was put in charge.

In 1957 the UTA introduced a new type of railcar, the Multi-Purpose (MP), and these cars remained in production until 1962. All were converted from former locomotive-hauled stock, a number of them being UTA 2951-built vehicles, as were some of the trailers. Each power car had one 175hp Leyland engine, which in some units was later replaced by either a 260hp AEC one or a 275hp Rolls-Royce engine.

The never very abundant UTA goods traffic was growing ever less, and these new cars were designed to be capable of hauling the remaining goods trains, which were not very heavily loaded, when they were not in use as passenger vehicles. It was certainly one way of getting the most out of one's motive power, but there was something slightly makeshift about the idea, and the (theoretically) complete cessation of internal freight haulage on the Six Counties lines much reduced the practice, although some units, working in multiple, continued to power the through freights to and from CIE. Like their GNR contemporaries, the UTA Multi-Purpose railcars had corridor connections at each end, and on express workings they were formed into five-coach sets. These consisted of two two-car units with a driving cab at each end of the unit, and a dining car in between, the total output of the train amounting to 1,100bhp. Seats were provided for 200 passengers, *plus* the dining car accommodation.

The arrival of the Multi-Purpose railcars meant the virtual end of steam working on the Londonderry line and the gradual withdrawal of the W class Moguls. One or two had a last fling on the other main line, between Belfast and Dublin, their unexpected appearance in the latter city so late in their careers adding another chapter to the story of the motive power employed on Ireland's international main line. The original W, No 91 *The Bush*, was among the final survivors. She and Nos 93/4/7/9/104 were withdrawn in 1965, leaving the WT 2–6–4Ts, one or two former GNR 0–6–0s (which shortly went to the scrap heap) and the old SL&NCR 0–6–4T *Lough Erne*, as the last active steam engines in ordinary service in Ireland.

The CIE locomotives remaining after the last of the Metropolitan-Vickers diesels had been delivered were finished off by an invasion from the other side of the Atlantic. A great deal of Ireland's present state of relative prosperity can be attributed to an ever-increasing tide of American visitors, washing dollars into the remotest corners of the country. So it was really only doing the decent thing to spend some of those dollars at General Motors, something that CIE in any case would have liked to do some years earlier. For its money CIE got 15 950hp Bo-Bo diesel-electric locomotives, with single cabs and of typically General Motors appearance.

Painted in a grey-and-yellow livery they were numbered B121–135, and went into regular service on February 20, 1961, on the Great Northern section and a day later on the Midland. To balance out the through working of some UTA steam engines to Dublin the new diesels went as far as Belfast, although some trains continued to change engines at Dundalk. Despite a plethora of diesel railcars the international main line still featured locomotive-hauled passenger trains. In August of that year I travelled on the midday train from Belfast, which at that time was still composed of GNR-built stock and in the charge of a 2–6–4T. The latter came off at Dundalk and its replacement was one of the new General Motors diesels, which did not greatly impress me for it looked but little larger than a shunter.

This was an example of looks falling short of performance, for by the end of the year it was clear that these small Bo-Bos were but little inferior to the much larger A Class Co-Cos. So CIE lost no time in ordering further

Rebuilt A Class Co-Co pulling out of Heuston Station. The rear vehicle is No 351, the President's saloon

examples, enough to ensure the complete displacement of steam. The second batch were fitted with cabs at both ends, a great improvement from an operational point of view but one which did nothing for the looks of the engine, for the narrow central section housing the works gave it a pinched-in appearance. The only angle of view which may be said to flatter them is the straight side which makes them look rather compact and powerful. All that, however, is very much like icing on the cake. What CIE wanted was a locomotive on which it could rely to perform the work allotted it economically and reliably, and this all three batches of General Motors engines have proved eminently fitted to do. No B141, the first of the second batch, was unloaded at North Wall at the end of November 1962, and she and a number of her sisters went into regular service on December 10. In all there were 37 of them, followed in 1966 by a further 12, Nos B181–192, virtually identical in appearance but with an engine uprated to 1,100hp. These final 12 are the latest engines in service with CIE and are likely to remain so for some while yet.

The General Motors B class, although not as powerful as the Metropolitan–Vickers As, took over most of the latter's passenger duties, working in tandem on the more exacting of them, and were to be seen over the entire CIE system and in the Six Counties. Their arrival was opportune, for by the early 1960s the A class was in some trouble, while it had soon become clear that the C class, with a rating little higher than that of a shunter, was underpowered and of use only on light goods and passenger duties, both of which were decreasing as branch lines shut. When new, the A class put in a great deal of hard graft and proved itself capable of working continuously for far longer periods than had been possible with steam.

Unfortunately after a few years a variety of troubles began to crop up, and the availability of the class, which had once been over 80 per cent, dropped until it was around 50 per cent. The trouble lay in the engines. These Crossley Vee-Eights were in a sense experimental, for although they were an adaptation of a proven and successful marine engine, their use in a moving locomotive was something new in 1955. Rigidly bedded down in the engine-room of a ship they had given little trouble, but when transferred to the vibrating, jarring frame of a railway locomotive they revealed weaknesses which, it would seem, had not been anticipated by their builders. Their mountings were not suitable, and despite numerous modifications made at Inchicore oil pipes were continually fracturing. With the advent of the General Motors Bs the As were largely removed from top link duties, and one could usually reckon on seeing anything up to 20 of them skulking about at Inchicore, awaiting or undergoing repair.

All this was costing CIE tens of thousands of pounds and was a situation which could not continue for long. The solution appeared early in 1968 when A58 emerged from Inchicore with a small "r" after her number and a beautiful new 1,325hp General Motors engine tucked away inside her in place of the old Crossley. She was put through extensive trials and by April was pronounced satisfactory; the go-ahead was then given to rebuild her 59 sisters on similar lines; no doubt by the time these words appear in print the re-engining programme will have been completed. The original generators are retained, with certain modifications, and practically the only external visible indication of the locomotive's new lease of life is the "r" suffix to its number and the twin headlights, similar to those fitted to the GMs, above the cab windows. The rebuilt As have been restored to many of the principal passenger duties, and with the subsequent uprating of A56r to 1500hp in the summer of 1970 she and other members of the class similarly treated are able to work most of these single-handed.

Meanwhile, in 1966 two of the C class were also re-engined, with German Maybach 950hp power units, putting them on a par with the earlier General Motors Bs. They were renumbered B233 and 234 and were allocated similar duties to the latter class, sometimes one of them working in tandem with an American engine. It was whilst double-heading, with B148, the 11.35pm Limerick–Dublin freight on July 29 1967, that B233 was involved in a collision with B172 at the head of the 9.25am Cork–Dublin freight at Limerick Junction. While there were no injuries to persons, 50 cattle were killed, a large proportion of the 43 wagons involved were destroyed, and the two General Motors locomotives received severe body damage, though No B233 was more or less unscathed. The cost of this accident totalled approximately £250,000, and it has been fortunate for CIE that such occurrences have been very rare. In their original form, however, the Cs seem unable to perform even the most menial tasks without a great deal of fuss, and I once watched one, running light, come staggering up from North Wall towards Glasnevin Junction enveloped in such a pall of smoke that the traffic standing on the bridge above momentarily completely disappeared inside it as the ailing C passed below.

Nothing more was done with the Cs until the latter part of 1970, when further members of the class were rebuilt, this time with the ever-popular General Motors 950hp engine. By that date the railcars, which had done a tremendous mileage, were due for a well-earned retirement, a number of them having already been taken out of service and laid up at Inchicore and Sallins. Their final express workings had been from Dublin to Sligo, in 1969, although they had a regular semi-fast turn between Belfast and Dublin lasting into 1970. From then on they were concentrated on the Dublin suburban services, augmented at peak hours and at summer weekends by trains of locomotive-hauled stock in charge of As and Ars, one or two General Motors Bs and the odd C. Although the AEC and BUT engines were by then pretty well worn out, the ever-thrifty CIE decided that further life was to be got out of the cars themselves. This would be done by converting them to locomotive-hauled push-and-pull units, powered by a rebuilt C class locomotive. The 950hp General Motors engine having at last gone out of production, more powerful 1,200hp versions of it would be fitted to those Cs not already converted. The refurbished railcars, minus their engines, and the Cs, now Bs, would thus provide the mainstay of the increasingly important suburban services, and this programme is at present being carried out.

Minor developments in the locomotive field on CIE in recent years have been the delivery of a further 14 Maybach-engined, Inchicore-built E class shunters in 1961, seven more small G class four-wheel diesels in 1962, and the withdrawal of one of the original CIE diesel shunters, No D302, in 1966.

In 1964 a new type of main line carriage entered service with CIE. This was the now familiar Craven coach, designed by that firm and sent across to Inchicore for completion. In appearance it is not unlike the British Rail Mark 11 carriages, and is constructed along similar lines, with an all-metal body welded to a corrugated steel floor, double-glazed windows, and an open interior layout. Originally all of these coaches were second class (now called "standard"), but a few have recently been upgraded to firsts, some merely by the painting of the figure "1" on the doors, but others by a complete and luxurious interior refurbishing. The Cravens were put to work on a variety of express duties, and after some initial heating and riding problems, the latter despite their B4 bogies, they have now settled down and are much appreciated.

Remarkable though it may appear, six-wheel carriages were still officially at work after the first of the Cravens had been delivered to Inchicore, and it was not until March 26, 1964, that the very last, former MGWR No 177M, was broken up. A few remain in departmental use, but otherwise bogie coaches at last are the rule in Ireland. Some of these are no chickens, for one or two ex-GS&WR arc-roofed non-corridors from the first decade of the century are still managing to find employment each summer in the Dublin area and down around Wexford. One would expect these, and the remainder of the GS&WR and GSR-built wooden-bodied carriages, to be withdrawn when the new Derby coaches enter service in the summer of 1971, but the old non-corridors have a seating capacity much in excess of more modern, open stock, and have proved so useful in conveying the regiments of young Dubliners who head for the delights of Bray at summer weekends that the operating department may consider them too precious to part with.

At the beginning of 1960 CIE possessed 194 steam engines, 52 of them of GNR origin. The newest was the remarkable turf-burner, No CC1, designed by Bulleid and completed at Inchicore at the end of July 1957. The attraction of turf as a fuel for locomotive purposes had lured the railways on previous occasions into dabbling with its possibilities, notably during World War II, and also in 1949, when the three narrow-gauge Bord na Mona well tanks were delivered. Nothing satisfactory had resulted, however, chiefly because turf as it burns breaks down into such quantities of ash as to be quite unacceptable in the limited confines of a railway locomotive's grate. Bulleid attempted to get over this by producing a revolutionary design running on two six-wheel bogies, with a very large grate, a central cab and totally enclosed boiler, working parts and bunker. No CC1 bore some similarity to Bulleid's Southern Railway Leaders of 1947–8, although in appearance it was rather squarer and therefore less handsome. It suffered a similar fate, coming too late to save the steam engine, and after running trials on the Dublin–Cork main line and North Wall–Kingsbridge transfer freights, was stored at Inchicore and eventually broken up.

Inchicore shed closed to steam in 1956, although the works continued to carry out repairs until 1961, while Limerick and Dundalk also overhauled steam engines in the late 1950s. Broadstone, although it had ceased to be a works and station back in the 1930s, survived for very much longer as a steam engine shed, becoming the last former Great Southern one in the Dublin area. It closed in 1961, but steam was still to be seen in the capital, at Amiens Street, until the spring of 1963, when steam locomotives were officially withdrawn from traffic. On March 31 the last 55 were put into store. Of these 21 were former GNR types, and there were three ex-GSR tank engines, two 0–6–0Ts and Bandon tank No 463; there was also ex-D&SER 2–6–0 No 461 and the rest were ex-MGWR and GS&WR 0–6–0s, 18 of them J15s.

The last time any of them had been in steam was the previous Christmas, when a number had done duty as carriage-warmers at Cork and Dublin. They were not all condemned, some being put into reserve in case their assistance should be called upon to supplement the diesels. It was soon realised that this was a most unlikely eventuality, and some of the 53 were sold to the UTA (only those of GNR origin) for further service, while others were broken up, at Inchicore and Mullingar. Nevertheless steam has never been officially superseded on CIE, and early in 1966 it was announced that J15s Nos 184, 185, 186 and 198, 2–6–0 No 461 and former GNR 4–4–0 No 131N, all of which were still in existence, would be retained for the use of the film companies which frequently do location work in Ireland and might require sequences with shots of steam trains in action. At the same time the turf-burner was dismantled, but not entirely broken up, for its boiler was retained and its chassis was converted into a well-wagon.

In Chapter 22 we left *Maeve* no longer in service but repainted in GSR livery and on exhibition to the public from time to time. Her surviving sister *Macha* pottered about Cork and Thurles in 1960 and 1961 on a variety of menial goods duties, and the last time I saw her she was in charge of a ludicrously lightweight train of some half-dozen wagons, but still in green livery and beautifully maintained. Soon afterwards, as there was no sense in using so large and sophisticated a locomotive on this sort of work, she was withdrawn. *Maeve* was last in steam in 1958. She was then stored at Thurles and taken with *Macha* to Inchicore in 1962. *Macha* was broken up, but *Maeve* was altogether too historic a locomotive to pass into oblivion or be reincarnated in the form of thousands of sardine tins, and at the suggestion of the Irish Railway Record Society, Dr Andrews, despite his acid comments about the West Clare being an expensive monument, agreed that *Maeve* should be preserved. On February 21, 1964, she was seen off at Amiens Street station by F. Lemass, General Manager of CIE, on her way to the Belfast Transport Museum. Her great weight presented problems when it came to crossing the Boyne Viaduct and she had to be separated from the diesel hauling her by a long line of empty wagons. At Portadown a UTA 2–6–4T took over, and after remaining for some time at Adelaide shed she was received in Belfast by the Lord Mayor at a ceremony at Great Victoria Street station and taken by road to her final home at the Museum. She was in quite reasonable mechanical condition when taken out of service, and could no doubt have been put back in steam without a great deal of expense, but the routes over which she could travel, virtually only the Dublin–Cork main line, were so restricted that there would have been little point in maintaining her in running order. So she is unlikely ever again to be anything other than a highly impressive static exhibit.

The future of four of the steam engines retained by CIE in 1966 was also assured, again partly through the offices of the Railway Record Society. One J15 No 186, was privately preserved by the Railway Preservation Society of Ireland, who also own the GNR 4–4–0 *Slieve Gullion*, while CIE itself agreed to be responsible for the other three engines. The GNR Q No 131 was repainted in that company's lined black livery; the D&SER 2–6–0 was restored to its original colours and at present remains at Inchicore despite various suggestions that it might go on permanent display at Wexford; while J15 No 184 was given a complete overhaul, painted in lined grey and put back into steam for an open day held at Inchicore in July 1968. She was a tremendous attraction, hauling a one-coach train up and down within the confines of the works, as was the Open Day itself, which has become an annual event and attracts crowds of football match proportions, well over 20,000 attending.

CIE has preserved three other steam engines. There is the West Clare engine at Ennis; at Mallow there is a GS&WR 0–6–0T, No 90, which was built in 1875 as an 0–6–4 tank steam carriage; while at Cork there is the historic No 36. The latter must rank as one of the most valuable pieces of industrial antiquity in existence, yet not much more than 20 years ago her continued survival was in some considerable doubt.

No 36 is a Bury 2–2–2, built in 1848 in the very earliest years of the GS&WR before the main line was completed. She is reputed to have been capable of exceeding 60mph down Ballybrophy bank although, as might be expected, she was not such a star turn at climbing; indeed, on wet days the only way she could be got to haul her train up the bank from Kingsbridge to Inchicore was for her fireman to walk alongside her tossing liberal amounts of sand under her driving wheels. The last of her class in service, she was stored at Inchicore after withdrawal for many years until 1948, when CIE decided she was taking up valuable space and made it known that they would like to get rid of her. She was offered as a free gift to anyone who would give her a home, and scores of replies were received from all over the British Isles. Transportation proved a stumbling-block in every case, and it did seem at one time that she might be broken up. This would have been vandalism on the scale of the destruction of the preserved GWR broad gauge single at Swindon in Churchward days, but fortunately CIE was persuaded to think again, and No 36 is alive and well and lives, here future assured, at Kent (formerly Glanmire Road) station, Cork.

This might be the place to mention the activities of the two principal societies for Irish railway enthusiasts. The oldest is the Irish Railway Record Society. Founded in 1946 its origins go back much further, to a little notebook which was passed around amongst a group of friends, each member adding his own observations whenever he travelled by train. From the late 1920s it took a more professional form in the shape of *Fayle's Journal*, a typed news-sheet edited by Hugh Fayle and produced at frequent intervals. The bound copies of this are now among the most prized possessions in the society's library, and are a mine of information of the most detailed character, invaluable to anyone wishing to find out what the Irish railways were up to in the 1930s and 1940s. Hugh Fayle was a photographer as well as a historian, and it is probably fair to say that more is owed to him than to anyone else for the comprehensive documentation of Irish railway history.

Although in no way an official body, the Irish Railway Record Society enjoys the best of relations with CIE. A number of employees of the latter are members, and J. J. Johnston, the one-time assistant CME, has long been a valued friend of the society as have several senior officials of CIE. The IRRS in custodian of much historical matter relating to public transport in Ireland, passed on to it by CIE. Its premises are situated in the buildings of the disused Drumcondra station in Dublin, recently made available to it by CIE and in process of renovation, an ambitious project undertaken with great gusto by some of the more energetic members.

The Railway Preservation Society of Ireland is a much younger organisation, but has achieved great things, the most notable being the preservation of several engines in working order, thus ensuring the continuation of steam on the main lines in Ireland. Its headquarters are in the North, which in its present state of unrest is not the best place to keep such large and easily vandalised objects as steam engines, and following the destruction of a preserved brake-van the society opened negotiations with CIE with a view to moving to the Republic, Sallins being mentioned as a possible new home. With the ready co-operation of CIE and the NIR, a number of runs behind steam are made each year and attract a great deal of interest, although it is a pity that the people who chase in cars all over the countryside after the trains cannot be persuaded to contribute something towards the cost of their entertainment, which is considerable. One of the first and most spectacular steam tours was a joint venture of several British and Irish societies covering eight days and 1,500 miles, in June, 1966. Five different UTA and four CIE steam engines were employed at various times on the train, and assistance towards its cost was given by Bord Failte Eireann (Irish Tourist Board), Guinness's and others; among the considerable amount of publicity the trip received was a 30min programme about it on Irish television on the opening night.

Apart from the added spice of steam in action from time to time, Ireland is a fascinating place for the railway enthusiast, with its mixture of British and American practice, its international route, and the still not entirely vanished reminders of the eccentricities which at one time were almost the rule.

CHAPTER TWENTY-FIVE

Irish Railways Today

IT MIGHT BE thought from the foregoing lengthy lists of new rolling stock introduced since World War II, particularly by CIE, that the railways were coining in money on a scale never previously experienced. But I hope I have done enough to show that the facts were quite the opposite; moreover in 1963 yet another report, brought out by CIE, suggested that the not very happy situation investigated by the Beddy Inquiry was now even less exhilarating. Inevitably it was stuffed full of statistics, all of which were very relevant and revealing, but I have neither the nerve nor the inclination to force yet more facts, figures and percentages down the reader's throat. If he is particularly interested, however, copies of the report, the "Pacemaker", while never sold to the public are available for scrutiny in the National and Trinity Libraries in Dublin. I will merely state that it has been suggested that the real purpose of CIE in commissioning the Report was to convince the Government that if it did not give the railways more financial assistance they would have to go out of business. As we have seen, this was no new threat, but this time the threat achieved its purpose, for 1963 may be said to have been the *nadir* for Irish railways, since which date the seemingly unstoppable slide into oblivion was firmly and, one may reasonably hope, permanently halted.

There have been but three closures in the South since then, and it does seem possible that there will be no more. There has been the reopening of most of the Waterford–Dungarvan line, the development of Foynes and its rail facilities, the new Silvermines branch, and various other indications that if anything the size of the railway network in Ireland is likely to increase rather than to contract in the future.

Successive bills and reports had charged CIE with the obligation to break even within a given period; on each occasion the period has had perforce to be extended, for the notion of solvency has become more and more a doubtful ideal rather than a practical possibility. By early 1964 the latest of these deadlines was approaching, and it was quite obvious that once again there was no chance of CIE meeting it. The Government had two alternatives; to shut down much that remained of the railway system, as outlined in the Pacemaker Report; or it could decide that social needs outweighed all other factors and that it must continue to give CIE a subsidy. If the Government took the latter course it knew that it would be setting a precedent, for no one was now under the illusion that any subsidy was merely a temporary arrangement until solvency was reached.

The Dail decided that Ireland did need its railways, and since then CIE has received an annual subvention of £2m, and in addition exchequer advances of £8m have been granted for capital replacement. In 1969 another Transport Bill was introduced into the Dail to augment the 1964 Transport Act and to provide further capital advances and subventions, and one cannot better illustrate the general attitude prevailing in relation towards the country's transport needs than by quoting from the speeches of members during the debate on the Bill.

The Minister for Transport and Power, Mr Lenihan, moved that £11m in Exchequer capital advances should be made to CIE (this was for all its

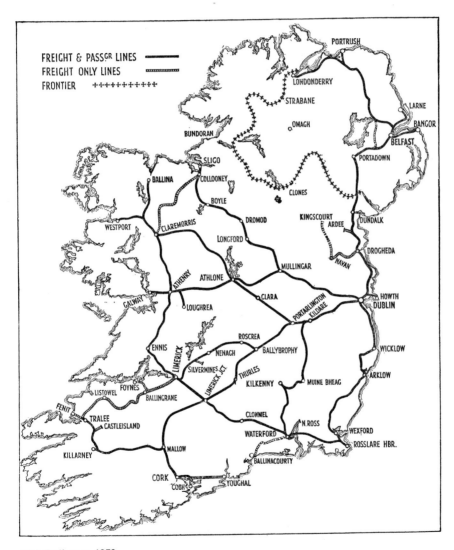

Irish Railways, 1972

needs of course, not just for the railways) and in addition proposed that a Draft Order to the 1964 Transport Act would increase the annual subvention of £2m (mainly to cover railway losses) to £2,650,000, this being necessary principally on account of inflation rather than any reduction in traffic. Mr Lenihan naturally had the support of his own party, Fianna Fail, but his measure also found favour with the chief opposition party, Fine Gael.

Its spokesman, George Russell, declared that it "confirmed the Government's changed attitude to CIE". There seemed, he said, to be a better and more progressive spirit through all ranks of CIE. Very keen and competent young men had been appointed area managers and they showed a great desire to give the best possible service to the public. Mr Russell went on to deplore the closing of the West Clare Railway and the loss of a "tremendous tourist draw, . . . for want of a comparatively small sum". Many other members expressed their approval of the Government's increasing support of public transport, and Dr Sheehy Skeffington regretted the closure of lines in the past, particularly the Harcourt Street one and the Howth trams. A number of members were concerned over the increasing traffic congestion in the streets of Dublin, and the part CIE might play in easing it; one, Professor Patrick Quinlan, estimated that road traffic in Ireland was likely to double within the next ten years. The Minister, closing the debate, agreed that the question of traffic in the centre of Dublin was the most pressing of Ireland's present day traffic problems, implying, as was undoubtedly true, that there was now virtually no opposition to the principle that the railways were a social service, subsidised out of the Exchequer in the same way as roads, education, public health and other essential needs of the community.

For the men employed on the railways this change in attitude has meant a great deal. For the first time since before World War I they may look ahead to an assured future and be reasonably certain that the threat of losing their jobs, ever present in a contracting industry, has gone for good. Long worn-out equipment is now being replaced and there is not likely to be any more of the sort of penny-pinching which resulted in the reduction of the amount of upholstery on the seat backs of main line carriages, in artificially low rates and fares necessitating cuts in the wages of already poorly paid workers, and in a decade without dividends for ordinary stock-holders.

CIE, as George Russell pointed out, is now able to compete with industry for the brightest young men on the management and research side, of which Ireland has a plethora. Graduates of University and Trinity Colleges in Dublin seldom have any difficulty in obtaining well-paid posts in Britain or the USA, but most would prefer to stay in Ireland, for a much smaller salary if necessary, if only jobs were available. By providing such opportunities CIE is serving a social need, as it is in the much larger field of the technician and the manual worker. On this ground alone a strong case could be made for granting CIE a substantial subsidy.

Perhaps the greatest achievement of the Irish railways in recent times has been the shedding of the image which clung to them for the best part of 50 years and more. It was one of antiquated eccentricity, of ornate and fusty gas-lit wooden carriages pottering along behind under-powered, fragile-looking locomotives, departures in the remote rural areas being dependent more upon the pigs being all aboard and the thirst of the crews adequately quenched in the nearest bar than upon the official timetable. The steam locomotive enthusiast, the lover of the quaint and curious, the fugitive from progress, found the railway scene in the South and West of Ireland a paradise. The local inhabitant found the motor car rather more to his liking, even if he had to go and work in England to earn sufficient money to buy one, and as it was the latter category of individual rather than any of the former which was much the most numerous it was his custom the railways preferred to cultivate. Each customer lost to the roads meant less income available for the replacement of worn-out rolling stock, and the scruffier this got so much the more people took to the roads, a vicious circle which spun inexorably faster with each succeeding year until by 1950 it had whirled the railways like a time machine into an age quite remote from that in which the rest of the world existed. Even the Great Northern Railway, which tried to put a bold face on its dire predicament by extending its beautiful sky-blue livery to most of its passenger tender engines, only succeeded in emphasising the period flavour of its trains.

It is different today. CIE was one of the first railways in Europe to abandon the steam engine completely, and on the NIR the new push-and-pull "Enterprise" is a highly sophisticated modern development. The three Hunslet/British Rail Bo-Bos which haul it confirm a trend which has been developing in Ireland of late, and has reversed that which came in during the 1930s and persisted for a good 30 years. The diesel railcar has served Ireland well, particularly in the North, where in recent years it monopolised all but a very few passenger services. It was never an ideal form of motive power for high speed long-distance running, but as there was very little of that it did not really matter. The one train serving Northern Ireland which does come into that category is the "Enterprise", and the various types of railcars used on it, whether of GNR or UTA origin, diesel-mechanical or diesel-electric, were never entirely suitable. It seemed not so long ago that the Northern Ireland authorities were content to let the service succumb to competition from the private car, but a most welcome change of heart overtook them and the result was on view to the public from July 3, 1970.

On that day the new "Enterprise" made a demonstration run from Belfast to Dublin and back, and on the day following went into regular service. The motive power is provided by two 1,350hp diesel-electric Bo-Bos, the first diesel locomotives intended for express working to be put into service by a Northern Irish railway. They are coupled to each end of the eight-coach train, one pushing and one pulling in each direction. During the winter months, when the traffic between Belfast and Dublin is lighter, a five-coach train usually suffices, worked by one engine, with a driving trailer at the opposite end. Unlike the newer CIE locomotives the NIR ones, of which there are three (one being kept as a spare), were built in England, at the British Rail Doncaster Works.

The electrical and traction equipment was supplied by the firm which built many of the NIR multiple-units, English Electric-AEI Traction Ltd, while the superstructure and bogies were designed by the old-established Hunslet Engine Company Ltd of Leeds, whose products were once familiar on the narrow-gauge in Ireland. They are sturdy looking, compact machines, hardly as handsome as the Swindon Westerns, which are supposed to have provided the inspiration for their appearance, but a distinct advance on their Republican General Motors brothers. They are painted maroon with a broad yellow V at each end, and bear the names of three of the Glover compound 4–4–0s which once worked the Dublin–Belfast expresses, *Eagle*, *Falcon*, and *Merlin*.

The coaches may be said to be in the NIR tradition. They were designed at Derby and are British Rail standard Mark 11Bs with certain modifications. For over 60 years British Rail and its predecessors, the LMS and the Midland, have built carriages for service in Northern Ireland and the Mark 11Bs are recognisably descendants of the later LMS open corridors, a number of which were put into service with the NCC and are still at work. The livery of the new coaches is a somewhat startling red, white and blue. Admittedly the red is a rather deep shade of maroon, and the white no more than a 1½in thick stripe dividing the other two colours, but nevertheless one cannot help wondering if someone in the North either had his tongue in his cheek or suffered from an excessive dose of patriotism when he was contemplating what colour scheme might most impress the Southern rebels.

At present the run between Belfast and Dublin is scheduled to take 2hr 15min, with two stops, but there is no doubt that two of the new engines, putting out a combined 2,700hp, the equal of a BR Brush Type 4 or a Western, could cover the 112½ miles in considerably less time, particularly when their speed limit is raised from 70 to 80mph.

The NIR has three other modern diesel locomotives, small 550hp diesel-hydraulics delivered in 1969, which are used for shunting and hauling ballast trains. The last spoil train ran on May 2, 1969, a ceremony being held to mark the occasion when steam engines Nos 4 and 53, the latter bearing a headboard proclaiming it to be the 7,600th such working since December 1967, ran to the site of the M2 Motorway at Greencastle. Now the last of the 2–6–4Ts has been handed over to the RPSI and the steam has gone from the NIR.

Much as one might regret the passing of the last main line steam engines in the British Isles the final elimination of the 2–6–4Ts has marked a turning point in the fortunes of the NIR. For two years now it has made a profit, and even though the £250,000 realised from the spoil contract will be missed its future seems considerably brighter. Nevertheless the Northern Ireland Development Programme for 1970–5 suggested that the Ballymena–Londonderry section, which is not particularly well patronised, might have only a limited life, but a subsequent Government White Paper squashed this idea, saying that for at least five years there was no possibility of any further closures in Northern Ireland. Someone a little more in touch with reality had no doubt grasped that there was a certain degree of dissatisfaction with the Government felt in Londonderry at the time. Perhaps he had even heard of the Bogside, of Bernadette Devlin and of unemployment figures in excess of 15 per cent, and had pointed out that to sever the city's last remaining rail link would hardly bring the crowds out in their thousands singing the National Anthem and offering to subscribe towards a statue of the Prime Minister!

Overall the situation looks fairly promising. At the beginning of 1970 the Minister of Development announced a ten-year plan for spending lots of money on the railways; such a statement a few years earlier would have landed its author in an institution for incurable imbeciles. A determined and successful campaign to bring passengers back to the railways is being waged, and some 70 conductor/guards were recently introduced, cutting out the necessity for a number of stations to be staffed, at least for part of the day. This latter move has not been altogether successful, as the unattended stations have attracted the attention of vandals, and a considerable amount of damage has been done to railway property. In a recent court case involving trespass on the railway the magistrate intimated that it was his opinion that the NIR were asking for trouble in leaving its stations unattended, and it may be that the savings made in wages will be frittered away by the cost of repairing the damage. No doubt the volatile political situation in the Six Counties is not conducive to law and order in other spheres, although it must be said that up to now railway property has escaped the spectacularly destructive treatment meted out to Belfast Corporation Transport Department buses.

Great changes are being wrought at York Road, Belfast, where the railcar and locomotive maintenance areas are right in the path of the M2 motorway. The station itself has been brightened up, although the refreshment room can still appear singularly unappetising on occasions, and many structural alterations have been carried out. It is proposed to reopen the Belfast Central Railway, linking the former GNR and County Down terminals with the Quay lines of the NCC, and there is talk, as there has been for a great many years past, of a Central station serving all the lines in Belfast and replacing York Road, Great Victoria Street, and Queens Quay. It would be a most welcome move, benefiting alike interchange passengers and commuters to and from the centre of the city, but the cost would be considerable and, rather like the Channel Tunnel, it is an ancient dream which has recently come rather nearer realisation but is still far from a certainty. New stations have been opened to serve various developments lately, including the university between Portrush and Coleraine, and the city of Craigavon, taking in Portadown and Lurgan, both of which stations are undergoing rebuilding, while a completely new one, Craigavon Central, has been constructed midway between the two. Freight traffic originating on the NIR no longer exists, officially, but CIE runs nightly trains between Dublin and Londonderry via the Antrim line and between Dundalk and Belfast. A new goods depot is to be built at Adelaide and it is not entirely beyond the realms of possibility that the NIR will be running its own freight trains again some day.

In Dublin, too, there is much talk of a Central station. A new road bridge is to be built across the Quays on the seaward side of the Loop Line bridge and it might be that this would eventually become a combined road and rail bridge. Connolly station (the former Amiens Street) would then be enlarged to cope with the traffic at present handled by Heuston (the former Kingsbridge), and the terminal platforms at Connolly would become through ones, with trains continuing on through where the concourse now stands over a new line to the proposed bridge, rejoining the present Loop Line in the vicinity of Tara Street. At the same time two former suburban services might be revived, the GS&WR one via Glasnevin and Drumcondra and the MGWR one from Maynooth. Congestion in the streets of Dublin has reached such a pitch that something drastic will have to be done very shortly, and there are many who feel that the cheapest and most effective method would be to make far greater use of the railways.

Outside Dublin a number of stations have undergone extensive face-lifts. The archaic layout at Limerick Junction has been improved, obviating the need for Dublin–Cork trains to reverse into the platform; Waterford Riverside (renamed Plunkett in 1966) has been almost completely rebuilt, and is now a very pleasant, airy structure, and other important stations such as Cork Kent (formerly Glanmire Road) and Galway Ceannt are now much more inviting than in days gone by.

In one sense Ireland was lucky to escape the Industrial Revolution, for although she was artificially held back during the 19th century and her people suffered great hardships, particularly during the famine, they were in some respects more fortunate than the British working class in that they were spared the degradation the latter was forced to endure in the great industrial towns and cities of England, Scotland and Wales. One shudders to think what might have happened to Cork, Waterford, Limerick or Londonderry when one looks at the only two centres of industry in Ireland, Belfast, and, to a lesser extent, Dublin.

Since the end of World War II there has been a marked increase in industrial activity in Southern Ireland; motorcar assembly, the manufacture of electrical appliances, pottery, mining, and so on, often backed by Japanese or German capital, now are carried on in conditions very different from those which obtained in the 1800s. The railways have taken a share of this new business (for example, one of the old Pullman underframes ended up as a bubble car transporter); but it is the mineral traffic which has proved particularly lucrative for CIE. Much of this originates from two sources, Silvermines and Bennett's Bridge.

To serve the former workings a 1¾-mile long branch line was opened in December 1966, some six miles west of Nenagh on the Ballybrophy–Limerick line. A total of 69 vacuum braked wagons, each of 20 tons capacity, was built to convey barytes and zinc concentrates from Silvermines to Foynes, where they are processed and then shipped out. The handling at both ends is done mechanically, and some 170,000 tons of barytes and close on 200,000 tons of zinc concentrates are handled annually. The traffic is not all one way, and nearly 100,000 tons of oil are conveyed by rail from Foynes to a cement works at Limerick each year. This type of traffic and that emanating from Bennett's Bridge, described in another chapter, could hardly be carried on if the railways were not able to handle it, and there is every likelihood that it will increase.

Mention of the vacuum-braked ore wagons leads to another development in the goods field, the freight-liner. This has meant all-braked trains and, as in England, the day must come when the loose-coupled pick-up goods train will be a thing of the past. At present CIE operates liner trains, partly in conjunction with British Rail (which still has a large depot at North Wall inherited from the LNWR), between Dublin and Cork, Limerick and Londonderry, and a Belferry liner train runs between Dublin and Waterford. At first all the wagons used on these trains were four-wheelers; but Inchicore has since built a number of bogie vehicles. Unlike the traditional main line goods trains which leave Dublin and the provincial centres in the early evening and travel through the night, the liner trains run during daylight hours, their much superior speed enabling them to be fitted into the passenger timetable. Nevertheless there would not appear to be a very strict adherence to the schedule of at least one of them, for on a number of occasions during the summer of 1970 I noticed the afternoon Cork train leaving the North Wall 30min or more late.

For a long time the Irish railways standardised on flat bottomed track, going over to bullhead quite late on; but flat-bottomed was reintroduced after 1945, and the latest development is all-welded track. At present there is very little of this, just a few miles on the Dublin–Cork main line, but if passenger speeds are to rise above the present 75mph maximum, as they undoubtedly will, there will have to be very much more.

Colour-light signalling is gradually becoming more common on both CIE and the NIR, and single line working has been speeded up by the introduction of mechanical exchange apparatus for ET staffs; on the Londonderry main line between Ballymena and Coleraine there is some 30 miles of track-circuited tokenless-block working. Automatic barriers are in operation at a number of level crossings on both CIE and the NIR, although the public understandably is still somewhat wary of them, and their installation has not gone ahead at the pace originally intended. Indeed at Sidney Parade on the Dun Laoghaire line the wiring was installed all ready for the barriers, only to be removed after vociferous protests from local residents, and a demonstration of the system to Dublin City Council, which then decided it did not like the idea.

Nevertheless great changes in signalling are in the air, and will result in a large degree of remote control. If it can find the money CIE would like to introduce continuous track-circuiting, which would result in perhaps no more than five or six signal-boxes in normal use, two or three on the Southern Section and one each on the Midland, South Eastern and Northern Sections. Provision would have to be made for shunting movements and a considerable amount of track alteration would be needed, but the only real obstacle to the implementation of the scheme is financial. This might well be overcome by the great saving in labour costs which would result. At first sight this might seem to be a contradiction of what I said a little earlier about the obligation of CIE to provide jobs for Irishmen who would otherwise be forced to emigrate, but if we look a little closer into the changing economic position of Ireland we shall see that this is not really so.

For the very first time the railways are finding difficulty in recruiting workers in certain fields. Much railway work is shift work, which most men do not prefer but used to put up with simply because this was a lot better than nothing. In the last few years, however, CIE has had to compete with the many factories which have sprung up in the Dublin area, and even the incentive of higher wages has not always proved equal to the lure of a regular five-day week daytime job. Outside Dublin CIE can still pick and choose its employees, but even there this situation may not last indefinitely. Permanent emigration to Britain has declined steadily since 1945, but Irishmen still come over for a limited period, perhaps if the farm is going through a bad patch, and do not mind undertaking, on a temporary basis, the rougher but highly paid manual jobs which exist in industry and civil engineering.

It used to be the case that the cost of living in Southern Ireland was generally lower than in Britain, although there were always exceptions. Before World War I the Chairman of the GS&WR was complaining that it was cheaper to have railway carriages built in Britain and pay the cost of shipping them across the Irish Sea rather than have them made at Inchicore. Nowadays, however, precious little costs less in the Republic than it does in Britain; rail travel certainly does not, and wages and salaries are generally comparable. Talk to the average Irishman about his first impressions of England and he may well express surprise at the low wages a sizeable section of the unskilled working class puts up with, whereas the rewards paid by the motor firms go soaring up at such a rate as to make him rub his eyes in amazement. The Republic of Ireland is much closer to a classless society than are most countries, and although there are still many families living in poverty the gap between the living standards of most working people and the really well-off is much less than it is in Britain.

So, as there is so much smaller a degree of industrialisation there is something of a shortage of skilled workers, and unless CIE can offer continuous employment in excess of basic rates it is unable to attract them. For this reason it is unlikely that any more carriages will be built at Inchicore; CIE's requirements are not such as to warrant a constant production line. It can keep a limited labour force continually at work on maintenance and repair, but modern methods of construction make it uneconomic to build carriages in ones and twos, and there are simply not the men available to be employed on a limited period basis who would be able to turn out a batch of 30 or 40 and then move on to employment elsewhere. When CIE announced towards the end of 1970 that it was spending over £2½m on 62 carriages, 22 steam-heating boiler brake-vans, and 11 electric generator-vans which would be built by British Rail Engineering at Derby, there was a strike at Inchicore in protest. Yet had the coaches been built there, assuming that they could have been, the cost would have been significantly higher.

These new carriages mark a big step forward for CIE. They are based on the current British Rail Mark 11D design, just as the NIR "Enterprise" set is based on the 11Bs, and will probably be used in complete sets. Hauled by two rebuilt 1,500hp A class diesels running on all-welded track, and controlled by continuous track-circuiting, they could one day be covering the 165 miles between Dublin and Cork in two hours.

It would now seem that the railways of Ireland have an assured future. The North has got itself into such a state of turmoil as to make any precise predictions liable to contradiction overnight. If unification of the 26 and Six Counties ever does come, as it surely must, the operation of a single railway system ought to have economic advantages; but this is a long way off. For the moment the unrest is doing the financial position of the North no good at all, and public transport is suffering along with everything else. The South had not been greatly affected, materially, apart from the Dublin–Belfast line which, despite the new "Enterprise" service is showing reduced receipts. One must assume that rates and fares will continue to go up as the cost of living rises, but this is unlikely to have any detrimental effect provided that the former do not overtake the latter. CIE has become very publicity conscious and its advertising agent, Arks Ltd of Dublin, was awarded the Rizzoli Trophy in 1970 by an international jury for the best series of advertisements to be run in the public press. This coincided with an increase in passenger traffic and is a measure of the impact that an original and attractive publicity campaign can have.

Ultimately, however, the greatest asset or liability of any large organisation is the impact its employees have on the public. Here both CIE and the NIR have a head start. The traditional Irishman was always portrayed in England as a jovial, uneducated simpleton, usually drunk, always ready for a fight, but equally eager to be on friendly terms with everyone. Like all such nationalistic generalisations it was a gross distortion of the truth, but in one respect it was accurate. The Irish are a friendly people. They may have little cause to love the English en masse, but the English visitor to Ireland will be made more welcome than almost anywhere else, and he will find the railwayman among those most delighted to see him. Whether it be a porter in the remote West, a ticket-collector in Dublin, an engineer at Inchicore, a locomotiveman at York Road, or a hostess on the "Slainte" express, the Irish railwayman seems to regard it as an essential part of his or her job to make the traveller's journey as enjoyable as possible, and this, in the end, is worth more than a whole collection of sophisticated technical advances.

Closures

LISTING THE closures of lines is a tricky business. In the first place one has to decide just when a line actually has gone out of business. Many continue to support a goods service long after passenger trains have ceased to run; the Palace East–Muine Bheag line for example saw its last regular passenger train in 1931 but goods trains continued until 1963. Even when regular goods services cease a line may still fail to succumb completely and draw a few last gasps in the shape of excursions and cattle specials. In some cases the abandonment order is promulgated immediately after the last scheduled trains have run, but in others it comes only after the track has grown rusty from years of total neglect. The GNR's Goraghwood–Markethill branch was one such, a number of small trees which had grown up between the rails having to be uprooted before the lifting train could perform its last rites and permit the track bed to return permanently to nature.

The dates I quote are either the last day any sort of train used the line or else the official date of closure, usually the day after all traffic ceased. However, finding either of these out has in some instances proved an impossible task. Sometimes I have been unable to get closer than the year of closure, and often in other cases when I have discovered a definite date in an authoritative account I have later come across a quite different one somewhere else.

Three instances may serve to illustrate this. *The Journal of the Irish Railway Record Society*, an excellent and highly informative magazine, stated that the Clonakilty branch was being lifted in 1954, yet according to CIE trains ran on it until March 1961. Again Pender and Richards in their generally precise and authoritative work *Irish Railways Today*, state that the former NCC Cookstown Junction–Cookstown line closed in 1950, yet a UTA working timetable for July 1957 lists one goods train each way each weekday over a large section of it. Then again CIE state that all goods and passenger trains had been withdrawn from the Kilmessan–Athboy branch by the end of March 1947, but in fact cattle specials continued to run over it for another six years. I quote these instances, not because I am suggesting that someone has done insufficient research, but precisely for the opposite reason, to illustrate that it is virtually impossible for even the most painstaking sleuth after facts and figures not to come unstuck on occasions. Therefore I trust the reader will understand when I commit myself to nothing closer than a month or even a year for a closure date, and I beg in advance to be forgiven for the inaccuracies which I am sure must exist amongst those I have managed to find sufficient courage to commit to print. In other words if your chances of inheriting a fortune from the insurance firm depend on proving that Great Aunt Kathleen was knocked down by the last train on the Kilmacwhatsit to Ballyhowsyourfather branch in 1929 please do not quote me as an authority.

Railway	Between	Date	Remarks
GNR	Keady and Castleblaney	10/8/24	
L&B	Listowel and Ballybunion	13/9/24	Monorail
NCC	Portstewart Station and Portstewart Town	1/1/26	Steam tramway
D&B	Blessington and Poulaphouca	30/9/27	Steam tramway
GSR	Kinsale Junction and Kinsale	1/9/31	Former CB&SCR
GSR	Monkstown and Crosshaven	1/6/32	Former CB&P, narrow-gauge
GSR	Monkstown and Cork	12/9/32	Former CB&P, narrow-gauge
D&B	Terenure and Blessington	31/12/32	Steam tramway
NCC	Ballyclare and Doagh	1933	Narrow-gauge
GNR	Markethill and Armagh	Feb./1933	Scene of worst accident on Irish railways
C&VB	Castlederg and Victoria Bridge	17/4/33	Narrow-gauge
GSR	Ballina and Killala	1/7/34	Former MGWR
GSR	Cork and Donoughmore	31/12/34	Former C&M, narrow-gauge
GSR	Coachford Junction and Coachford	31/12/34	Former C&M, narrow-gauge
GSR	Galway and Clifden	24/4/35	Former MGWR
L&LSR	Buncrana and Carndonagh	2/12/35	Narrow-gauge
NCC	Rathkenny and Retreat	19/4/37	Narrow-gauge
GSR	Westport and Achill Sound	30/9/37	Former MGWR
GSR	Castlegregory Junction and Castlegregory	15/4/39	Former T&D, narrow-gauge
NCC	Ballymena and Rathkenny	1940	Narrow-gauge
L&LSR	Gweedore and Burtonport	1/6/40	Narrow-gauge
CV	Maguires Bridge and Tynan	31/12/41	Clogher Valley, narrow-gauge
NCC	Ballyboley and Ballymena	1942	Narrow-gauge
GSR	Birdhill and Killaloe	24/4/44	Former GSWR
GSR	Woodenbridge and Shillelagh	24/4/44	Former DSER
CIE	Crossdoney and Killeshandra	25/1/47	Former MGWR
CIE	Streamstown and Clara	27/1/47	Former MGWR

CIE	Fermoy and Mitchelstown	27/1/47	Former GSWR
CIE	Schull and Skibbereen	1/2/47	Narrow-gauge
L&LS	Letterkenny and Gweedore	1/6/47	Narrow-gauge
CDJ	Glenties and Stranorlar	13/12/47	Narrow-gauge
B&N	Bessbrook and Newry	10/1/48	Electric tramway, narrow-gauge
GC	Portstewart and Giants Causeway	1949	Electric tramway, narrow-gauge
UTA	Comber and Newcastle	15/1/50	Former BCDR
UTA	Ballynahinch Junction and Ballynahinch	15/1/50	Former BCDR
UTA	Downpatrick and Ardglass	15/1/50	Former BCDR
UTA	Ballymacarrett Junction, Comber and Donaghdee	1950	Former BCDR
UTA	Larne and Ballyclare	3/7/50	Last former NCC narrow-gauge lines
UTA	Ballymoney and Ballycastle	3/7/50	
DN&G	Dundalk and Greenore	31/12/51	Last English owned lines in Ireland
DN&G	Newry and Greenore	31/12/51	
L&LS	Derry and Buncrana	10/8/53	End of L&LS system
L&LS	Tooban Junction and Letterkenny	10/8/53	End of L&LS system
CIE	Cork and Macroom	1/12/53	
CIE	Kilmessan and Athboy	15/1/54	Former MGWR (abandonment date, regular services ended 10/3/47)
CIE	Goolds Cross and Cashel	Sept, 1954	Former GSWR
CDJ	Derry and Strabane	31/12/54	Narrow-gauge
UTA	Magherafelt and Cookstown	1/5/55	Former NCC
UTA	Limavady Junction and Dungiven	1/5/55	Former NCC
UTA	Castlewellan and Newcastle	1/5/55	Former BCDR (worked by GNR)
GNR	Castlewellan and Scarva	1/5/55	
GNR	Goraghwood and Markethill	1/5/55	
GNR	Knockmore Junction and Banbridge	29/4/56	Except for 1½ miles siding Knockmore to Newforge
GNR	Portadown and Tynan	1/10/57	
GNR	Armagh and Keady	1/10/57	
GNR	Omagh and Newtonbutler	1/10/57	
GNR	Bundoran Junction and Bundoran	1/10/57	

GNR	Fintona and Fintona Junction	1/10/57	Horse worked tram
SLNCR	Collooney and Enniskillen	1/10/57	
CIE	Harcourt Street and Shangannagh Junction	30/12/58	Former DSER
CIE	Sallins and Tullow	15/3/59	Former GSWR
UTA	Ballyhaise and Belturbet	1/4/59	Former GNR
CIE	Sutton, Hill of Howth and Howth	1/10/59	Former GNR tramline
UTA	Kilrea and Cookstown Junction	1/10/59	Former NCC

Remaining section of Derry Central Line, i.e. Kilrea and Macfin and Magherafelt and Draperstown was closed by 1957. Magherafelt and Drapers-town passenger service ended 1/10/30, goods continued, Kilrea and Macfin goods and passenger services still extant in 1949.

UTA	Coalisland and Cookstown	5/10/59	Former GNR
CDJ	Strabane and Killybegs	31/12/59	Last sections of County
CDJ	Donegal and Ballyshannon	31/12/59	Donegal system
UTA	Dundalk and Clones	1/1/60	Former GNR
CIE	Inny Junction and Cavan	1/1/60	Former GNR
CIE	Claremorris and Ballinrobe	1/1/60	Former MGWR
CIE	Headford Junction and Kenmare	1/1/60	Former GSWR
CIE	Clones and Monaghan	1/1/60	Former GNR
CIE	Inniskeen and Carrickmacross	1/1/60	Former GNR
CIE	Farranfore and Valentia	1/2/60	Former GSWR
CIE	Waterford and Tramore	31/12/60	Former W&T
CIE	Ennis and Kilrush	1/2/61	Former West Clare. End of narrow-gauge
CIE	Moyasta and Kilkee	1/2/61	Former West Clare. End of narrow-gauge
CIE	Dromod and Belturbet	1/2/61	Former Cavan & Leitrim. End of narrow-gauge
CIE	Ballinamore and Arigna	1/2/61	Former Cavan & Leitrim. End of narrow-gauge
CIE	Clonakilty Junction and Clonakilty	31/3/61	Former CB&SCR
CIE	Ballinascarthy and Courtmacsherry	31/3/61	Former T&C
CIE	Cork and Bantry	31/3/61	Former CB&SCR
CIE	Drimoleague Junction and Baltimore	31/3/61	Former CB&SCR
UTA	Knockmore and Newforge	1962	Former GNR
	Derry Port and Harbour Commissioners Tramway	31/8/62	

CIE	Clara Junction and Banagher	31/12/62	Former GSWR
CIE	Portlaoise and Kilkenny	31/12/62	Former GSWR
CIE	Portlaoise and Mountmellick	31/12/62	Former GSWR
CIE	Castlecomer Junction and Deerpark Colliery	31/12/62	Built by Government, operated by GSWR
CIE	Roscrea and Birr	31/12/62	Former GSWR
CIE	Palace East and Muine Bheag	2/2/63	Former GSWR
CIE	Nesbitt Junction and Edenderry	2/2/63	Former MGWR
CIE	Athy and Ballylinan	2/2/63	Former GSWR
CIE	Clonsilla and Navan	2/2/63	Former MGWR
CIE	Navan and Oldcastle	2/2/63	Former GNR
CIE	Macmine Junction and New Ross	2/2/63	Former DSER
CIE	Kilfree Junction and Ballaghadereen	2/2/63	Former MGWR
CIE	Banteer and Newmarket	2/2/63	Former GSWR
UTA	Goraghwood and Warrenpoint	4/1/65	Former GNR
UTA	Dungannon and Coalisland	4/1/65	Former GNR
UTA	Portadown and Derry	15/2/65	Former GNR
UTA	Coleraine Harbour Branch	12/9/66	Former NCC
CIE	Mallow and Waterford	25/3/67	Former GSWR/FRRH, Waterford to Ballinacourty later reopened for dolomite traffic
CIE	Thurles Junction and Clonmel Junction	25/3/67	Former GSWR
CIE	Patrickswell and Charleville Junction	25/3/67	Former GSWR
CIE	Royal Dublin Society Siding	August 1971	Former DSE (used for Horse Show traffic)

Liveries

Narrow-Gauge

NCC: as for broad-gauge (Ballycastle, absorbed into NCC 1924, locomotives light green; carriages dark brown with light brown upper panels).

Castlederg and Victoria Bridge: locomotives and carriages dark red.

County Donegal: Pre-1933 locomotives black; carriages maroon. After 1933 locomotives black; carriages scarlet and cream, railcars scarlet and cream from outset. From early 1940s locomotives red.

Londonderry and Lough Swilly: Pre-1933 locomotives black with vermillion lining; carriages chocolate and cream. Later carriages black then grey, and at end some engines at least in dark green with yellow lining.

Clogher Valley: Locomotives at one time green, in last years reddish brown; carriages dark red.

Bessbrook and Newry: All cars red and cream, apart from Nos 7/8 (Ex-Dublin and Lucan) which retained their former green and white.

Giant's Causeway: Cars and trailers cream predominant colour with brown surrounds and lining.

GSR lines before 1925

Tralee and Dingle: Locomotives black lined in chocolate, yellow and red; carriages brown lined yellow and red.

West Clare (including South Clare): Locos black lined in red, white and vermilion, underframes mid-brown; carriages, first-class dark blue with white lining, third-class dark red with black lining. (Preserved No 5 in earlier green livery).

Cork, Blackrock and Passage: Locomotives black with vermilion and white lining, carriages dark green.

Cork and Muskerry: Locomotives and carriages green.

Schull and Skibereen: Locomotives and carriages green.

Cavan and Leitrim: Locomotives green with red lining, carriages brown.

Listowel and Ballybunion: Locomotives dark green with black lining, carriages reddish-brown.

Broad Gauge

GS&WR: Locomotives dark grey (often quoted as black, presumably because it weathered until the difference was almost imperceptable) with red and white lining; carriages claret (deep purple) with yellow and red lining, gold lettering and numbers, with company crest in centre of lower panels. No indication of ownership on locomotives or tenders, brass number plates. Wagons grey.

MGWR: Locomotives in last years black with red lining, brass numberplates or shaded yellow painted numbers on cab and tank sides and back of tender, MGWR initials and company crest on tender sides. Locomotives previously green, and for a short while, blue. Carriages dark brown with gold lining, lettering and numbers. Wagons principally slate grey.

GNR: Locomotives 1916–28 black with red lining, "Great Northern" on tender and tank sides, crest on splashers of passenger engines. 1928 onwards black with no lining, initials "GNR" on tender and tank sides, no coat of arms. Compounds came out in 1933 in black with double red lining, "Great Northern" in full with crest between on tender sides. In 1935 repainted in sky blue with black and white lining, initials "GN" on tender with crest between, and crest also on splashers. Similar livery borne by rebuilt S and S2s from 1938, also new VSs and Us on delivery, and eventually, after 1948, all 4-4-0s except smallest. Carriages varnished mahogany, until 1928 lined in straw. Numbered and lettered in gold, shaded blue, crest on sides. Metal panelled stock orange-brown after brief period of imitation wood graining. Railcars blue lower and cream upper panels. Wagons grey.

DSER: Locomotives black with red and gold lining, painted yellow numbers, crest on upper cab panels. Carriages crimson lake with gold lining and lettering.

CB&SCR: Locomotives and carriages olive green with yellow lining.

Cork and Macroom Direct: Locomotives light green with yellow and black lining.

Dublin and Blessington: Locomotives black with red and gold lining; carriages crimson lake with gold lining.

NCC: Locomotives very deep olive green (invisible green) with yellow lining, initials "MRNCC" on tender and tank sides. From 1924 locomotives gradually painted Midland red with LMS crest on cabside and initials "NCC" on tank and tender sides. From 1946 Midland red replaced by black with straw lining. Carriages green until 1924, then crimson lake, lining and lettering gold, black and yellow.

B&CDR: Locomotives dark green, lighter shade from 1936; carriages dark brown.

GSR: GSWR livery continued for locomotives, carriages and wagons, except that corridor coaches gradually painted chocolate and cream. From 1936 all carriages painted in red livery almost identical to that of LMS with crest on lower panels. Earlier Drumm trains in chocolate and cream, later all dark red. 800 class engines blue-green with black and yellow lining, "GS" initials on tender with crest in between.

UTA: Continuation of later NCC lined black for locomotives with crest on tender and tank sides. Carriages, railcar and locomotive hauled, dark green. 1965–6 GNR Section railcars blue and cream (livery of Enterprise 1965–7), NCC Section cars dark red and pale grey, Bangor line cars olive green and cream. Some other stock maroon but most remained dark green.

CIE: Locomotives continued in GSR dark grey but with CIE emblem on some tender sides. From 1946 GSR numberplates replaced by large yellow unshaded painted numbers (except for 800 class). From early 1947 all 4-6-0s,

Woolwich 2–6–0s, three 4–4–0s and DSE suburban section tank engines painted green, lined black and yellow. In last years most surviving steam locomotive unlined black. First diesels silver (or aluminium), some around 1960 in light green. Single cab GM B class originally grey. Experimental deep orange (officially gold) broad lower band, black middles, white upper band and black roof tried out in summer 1961 and later adopted as standard. Many variations on this have been applied including all black, and yellow fronts, but most locomotives now have standard three tone with broken wheel emblem. The re-engined As look much more handsome than in previous liveries and are kept commendably clean.

Carriages were dark green with winged wheel (flying snail) emblem, pale green broad stripe above and below windows. Lighter shade with pale green waist band and numbers, no emblem, came in with Park Royals in 1955; also applied to railcars. At the end of 1955 unpainted aluminium coaches and vans were introduced, with large red 1s and 2s to indicate classes and small red running numbers (these had a habit of rapidly wearing out). From 1958 ail carriages repainted in standard green. New livery introduced in 1961 concurrent with that for locomotives, deep orange lower panels, white waist stripe, black upper panels, roof, and ends. The purpose of the black upper panels was to suggest some sort of conformity between modern steel sided stock and older wooden panelled stock, which still existed in some numbers at the time, the white band appearing at the same level on all carriages, regardless of where their actual waitline occurred. CIE carriages are repainted every two years, and are overhauled every five to six years, and as they are well cared for in between, the upper black panels look better than might be supposed. Nevertheless one may express the hope that something less sombre may take its place when the few remaining wooden bodied carriages disappear. Incidentally it was intended to repaint CIE buses in black and orange when the former green livery was abandoned but somehow or other the double deckers became blue and cream, the single deckers red, and the coaches chocolate and cream.

Wagons are reddish brown, departmental stock grey, although there have been some experimental goods stock liveries of late.

NIR: Railcars maroon, locomotive hauled stock remained UTA green. Locomotives black, one or two 2–6–4Ts acquired ugly NIR symbol on tank sides. Enterprise stock maroon lower panels, white band, deep blue upper panels. Enterprise locomotives maroon with yellow V front, brass nameplates, painted numbers, NIR symbol on sides.

Preserved Rolling Stock

Locomotives

Company		*Location*
GNR	JT class 2–4–2T No 93 built 1895	Belfast Transport Museum
GNR	V class compound 4–4–0 No 85 *Merlin* built 1932	at present at Lisburn but will be at either Whitehead (RPSI) or Belfast Transport Museum by time of publication (RPSI owned)
GNR	S class 4–4–0 No 171 *Slieve Gullion* built 1913	RPSI (in steam)
GNR	Q class 4–4–0 No 131 built 1901	CIE (Dundalk)
GSR	B1a class 4–6–0 No 800 *Maeve* built 1939	Belfast Transport Museum
GSWR	J15 class 0–6–0 No 184 built 1880	Inchicore (in steam)
GSWR	J15 class 0–6–0 No 186 built 1879	RPSI (in steam)
GSWR	Bury 2–2–2 No 36 built 1848	Kent station, Cork
GSWR	J30 class 0–6–0T No 90 built 1875 (as rail-motor)	Mallow
DSER	2–6–0 No 15 built 1922	CIE (Inchicore)
NCC	U2 class 4–4–0 No 74 *Dunluce Castle* built 1924	Belfast Transport Museum
NCC	WT class 2–6–4T (proposed)	Either Belfast Transport Museum or RPSI
BCDR	1 class 4–4–2T No 30 built 1901	Belfast Transport Museum
SLNCR	0–6–4T *Lough Erne* built 1949	RPSI member Mr R. Grayson
Guinness 0–4–0ST No 3 built 1919 (Hudswell Clarke)		RPSI
Londonderry Port and Harbour Commissioners No 1 0–6–0T built 1891 (Stephensons)		Belfast Transport Museum

Narrow-Gauge Locomotives

Cavan and Leitrim 4–4–0T No 2 *Kathleen* built 1887	Belfast Transport Museum
Cavan and Leitrim 4–4–0T No 3 *Lady Edith* built 1887	USA
West Clare 0–6–2T No 5 *Slieve Callan* built 1892	Ennis
Tralee and Dingle 2–6–2T No 5 built 1892	USA

213

County Donegal 2–6–4T No 2 *Blanche* built 1912   Belfast Transport Museum
(also two 2–6–4Ts, purchased for preservation
in USA but still at Strabane)

County Donegal No 11 *Phoenix* 36hp four-   Belfast Transport Museum
wheel diesel

Larne Aluminium Works No 1 0–4–0T   Lord O'Neill
built 1906 (Peckett)

Larne Aluminium Works No 2 0–4–0T   Belfast Transport Museum
built 1906 (Peckett)

Bord na Mona—three 0–4–0WTs (Barclay)   Two with the Irish Steam
Preservation Society, one
(much rebuilt) with the
Talyllyn

Guinness No 20, 2ft gauge 0–4–0T built 1905   William Spence & Son,
Dublin, now in Belfast
Transport Museum

Carriages and Wagons

NCC   Railcar No 1 (Proposed)   Belfast Transport Museum
GNR   Four-wheel railbus No 8178 built   Belfast Transport Museum
          1932 (in running order)
DWW   Third-class open sided four-wheel   Belfast Transport Museum
          coach built 1840
DNGR   1st/2nd six-wheel coach No 1 built   Belfast Transport Museum
          1904
MGWR   "Dargan saloon", six-wheel coach   Belfast Transport Museum
          built for William Dargan, 1844
Tralee and Dingle coach   USA
County Donegal railcar No 1   Belfast Transport Museum
County Donegal railcar (ex-Clogher Valley) No 10 Belfast Transport Museum
County Donegal directors coach No 1   Belfast Transport Museum
County Donegal coach No 3 (former D&B)   Belfast Transport Museum
Cavan and Leitrim coach No 6   Belfast Transport Museum
The RPSI also have one or two items of 5ft 3in goods stock, i.e. two GNR
bogie grain wagons, a Shell tanker, a GNR flat wagon, a GNR 6-wheel
brake van damaged by vandals

Tramcars

GNR   Fintona horse tram   Belfast Transport Museum
Belfast Corporation horse tram No 118   Belfast Transport Museum
Belfast Corp electric (ex-horse) tram No 249 Belfast Transport Museum
Belfast Corporation electric tram No 357   Belfast Transport Museum
GNR   Howth tram No 4   Belfast Transport Museum
GNR   Howth tram No 7   Crich
Giant's Causeway toast-rack trailer car No 5 Belfast Transport Museum
Bessbrook and Newry electric tram No 2   Belfast Transport Museum
NCC   Portstewart ST steam engine No 2 Belfast Transport Museum

The McKinsey Report

SINCE COMPLETING the manuscript for this book two important reports on Irish transport have been published, and it was felt that at least a summary of their findings ought to be included, as an appendix, to bring the story of the railways up-to-date.

Foras Forbartha (The Development Corporation), headed by Kevin Heanue, carried out a survey of traffic problems in Greater Dublin and came out with a plan for Dublin transport until 1991, the chief features of which were the up-grading of rail and bus services at the expense of the private motorist, and a five mile Underground system connecting the city centre with the four main trunk lines. Whilst generally welcomed, the cost would be considerable, and we shall have to see whether the Underground railway proposal goes the same way as did Jim Larkin's of 30 years ago. Mention should also be made in passing of a £60 million road building scheme, including a new bridge over the Liffey, further east than any of the present ones; again most people, other than those residents who would lose their homes, found it very acceptable but wondered where the money was going to come from.

The report most likely to bear upon CIE's immediate future is that of the findings of McKinsey, an American firm of consultants, commissioned by the Government to look into the workings of CIE, and particular apposite at this time, as in the year ending March 31, 1971 CIE made a loss of £541,000 despite a Government subvention of £5.63 million, and estimates for the current year suggest that something of the same order can be expected.

McKinsey's six main conclusions are as follows:

(1) CIE's current financial problems, like those of public transport companies in other countries, result largely from two factors. First, costs are rising rapidly at a time when many opportunities to improve productivity have already been exploited. Second, growing private transport competition—from both motor cars and lorries—is limiting the possibility of increasing rates in line with cost increases.

(2) The railway is the main current cause for concern. Losses on the commuter services are so large that from a purely commercial view they should be terminated immediately. From the same commercial view many freight services should be run as wasting assets.

(3) Analysis of social costs and benefits, however, shows that many railway services make a major contribution to the community. It has been concluded that these services should be retained and developed further to play an important continuing role in the future national transport system.

215

(4) Even after the effects of social costs and benefits are included the continuation of some railway services cannot be justified. Restricting of the railway is necessary, therefore, to eliminate these services and improve the railway financial results by about £1m annually.

(5) Major changes are required in the methods used to provide financial support to CIE from the Exchequer with future emphasis on grants made for specific purposes.

(6) Finally some changes to CIE's management structure and processes should be made, to adapt them to the changing environment in which CIE now operates.

One's first reaction to the foregoing is that the Government might have found all that out by sending a man with a notebook down to the main Dublin termini for the day and asking a random selection of regular commuters and main-line travellers for their views. One's second is that at a price of £3 for a 122-page paperback without any pictures they were perhaps trying to cover CIE's losses on this alone. However, to be less flippant, certain points emerge. The first two conclusions are identical to those arrived at in all previous reports and would have applied with as much force at any time in the last 50 years. The third is made with rather more emphasis and conviction than in the past, and is now generally accepted. The fourth is arguable, a suggestion that the route from Wexford to Dublin should be by way of Waterford and Cherryville Junction hardly seems practicable, and I doubt if anyone in Ireland could find the wherewithal to finance a preservation society to run the Cobh Junction to Youghal line as the report suggests. There are other, obvious lines, such as the North Kerry and the Limerick—Galway which from a financial point of view might certainly be closed, but to do so would strongly reinforce the view held in the West that certain lads up in Dublin don't believe in spending money on anything outside a radius of 30 miles from O'Connell Street. The fifth point seems reasonable enough, for as the report goes on to say, the danger of giving any state body a lump sum and saying do what you think best with it, usually results in those activities which lose the most being the most neglected, even though they are of the greatest benefit to the community. A specific recommendation made under the sixth conclusion is that there should be a head of railways, under the General Manager of CIE, and there is also a suggestion that both bus and rail services in Greater Dublin should be controlled by a single department, thus enabling buses to act as feeders to the railways, relieving duplication of facilities and making it possible to charge more realistic fares on some train journeys which are at present kept artificially low in order to compete with the buses.

One recommendation not made, despite being widely predicted, is the breaking up of CIE into separate bodies, although the report also makes it clear that many local decisions can only be made on the spot by the people there. On the whole the report contains a great deal of commonsense, is rather more lucid and written in a less turgid style than some of its predecessors, is much less revolutionary than some people expected and seems to have a pretty good grasp of the Irish situation. It is now up to the Government to decide what to do, if anything, about it, and as this boils down to a question of priorities, how much money is available, and the amount of pressure the various interested parties are able to exert, one can only sit back and await the outcome.

Bibliography

A History of Railways in Ireland, J. C. Conroy 1927
The Irish Answer, Tony Gray, Heinemann 1966
Seven Lean Years, CIE 1946
Around the Bend, CIE 1946
Fifty Years of Railway Life, J. Tatlow 1920
Irish Railway Album, C. P. Boocock, Ian Allan 1968
Narrow Gauge Railways of Ireland, R. W. Kidner, Oakwood Press 1965
Twentieth Century Irish Locomotives, W. E. Shepherd, Union Publications 1967
ABC Irish Locomotives, R. N. Clements and J. M. Robbins, Ian Allan 1949
Fiery Cross, Joseph Deasy, New Books Publications 1963
Labour in Irish History, James Connolly, New Books Publications 1967
Journal of the Irish Railway Record Society, 1946 onwards
Report on Transport in Ireland, The Stationery Office, Dublin 1948
Report of Committee of Inquiry into Internal Transport, 1957, The Stationery Office, Dublin
Benlon Report on Internal Traffic in Northern Ireland 1963
Fayle's Journal, edited by C. J. Coghlan, K. A. Murray and Hugh Fayle 1929–46
Narrow-Gauge Railways of Ireland, Hugh Fayle, Greenlake Publications 1946
History of the GNR, GNR 1946
Pacemaker Report, CIE 1963
"Minutes of GSR Board of Directors"
"Annual Reports of Irish Railway Companies," 1916 onwards
"Bord na Mona annual reports"
Irish Statistical Bulletin
Irish Railways Today, Pender and Richards, Transport Research Associates, Dublin 1967
Various issues of:
Locomotive Railway Carriage and Wagon Review; Railway Magazine; Trains Illustrated; Modern Railways; Railway World; The Irish Times; Irish Press; Irish Independent; The Kerryman

This bibliography is by no means complete but it covers the period pretty well without undue emphasis on the rolling stock aspect.

Index